FAMOUS
1914-1918

Also by Richard van Emden:

The Last Fighting Tommy
Britain's Last Tommies
Boy Soldiers of the Great War
All Quiet on the Home Front
Last Man Standing
The Trench
Prisoners of the Kaiser
Veterans: The Last Survivors of the Great War
Tickled to Death to Go

Also by Victor Piuk:

A Dream Within the Dark

FAMOUS
1914 - 1918

**Richard van Emden
and
Victor Piuk**

Pen & Sword
MILITARY

Published in this format in 2008 by
Pen & Sword Military
An imprint of
Pen & Sword Books Ltd
47 Church Street
Barnsley
South Yorkshire
S70 2AS

ISBN 978 1 84415 642 9

Printed and bound in England
by CPI UK

FSC
Mixed Sources
Product group from well-managed
forests and other controlled sources
Cert no. SGS-COC-2953
www.fsc.org
© 1996 Forest Stewardship Council

Pen & Sword Books Ltd incorporates the Imprints of
Pen & Sword Aviation, Pen & Sword Maritime, Pen & Sword Military,
Wharncliffe Local history, Pen & Sword Select, Pen & Sword Military Classics
and Leo Cooper.

For a complete list of Pen & Sword titles please contact
PEN & SWORD BOOKS LIMITED
47 Church Street, Barnsley, South Yorkshire, S70 2AS, England
E-mail: enquiries@pen-and-sword.co.uk
Website: www.pen-and-sword.co.uk

Dedicated to Daniel and Juliette Cullen

CONTENTS

INTRODUCTION

The utter stupid waste of war, not only material but moral and spiritual, is so staggering to those who have to endure it. And always was (despite the poets), and always will be (despite the propagandists...).

JRR Tolkien

It is odd to start a book by apologising for its title. The idea, to write about the Great War experiences of men who later went on to national, frequently international, fame and sometimes fortune, seemed attractive, indeed, it was surprising that no one had written such a book before. 'Famous 1914-1918' was the obvious title, pithy and to the point, and the very word famous, particularly in the context of the Great War, would capture attention and, hopefully, interest.

Nevertheless, we apologise. Fame was rarely what any of these men sought; for some, it was an unwarranted intrusion into their lives. They wrote, acted, sculpted, led great institutions or helped safeguard the country's future not because they sought celebrity, or even its trappings, but because they worked hard at what they wanted to do and happened to be very good at it. In recent years, the cult of the celebrity has come a long way (down) from the days when fame was incidental to an individual's body of respected work, and considered a by-product, bringing mixed blessings. Today, popular culture has made fame accessible, egalitarian and utilitarian, often sought for its own sake.

The book tells the Great War stories of twenty-one of the best known men of the twentieth century. They are famous for a variety of reasons: for their work in literature and art, or for rising to the top of the political tree. Several went on to international acclaim as actors; another to posthumous fame for (perhaps) conquering Mount Everest thirty years before anyone else. They came from all walks of life but they all had one thing in common, a talent that set them apart from their peers and that would bring them to the pinnacle of their chosen professions. Only two of our subjects do not fit this scenario: John Reginald Halliday Christie, the infamous murderer of 10 Rillington Place, and Ned Parfett, the newspaper boy photographed outside the offices of the White Star Line. It was the day after the catastrophic demise of RMS *Titanic,* and his image has become inextricably linked to the most famous of all maritime tragedies.

Over ninety years ago, such men as these enlisted to fight. Perhaps one of the most remarkable aspects of the Great War was the almost universal desire to serve the country in its time of need. The voluntary nature of recruitment into the armed services between 1914 and the introduction of conscription in 1916 drew men into uniform from every social milieu, and without prejudice to one class of scholar, worker or artisan. Every trade, every occupation, enlisted; every class was represented, from the sons of serving or former Prime Ministers to the poorest Barnardo's boy: they were all there.

There were many reasons why they chose to enlist. Patriotism was accepted as the over-arching reason, but thousands enlisted simply for three square meals a day. Others were pressurised into joining up, even shamed, while some wished to escape problems at home, or merely sought a great adventure with their mates. Nevertheless, whatever the real motivation, the popular clarion call was that Britain had to be defended against an over-bearing and aggressive Germany, and national sovereignty and the international rule of law had to be respected. Most men, whatever their true, perhaps unconscious, rationale for serving, would have broadly agreed with the publicly-stated reasons for declaring war on Germany.

When the desire to serve cut across all social and economic boundaries, it naturally attracted men from occupations not normally associated with wearing the King's uniform. Footballers, international rugby players, many playing at the highest levels of the game, joined up, as did boxers, cricketers, even a Wimbledon Champion. Artists, composers and actors did likewise. Some battalions became synonymous with particular occupations. There was a Stockbrokers' Battalion, and ones for artists, civil servants and former public school boys. There was more than one battalion for sportsmen too: the 17th Middlesex Regiment, known as the 1st Sportsman's Battalion, included such men as Walter Tull, not only the first black officer in the British army but also a well known footballer for Tottenham Hotspur. It is fair to say that there was no stratum of society, no professional body of men, that did not feel that, when duty called, their time and possibly their lives belonged to their country.

In 1914, fame was far more elusive than it is today, and tended to be built gradually over an extended time, as peer respect grew and the national press began to take notice. Even so, there were few available paths along which an individual's growing fame could be disseminated; in the absence of radio and television, and with the film industry still in its infancy, newspapers and word of mouth were the predominant media for spreading information.

If the avenues to establishing a name were few, then the number of short-cuts to fame and fortune were even fewer. The army, however, was one possible route to public acclaim, at least amongst those who became officers. While it was popularly believed to employ ruffians and vagabonds in its ranks, it was still revered as an institution that maintained British power and influence internationally, and was a great source of pride amongst British people. The British army and navy were celebrated in schools and, with the dearth of popular alternatives, the images of 'famous' generals adorned school walls, and bronze statues cast in their image commemorated their great leadership and, as a consequence, their battlefield success.

The majority of the men in this book served their country and then became famous, not for their wartime activities but because in the post-war world, with the development in the scope and role of the media, they were outstanding in their own right, as actors, writers, sculptors, politicians. There are a couple of exceptions. Winston Churchill was already well known as the former First Lord of the Admiralty when he chose to serve in the trenches. The public's awareness of him began nearly two decades before when, as a journalist, he was present at the Battle of Omdurman, subsequently writing *The River War* about the re-conquest of Sudan. A little over 18 months later, as a war correspondent, he was captured by the Boers in South Africa, only to escape in a *Boys' Own Paper* style adventure that was widely reported at home. Another was A A Milne, an increasingly well-known playwright and, at 34 years of age, the deputy editor of *Punch* magazine.

Many of those whose wartime stories we have followed in this book, such as Basil Rathbone, and indeed those we have not, such as Ronald Colman, Charles Laughton, and Claude Rains, had a presence that, with the advent of the cinema, circled the globe, bringing their name and image to a vast audience, a level of popular exposure that was unobtainable fifty years earlier. Nevertheless, fame, of course, is transitory even for those considered legendary in their day. Men such as Ronald Colman are far less well known than they were fifty years ago. Basil Rathbone, but for his exploits as Sherlock Holmes, would probably have faded in the public consciousness too.

Vic Piuk and I drew up a list of as many 'famous' people as we could think of who were born towards the end of the nineteenth century and therefore old enough, and indeed young enough, to have served in the Great War. The age for enlistment in 1914 was nominally 19-30, extended soon after the outbreak of hostilities to 35 years. In searching for suitable candidates for study, we were looking in a demographically narrow belt, men born broadly between 1880 and 1900.

To be considered, each person had to be famous not just in the past but also today. To an extent, this was a subjective assessment. We considered including the writer Hector Hugo Munro, better known by his pen name Saki. His fame was already established by the time he served and died in the Great War but we felt that his name was now not familiar enough to justify a chapter. A biography of Saki, published recently and reviewed in the national press, undoubtedly contests our perception that he is largely forgotten. Even so, there was no point in writing about a household name of the 1920s or 30s, if his name drew little more from readers today than a shrug of the shoulders.

For this reason, no sportsmen are included in this book. Men and women who achieved short-lived fame during their playing days often won swift anonymity after retirement. This is especially true for those who played team games, where a significant turnover of players was the norm. For a footballer or cricketer to have served his country in the Great War and then played sport at the highest level, he would, almost by definition, have retired by the mid 1930s. Only a very few sporting greats can expect to be in the public consciousness seventy years later, and in the event few are. The chief criterion for appearing in our book was that the majority of people *today* should be aware of their names and, hopefully, familiar, to a greater or lesser degree, with their work.

In an unscientific straw poll, we asked friends and family of varying ages how many of the twenty-two characters who appear in this book they were familiar with. The number 'known' ranged from twenty (friends and family who were aged thirty-five or above) to as few as eight amongst teenagers aged fifteen and sixteen years old. Everyone asked was aware of Churchill, Tolkien, and A.A Milne; the majority knew the names of Macmillan, Priestley, Montgomery, Vaughan Williams and C.S Lewis; fewer knew the names of Mallory, Rathbone, Bruce and Christie.

Just as some names crossed generational boundaries, others halt abruptly at a certain time. A name might be perfectly familiar to a middle aged or older individual but completely unrecognisable to a child or young adult. This cannot be said of the characters in *Dad's Army*, the hit comedy series which remains a staple diet of BBC repeats. In the case of the Home Guard of Walmington on Sea, it was not always clear who was more famous, the actor or the character he played. The names of Arnold Ridley and John Laurie are instantly recognisable to an older generation, but their alter egos, Private Charles Godfrey and Private James Fraser, are known to almost everyone. Both these men served in the Great War, Ridley as a Private in the 6th Battalion [Bn] Somerset Light Infantry, and Laurie as an acting Lance Corporal in the Honourable Artillery Company. Arnold Ridley has a chapter in this book while John Laurie, who does not appear to have ever spoken about his service, sadly does not.

We regret that this is a male-dominated book. Both Vic and I tried hard to discover any women who might have become indirectly involved with the fighting at the front, almost inevitably as nurses. Names were few and far between excepting the obvious, Naomi Mitchison and Vera Brittain, but they became famous largely owing to their service in the war and their subsequent writings on the subject. There were several with tenuous links to the war, Amelia Erhardt, Agatha Christie, and the 'Unsinkable' Molly Brown, of *Titanic* fame are examples, but their involvement was too transitory or peripheral to warrant more than a mention, let alone a chapter.

Sometimes individuals were discounted because we already had enough characters from that arena or sphere of work. Almost an entire generation of politicians served, including Anthony Eden, Winston Churchill, Clement Atlee and Harold Macmillan, but four politicians would have been too many for this book and so only two appear. Equally, almost every senior officer in the Second World War fought in the First, from Bomber Harris to Claude Auchinleck, from Bernard Law Montgomery to Archibald Wavell; the list goes on and on, but only Montgomery is featured here.

There were those about whom, for one reason or another, we were unable to find much information. Unfortunately, these were usually men who served as privates or NCOs. Their names, unlike the names of those who served as officers, would not as a rule appear in battalion war diaries or regimental histories, and, if they never spoke to biographers or wrote about their service themselves, they left little on which to base any research; John Laurie is a case in point.

Then there are those whom most people will never have heard of and yet their image is very familiar. Private George Scorey, of the 2nd Dragoon Guards, is unknown except for his distant image. He is the policeman sitting astride the famous white horse at Wembley Stadium during the pitch invasion before the 1924 FA Cup Final. William Wells, better known as Bombardier Billy Wells, the heavyweight boxing champion, is known now as the man who struck the gong as a prelude to all J. Arthur Rank films. Both he and his brother served in the Great War. Neither Scorey nor Wells appears here but newspaper boy Ned Parfett does. Thanks to the kind co-operation of his family, his story can be told.

The majority of our characters left a reasonably detailed record of their service, JB Priestley wrote of it, as did Harold Macmillan, Dennis Wheatley and Basil Rathbone. Others such as Nigel Bruce were harder to piece together. An unpublished memoir by Bruce was left to his daughter, but her whereabouts are currently unknown. It has been possible to recreate his story from the scant records left in his officer's papers, (he served as a private in France but was later commissioned) along with information obtained from his unit's war diary and from memoirs written by comrades who were serving in the same part of the line. The story of George Mallory is told almost entirely through his personal letters which survive at Magdalene College, Cambridge. The complete War Diary of the unit with which he served, the 40th Siege Battery, Royal Garrison Artillery, sadly no longer exists.

Every year of the war is covered by one or more of the twenty-one names, although only one theatre, that of the Western Front. A few that we might have included, such as the Labour Prime Minister Clement Atlee, served elsewhere, in his case Gallipoli, but on reflection we decided to remain in what was the principal crucible of the war, France and Flanders. Of those we chose, over half were wounded or invalided out of the army for health reasons; a dozen went over the top or were otherwise involved directly during an action in which their unit attacked the enemy lines. Most lost very close friends or brothers during the war.

Most went on to profess that they had been deeply affected by what they had seen and experienced, and that the war had a direct influence on the way they wrote, commanded, governed, even acted, and in one case, that of John Reginald Christie, murdered. These men survived the war, but they never quite escaped it.

The original idea was that each chapter would fit a pre-set blueprint. Each character would have one incident that could be studied in detail, followed by a précis of their remaining service followed by a short description of their childhood and subsequent post-war career and fame.

In studying any one incident in detail, we have drawn on a number of sources to explain and describe events beyond those recalled by the characters themselves. This means studying war diaries and unit histories not only to flesh out the story itself but also to verify the sequence of events and the overall effect and result of actions in which our famous people were involved. Records held at the National Archives, the Imperial War Museum and the Liddle Collection at Leeds University have proved particularly useful.

The scope which we have employed when describing an event has had to be limited by space in the book. An attack in which Arnold Ridley, AA Milne or Harold Macmillan was involved might employ a number of neighbouring divisions, each with its own objective within a broader overall plan. It would be too easy to become bogged down in strategy and tactics, referring to battalions or brigades which are not directly relevant to our subject. For that reason, we have narrowed descriptions of battle to those that our subject would have seen, and refer to other units only as they are or become directly relevant in a battle. For readers interested in the broader strategy at a particular juncture, there are many other books available that will supply a more complete picture.

The structure which we set ourselves has been broadly adhered to, though there are exceptions. Occasionally, such as in the career of Dr Alexander Fleming, no one story or event stood out for particular attention. However, Fleming's outstanding contribution to world health and his international fame ensured that such a fascinating man automatically received his place.

In the same vein, where the war had an obvious and profound influence on an individual's later life and fame, and where this influence was recorded, we felt that their story should be broadened to add this element to the overall picture, beyond that originally envisaged. Arnold Ridley's post war trauma was particularly enlightening and his character as Charles Godfrey in *Dad's Army* appeared to have been written with so much of Ridley's own character entwined that it was worth further exploration. Nicolas Ridley, Arnold's son, added fascinating extra material, recalling his childhood with his father and the extent to which his father was still haunted by the war years.

How close Arnold Ridley came to death is evident in his story. He nearly died, as did a number of others who lived to enrich and expand British culture. And this is what was also disturbing about the research we undertook. Any one of these men could so easily have been a fatality. It is not only a question of asking where Britain would have been had Churchill been killed in 1916 or how much longer the Second World War might have lasted if Montgomery had not survived his bullet wound in 1914, but what unimaginable loss of human life would have resulted if a German aeroplane had dropped a bomb and accounted for Alexander Fleming at Wimereux in 1918.

Looking over a cultural precipice, can we imagine how much poorer the world would be without *The Lord of the Rings* trilogy, the sculptures of Henry Moore or the music of Vaughan Williams? Television without the influence of Lord Reith or the law without Lord Denning – it is unimaginable.

Then one is inescapably drawn to the terrible alternative. If they were lucky enough to survive, which man died who might have made an equally remarkable contribution to society? Who died in a dugout on the Somme, on the barbed wire at Ypres or in a Casualty Clearing Station near Arras who might have changed the world? So many of those who appear in this book lost not just one but two, three, even four friends they venerated, held up to be better than they were, were considered more gifted, more intelligent, more skilled. Everyone in this book lost someone precious to them; what *they* would have become had they survived, we shall never know.

We are aware of the extensive and growing interest in the Great War, as we are of the on-going fascination with the lives of those we have covered in this book. Well over 250,000 Britons visit the battlefields each year, and with this in mind we have included a number of maps identifying the location where our characters fought. These maps are intended as a battlefield guide. However, the battlefields have, by and large, been returned to farm land, and respect for a French or Belgian landowner's property should always be kept firmly in mind. They will not thank anyone for trampling their crops to see where Milne, Priestley or Macmillan went over the top.

Finally, it has been an honour to examine the lives of these great men, with the obvious exception of Christie, and to handle original letters and manuscripts was at times both exhilarating and humbling. Holding the small bundle of letters recovered from George Mallory's body, found just below the summit of Mount Everest in 1999, was extraordinary, no less extraordinary than their remarkable state of preservation. It is no exaggeration to say they looked as if they were written yesterday. It is also true to say that it has been a thrill to hold the officer enlistment papers of the 'famous' held at the National Archives (NA). JRR Tolkien's papers at one point rested on top of those of Dennis Wheatley and JB Priestley. There was an undoubted nostalgic thrill, too, when the service papers of Basil Rathbone and Nigel Bruce, Sherlock Holmes and Dr Watson, were put side by side in the NA's reading room, a strange association that even the great sleuth could not possibly have foreseen.

Richard van Emden and Victor Piuk

June 2008

CHAPTER ONE

A A Milne

—⚹—

If a special order had gone round the British Army: 'For your information and necessary action: Milne is joining us. See that he is given the easiest and best time possible, consistent with ultimate victory,' I could not have had more reason to be grateful to my commanding officers.

AA Milne, *It's Too Late Now*

IT IS HARD TO IMAGINE any connection, no matter how unlikely, between Jane Austen and the pock-marked Somme battlefield, but there is one, albeit rather tenuous. During the carnage of the Great War, almost anything was possible *in extremis* and in August 1916, in a dugout just hours before an attack, there seemed to be nothing more apposite than for the author AA Milne to talk about literature, and great literature too. Overhead, as he spoke, the enemy shells slammed into the ground, and intermittent machine gun fire spattered the trench parapet.

Before he enlisted in the army, Alan Alexander Milne, creator of Winnie the Pooh, was already known as a playwright and assistant editor of *Punch* magazine. Yet the international acclaim that would make him one of the most familiar writers of the twentieth century to children and adults alike was still a decade away. Not that either fame or fortune was on his mind on 12 August 1916. Survival was uppermost in his thoughts, and as the battalion was due to go over the top in a few hours, it was by no means certain that he would live to see the next dawn.

Milne was serving as a Second Lieutenant in the 11th (Service) Bn Royal Warwickshire Regiment. It was his first time up the line and an attack on a heavily defended German trench was set for later that evening. As the battalion's new Signalling Officer, (the previous incumbent had been wounded in the head only a few hours before) Milne was supposed to be asking the men under his command a thousand and one technical questions. Instead, he found himself engaged in a long discussion about literature with Lance Corporal James Grainger, formerly a Welsh miner and now an experienced soldier, who had served with the battalion since it came to France, a year previously. He would be the perfect person to help turn Milne's theoretical knowledge of signalling into something more practical for a battlefield. Instead the quiet, genial NCO was more than happy to trade ideas about the novel and in particular Jane Austen, for whom they shared a passion.

For over two weeks, British forces had been attacking a German line known as the Intermediate Trench. This had appeared on aerial reconnaissance photographs taken on 21 July, and was situated midway between the village of Bazentin-le-Petit and a low ridge beyond. Ever since the photos had been reviewed, the capture of this long trench had become critical to the wider objective of taking the ridge and High Wood, which dominated the surrounding landscape. Battalion after battalion had been sent in to take the Intermediate Trench, which the Germans defended tenaciously. The most recent attacks, in early August, had seized two-thirds of the trench but a further three hundred yards were still in enemy hands, a sandbagged and barbed wire barricade being all that separated German from Briton in the same trench. The 11th Warwicks, with support from other battalions in the Division, were to attack at 10.30pm on the night of 12/13 of August and seize the remaining portion of the line. A bombardment would precede the attack.

Two days earlier, on 10 August, the battalion had taken over five hundred yards of the front line, just to the north of Bazentin-le-Petit.

Much to Milne's frustration, after 18 months' training as a signalling officer, he had been given command of an infantry platoon. However, he had been told that he could accompany the existing Signalling Officer, Kenneth Harrison, and three other men, into the line to gain some practical experience. The plan was to run out telephone cable through to the front line trenches by a devious route so that during the forthcoming attack communications with battalion and brigade headquarters could be maintained. On the day before the attack, Milne followed Harrison, laying cable as they went, but as they neared the front line a salvo of German shells burst overhead. Harrison was struck on the back of the skull by a shell splinter that punctured his helmet and entered his head. Surprisingly it was not, at first glance, a serious wound. Nevertheless, he was sent down the line and eventually to England. He never returned to France. Milne was now the new Signalling Officer, in which capacity he had gone to the signallers' dugout to introduce himself to Lance Corporal Grainger and the other men in the section.

The following morning, 12 August, Milne set out at 4am and laid another telephone line, 'elaborately laddered according to the text books, and guaranteed to withstand any bombardment'. He then returned to battalion headquarters to await the start of the battle.

In the event, two companies would lead the way, attacking over ground that varied between 150 yards and 200 yards in width. They would be supported, if required, by two further companies, while battalions on both flanks would lend assistance, the 10th (Service) Bn Loyal North Lancashire Regiment bombing down the Intermediate Trench from the section already captured. Once in the trench, the men of the Warwickshire Regiment would consolidate the position.

Heavy calibre guns unleashed the preliminary bombardment during the afternoon, ending at 7.00pm just as the sun set. These guns were followed by lighter artillery which would pound the objective and sweep the ground behind to stop enemy reinforcements. However, the heavy bombardment was the last thing the Warwicks' Commanding

Officer, Lieutenant Colonel Charles Collison, wanted. 'Not only would it render the trench uninhabitable to our men, should they succeed in taking it,' he later wrote, 'but it was plain intimation to the Hun that we contemplated some action against him in the near future.' He contacted brigade and asked for the guns to cease fire but his request was refused.

At 9pm the Germans retaliated, plastering the British communication trenches and the Warwickshires' battalion headquarters with shells of every size. The headquarters was an old German dugout deep below ground, and facing, of course, the wrong way. Here, Milne sat round a candlelit table with the commanding officer and two other officers, a major and the battalion adjutant. All communication with the front line was cut almost immediately, to be followed by the line to brigade headquarters.

> We sat there completely isolated. The depth of the dugout deadened the noise of the guns, so that a shell-burst was no longer the noise of a giant plumber throwing down his tools, but only a persistent thud, which set the candles dancing and then, as if by an afterthought, blotted them out. From time to time I lit them again, wondering what I should be doing, wondering what signalling officers did on these occasions. Nervously I said to the Colonel, feeling that the isolation was all my fault, 'Should I try to get a line out?' and to my intense relief he said, 'Don't be a bloody fool.'

It had been difficult for the infantry to keep their composure. For over half of those waiting to go, this was only their third week in France. They had arrived at the end of July in a draft of 388 men. The War Diary notes that only 63 of these men had ever seen action before, and of the rest, most had received just 13 or 14 weeks' training. Few had ever thrown a Mills Bomb and none had fired a Lewis Gun. These men, led mostly by new officers, had been set the already difficult task of taking the Intermediate Trench – and that was before the German bombardment.

Colonel Collison wrote:

> The delivery of an assault under such conditions was a test that would have tried veteran troops, but the bravery and devotion of the officers, and the steady valour and example of the old remnants of the original battalion provided the necessary impetus, and punctually to time the leading line of stormers left the trenches and advanced against the enemy.

The men made their attack behind a shrapnel barrage that lifted as they went forward. Almost immediately they came under intense enemy machine gun and artillery fire, and although a few pressed on, none of the men got to within twenty yards of the German trench. On the left, part of one company became so confused in the dark that it ended up jumping into a British sap that ran at right angles to the objective.

Soon afterwards Private Hunt, one of two headquarters orderlies, arrived with a message. The attacking companies were in no need of support or assistance. 'This was very welcome news, as it was naturally inferred that the attack had succeeded,' recalled Collison in a memoir in 1921. 'These hopes, however, were soon dashed.'

The attack had failed completely. At 2am a runner reached battalion headquarters to explain the situation, reeling off the names of a few of those who had died, some of whom Milne recognised. The Major then stood up and buckled on his revolver; he would go and reorganise the surviving troops. It was a signal for Milne to stand up and buckle his revolver on too. The Colonel spoke to them: 'Use your common sense,' he said. 'I simply cannot lose three signalling officers in a month.' Milne promised, while wondering what the difference between common sense and cowardice was.

Milne told his sergeant that he intended to run a telephone cable up to the front line so communications could be restored and that he needed two men to go with him. 'I knew nothing of the section then, save that there was a lance corporal who loved Jane Austen, unhelpful knowledge in the circumstances.' The Major, followed by Milne, led the way, followed by a sergeant and a signaller who laid out the telephone line neatly and skilfully.

> We passed one of the signal stations, no longer a station but a pancake of earth on top of a spread-eagled body; I had left him there that evening, saying, "Well, you'll be comfortable here." More rushes, more breathers, more bodies, we were in the front line,' wrote Milne. The Major hurried off to collect what men he could, while I joined up the telephone. Hopeless, of course, but we could have done no more.

Milne pressed the buzzer and, much to his surprise, got through to the Colonel, telling him what he knew, and asking for a small counter-bombardment.

> Then with a sigh of utter content and thankfulness and the joy of living, I turned away from the telephone. And there behind me was Lance Corporal Grainger.

> "What on earth are you doing here?" I asked.

He grinned sheepishly.

> "You weren't detailed, were you?"
> "No, sir."
> "Well, then."
> "I thought I'd just like to come along, sir."
> "But why?"

He looked still more embarrassed.

> "Well, sir, I thought I'd just like to be sure you were all right."

> Which is the greatest tribute to Jane Austen that I have ever heard.

The battalion lost around sixty killed, and just over a hundred wounded. Of the five officers who led the attack, three were killed and two severely wounded, and the officer commanding the supporting company was evacuated with shell shock. Colonel Collison wrote a report for the divisional commander. Rightly proud of the efforts made, he defended his men against any possible accusation that they had not tried hard enough. 'I may mention that I saw no man lying otherwise than with his face to the enemy.' For a man whose dislike of the enemy was well-known, he gave them, on this occasion, the respect they deserved. 'One must allow him the credit of a very stout defence.'

The last section of the Intermediate Trench was never captured but was surrendered on 26 August by 130 men of a Bavarian Regiment. Milne later wrote how he had grown to loathe the war. 'It makes me

The Disastrous attack of 11th Bn Royal Warwickshire Regiment on Intermediate Trench, 13 August 1916.

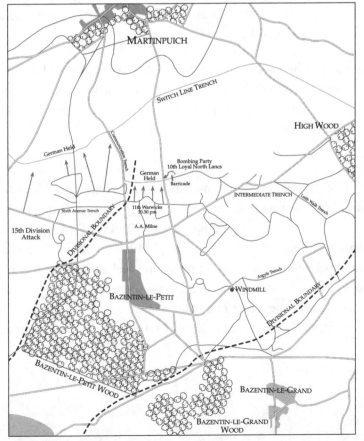

almost physically sick to think of that nightmare of mental and moral degradation, the war.' It was hardly surprising. Just three weeks into his service in France, he had seen enough death and injury to last a lifetime. Even out on rest, when he had first joined the battalion in a wood well behind the lines, long range artillery had speculatively dropped several high explosive shells amongst the trees, killing and maiming over fifty men including three officers. In the two weeks since then, another nine officers had gone, almost half the battalion's complement.

However, there was one death which perhaps touched Milne as much as any other, and it was that of the young officer with whom he had first travelled to France.

The two men had embarked on 20 July 1916, landing the following day. With Milne was Ernest Pusch, a nineteen year old subaltern with no experience of front line life. Milne recalled that he was a quiet boy and that he was rather embarrassed by 'an under-garment of chain mail,' which his mother had provided and made her son promise to wear. It was recalled Milne,

> ...such as had been worn in the Middle Ages to guard against unfriendly daggers, and was now sold to over-loving mothers as likely to turn a bayonet-thrust or keep off a stray fragment of shell; as I suppose, it might have done.

Although he faithfully wore it, Pusch was embarrassed and bothered about the garment in almost equal measure. He may have felt, believed Milne, that it was somehow unsporting, even a little cowardly, something that was not quite done. He asked Milne's advice, 'charmingly, ingenuously, pathetically.' Milne told him to wear it and to tell his mother how secure it made him feel and that he was bound now to come home. It was nevertheless pathetic. 'You may laugh or cry as you will,' he wrote in a letter home.

Milne and Pusch joined a draft of seven other second lieutenants, all of whom were being sent from the base to the battalion. All nine were new to active service conditions and nerves were no doubt jangling as they arrived in the early evening of 25 July to be detailed off to their respective companies. The battalion was resting after its exertions earlier that month, although the sound of battle continued in the near distance, the guns thundering away day and night. With the battalion replenished by new drafts, it could move back up, close to the front line. On 6 August, Milne was sent forward with A and C Companies, along with the men of battalion headquarters to the southeast edge of Bazentin-le-Petit Wood, while D Company, with Second Lieutenant Pusch, was ordered to a position close to the edge of Mametz Wood, a few hundred yards to the south. The shelling was incessant, with the artillery duelling with each other throughout the night and the following day, neither side gaining the ascendancy. On 8 August, Mametz Wood was pounded again.

Milne never knew whether his young friend had taken his advice and worn the protective chain mail.

> Anyway it didn't matter; for on the evening when we first came within reach of the battle-zone, just as he was settling down to his tea, a crump [shell] came over and blew him to pieces.

In the statutory letter written to the officer's parents, Colonel Collison, the Battalion Commander, assured them that he had died as gallantly as he had lived, an English gentleman. Such kind platitudes were not untypical of the time, but in this case they were also inevitable as there had been no chance for the Colonel to get to know this junior subaltern.

Ernest Pusch was buried 900 yards southwest of the church in the Somme village of Bazentin-le-Grand but was later exhumed and taken to Flat Iron Copse Cemetery where he lies today. His death, so soon after arriving at the battalion, would have been a terrible blow to his family back home in any case, but as Milne was only too keenly aware, it was much worse than that.

On his way to France, Ernest Pusch had chosen to confide in Milne. He was not long out of school, and was the younger of two brothers. His elder brother, Frederick, he explained, had been killed just four weeks earlier. Little wonder, in her great anxiety, that Ernest's mother had done everything in her power to preserve her remaining son's life. Frederick had served in France since March 1915 and had won the Distinguished Service Order. On 24 June 1916 he had been transferred to a new battalion, the 1st Irish Guards, and just three days later he had been shot dead by a sniper as he went to the rescue of a wounded man. Frederick's parents, Emile and Helen, were still dealing with the effects of his death when they received the news of Ernest's.

The death of Ernest Pusch must have shaken Milne, coming so soon after they arrived at the battalion. Two weeks later it may have seemed like a distant memory, so much had happened in between.

* * *

On the outbreak of war, AA Milne was thirty-two and just above the age limit imposed by Kitchener for civilians to join his new civilian army. The fact that Milne enlisted at all was due to a change of heart, for before the war he was a pacifist. He was persuaded by the notion that it was a just war, 'a war against war,' and hoped that its prosecution would finally persuade all right thinking people that fighting was nothing short of lunacy, putting an end to any notions of war being heroic and with it the sentimentality that seemed to follow in its wake, the popular triumphalist recollection of battles and campaigns.

It was as a result of an introduction, by a distant relative of the poet Robert Graves, that Milne was commissioned into the army in February 1915, leaving work to join his unit, The Royal Warwickshire Regiment, on the Isle of Wight. By his own admission, Milne hated the basic training, but soon after, 'through a variety of accidents' he was offered the chance of becoming a signalling officer, attending a nine weeks' course at Weymouth.

The new appointment suited his personality perfectly. Participation in the Great War, for people like Milne, was not so much a great sacrifice of his life but, he argued, of his liberty. Since leaving university, he had been the master of his own time and under no one else's discipline. All this freedom was given up by enlisting. Becoming a signalling officer offered him a window on his old life:

> As a specialist officer I was, I thanked heaven, independent again. Nobody in the battalion could tell me anything about signalling; I was excused – or excused myself, it was never clear which – orderly officer's duty; never saw my company commander from one week to another; and having the whole battalion behind me on route marches could almost imagine that I was taking a brisk country walk in civilian knickerbockers.

One unforeseen advantage to the course was that Milne became proficient enough to be held back as a qualified instructor for the best part of a year. It was a fortunate appointment, for otherwise he would have been sent to the 2nd Bn Royal Warwickshire Regiment in France, a unit that was almost destroyed in the advance made at Loos in September. In the event, it would be another nine months before he would have to serve overseas.

After the attack on the Somme in August 1916, Milne served a further three months on the Western Front. His battalion, which had been attached to the 34th Division, had suffered terribly in the first weeks of the campaign and after the latest mauling it was taken out of the battle and sent north. Here it rejoined the 37th Division holding the much quieter trenches near the old Loos battlefield. Out on rest, the battalion undertook training; back in the line, they suffered few casualties, around a dozen killed in the following two and a half months. Milne was fortunate also that when the battalion was next due to go over the top back on the Somme, it was already autumn, and the weather had deteriorated to such an extent that the attack, close to the recently captured village of Beaumont Hamel, was postponed. When a date was finally set and the battalion was due to move up into position, Milne was already in hospital, having contracted trench fever. His temperature soared to 105 degrees and he was evacuated to England and out of the war.

Back home, Milne was sent to a newly-established signalling school, where he was placed in charge of one of four companies, teaching, as he put it, 'ploughboys the theory of induced currents.' Indifferent health, largely brought on by overwork, kept him on 'light duty' at home. He was admitted to a convalescent hospital at Osborne on the Isle of Wight in September 1917, 'in a generally debilitated condition,' noted a medical report; the war, as Milne knew, had taken its physical toll. Nevertheless, during this time he and his wife managed, at great speed, to write a play, *Belinda*, which reached the stage in 1918. In the same year, he was transferred to the War Office where his literary abilities were put to work on propaganda. 'I had a room to myself and wrote pretty much what I liked,' he recalled, adding that 'if it were not patriotic enough, or neglected to point the moral with sufficient hardihood, then the major supplied the operative words in green pencil.' It was in this job that he would see out the War when, aged 36, he would be free to return to work, a civilian once again.

* * *

Alan Alexander Milne was born in 1882, in Hampstead, London, where his father, John Milne, ran a small independent school at which HG Wells was one of the teachers. Alan's mother had been keeping a School for Young Ladies when she met her future husband; she left this on her marriage, and worked hard to help him get his school on a sound financial footing and to bring up their three sons, of whom Alan was the youngest.

Perhaps not surprisingly, given this heredity, he could read by the time he was three years old, and delighted in showing off at the expense of his older brothers, of whom, in spite of this, he was very fond.

After being a pupil at his father's establishment, the young Alan went to Westminster School and, on a mathematics scholarship, to Trinity College, Cambridge. At school, he and his brother Ken found a mutual enjoyment in writing light, humorous verse; at Cambridge, Alan wrote for, and edited, the student magazine *Granta*. He decided – to his father's horror – that he would be a writer.

Encouragement – and practical advice – came to the young man from his father's former employee, HG Wells, and gradually Alan became accepted as a freelance writer. His goal was to write for *Punch*, but for the present his living was precarious. During this time, in the hope of getting material for an article, he spent a night alone on an uninhabited island (very close to the British mainland), and decided to stalk and shoot a rabbit. He recorded that 'the rabbit looked up at the noise, noticed me, and trotted back into its hole to tell the others'. It was not a promising incident for a future army officer.

Fortunately, Alan's writing fared better, and at the age of twenty-four, he became Assistant Editor of *Punch*; in 1910, he published *The Day's Play*, a collection of *Punch* articles. In 1913, he married the Editor's god-daughter, Dorothy, known as Daphne. Happy though he was at *Punch*, he decided to be a dramatist, and had his first short play accepted; before he could celebrate, war had broken out. Believing ('with other fools' he wrote later) that this was the war to end all wars, he joined up and became what he called 'an amateur soldier'.

At the start of his war, Milne was able to continue writing, indeed, the Colonel's wife and Daphne got together to organise an entertainment for the troops, and the Signalling Officer was detailed to write a short play for the Colonel's children (and Daphne) to perform. As he felt that after a day's soldiering he would be too tired for writing, the faithful Daphne suggested that he dictate the play and she would write it down; in this way, they produced not only the play but also a book, a long fairy story called *Once on a Time*. Milne thought that life was perfect: 'spring was here, and now, save for this trivial business of soldiering, I was free, I could take a holiday, I could rest.' His collaborator had other ideas, and he continued to write, producing a play which had just been accepted when 'there was a heavy knocking on the front door...I went down, knowing what it was...I was for France in forty-eight hours.'

When he was demobilised, Milne half expected to go back to his job at *Punch*, while at the same time hoping to make a career as a playwright. Understandably, the Editor felt that he should have been using his spare time to write *Punch* articles rather than plays, and they parted company. Two events in his life were to herald his future: the birth in 1920 of his only son, Christopher Robin, and the publication in 1923 of a children's poem, *Vespers*, which featured his son.

A book of children's poems, *When We Were Very Young*, followed, with illustrations by the famous *Punch* illustrator EH Shepard. It included the first appearance of Winnie the Pooh.

The source of the name is interesting. Reputedly, it was a Canadian black bear named Winnipeg Bear, used as a military mascot by the Royal Winnipeg Rifles, a Canadian Infantry Regiment, and eventually, after the War, left to London Zoo. The bear became known as Winnie the Pooh probably about 1915. It was only ten years later that he achieved a new lease of life as the main character, along with his friend Christopher Robin, in Milne's book of the same name.

Interestingly, Milne saw the Winnie the Pooh books as primarily for grownups rather than children, and they continue to have a wide readership. Their overwhelming success brought serious problems: their author tried to shield his son from the publicity the stories generated, but inevitably failed to do so; he was himself extremely annoyed that his children's books so overshadowed the rest of his writing, but they have of course continued to do so.

In 1952, Milne had a brain operation that left him an invalid. He died in 1956. His widow sold the rights to the Pooh characters to the Walt Disney Company, and destroyed his papers.

CHAPTER TWO

George Mallory

I don't object to corpses so long as they are fresh – I soon found that I could reason thus with them. 'Between you and me is all the difference between life and death. But this is an accepted fact that men are killed and I have no more to learn about that from you, and the difference is no greater than that because your jaw hangs and your flesh changes colour or blood oozes from your wounds.' With the wounded it is different. It always distresses me to see them.

George Mallory, letter to his wife, Ruth Mallory, 15 August 1916.

IN JANUARY 1919, GEORGE MALLORY was feeling frustrated. He had served since mid-1916 on the Western Front, fighting throughout the Battle of the Somme. Now, like so many men, he was desperate to be demobilised and to get back to his young family. But his mind was not just on his wife and two young daughters, but also on the activity that had dominated his pre-war years: climbing. At a camp near Calais, he wrote a letter to his wife, Ruth:

> The low hills near here were looking very green and pretty this morning and even such little hills when one is living in dead flat country makes me think of high mountains. My imagination has been wandering in the idle leisure among the Alps and planning wonderful expeditions up great mountains.

Did Mallory, in June 1924, actually get to the top of Mount Everest? It is a matter that has perplexed the best mountaineering minds. The only certainty is that thirty-seven year old George Mallory, and twenty-two year old Andrew Irvine, two of the best climbers of their generation, died close to the summit of the 29,028 foot mountain. In 1999 Mallory's body, fully clothed and almost perfectly preserved, was found, but not the camera which might prove one way or the other, whether he and Irvine, in climbing parlance, 'summitted'.

It is fascinating to read the letters he exchanged with his wife during the war – there were hundreds in both directions – but it is noticeable just how little he mentioned his passion for mountaineering. Once abroad, he was happy to serve his country in its hour of need and was in no doubt as to the justice of the cause. 'This is a great adventure and a rich adventure for me, dearest, and you'll love me more for it, I hope, when we meet again,' he wrote in May 1916, shortly after arriving in France. 'I'm prepared for whatever may happen.' Nevertheless, for a man so devoted to his sport, it is surprising that his letters did not slip back more often to his climbing days in the Lake District and the Alps. One of Mallory's few allusions to mountaineering came in a letter of November 1916.

I suppose I shall be going to the OP [Observation Post] tomorrow; it is my turn, and that will probably mean spending half the day up to my knees – or thighs perhaps – in slimy mud. Will you please send out my climbing boots; they ought to be very useful in these conditions.

* * *

Second Lieutenant George Mallory had been in France only a few weeks when his unit, the 40th Siege Battery, Royal Garrison Artillery [RGA] was directed to the Somme Battlefield and to the forthcoming offensive, the 'Big Push' as it became known. This all-out offensive would, it was hoped, decisively break the German line and begin to loosen the stranglehold the enemy had kept on occupied northern France. Mallory had crossed to the continent on the night of 4 May and was sent to the battery which consisted of four 6-inch Howitzers. His enthusiasm for the struggle ahead was evident in his letters, as he wrote on 11 June:

> It is extraordinary how the desire is growing within me to take part in a big offensive. I feel we must do it and when we do I want to be there – not for the excitement but because I want to fight in this cause.

Two weeks later, the preliminary bombardment was under way. Some 1,437 guns in all, from the lightest field guns to 15-inch howitzers, were ranged against the enemy. The bombardment began on 24 June, and the following day Mallory wrote a letter to Ruth. He had been on duty from lunch time and remained busy all night, at one time arranging for the ammunition to arrive at the guns, then attending to the endless figures needed for each gun's calibration, checking over the numbers in the map dugout with an acetylene lamp for company.

> It was very noisy. Field batteries again firing over our heads (of course there are plenty in front of us too) and most annoying of them a 60-pounder which has a nasty trick of blowing out the lamp with its vigorous blast. I took a good look round in the middle of the night from the top of our bank, it was a moving sight to see the flashes of many guns like numerous flickers of lightning.

The Germans returned very little in retaliatory fire, at least where Mallory and his team were working. Then, just before dawn, 40th Siege Battery began its contribution to the offensive, each gun firing for ten minutes 'at a rapid rate and with their biggest charge'. A second shoot was ordered for 5am, after which the battery fell silent. 'I am feeling quite strong and full of hope,' Mallory noted.

In the end, the infantry assault that had been timed for 29 June was postponed owing to heavy rain, and after a two-day delay, zero hour was set for 7.30am, 1 July. Mallory's battery had been firing for almost a week but now their targets changed in order to support the men going over the top.

> Our part was to keep up a barrage fire on certain lines, "lifting" after certain fixed times from one to another more remote and so on. Of course we couldn't know how matters were going for several hours. But then the wounded – walking cases – began to pass and bands of prisoners. We heard various accounts but it seemed to emerge pretty clearly that the attack was held up somewhere by machine-gun fire and this was confirmed by the nature of our own tasks after the "barrage" was over. To me, this result together with the sight of the wounded was poignantly grievous. I spent most of the morning in the map room by the roadside, standing by to help Lithgow [the Commanding Officer] to get onto fresh targets.

The bombardment had largely been a failure. Over 1.7 million shells of all sizes had been expended but a large proportion failed to explode and many burst harmlessly above ground, spattering the land either side of the trenches. Even those that arrived on the enemy line did little or no damage to the defenders, as the majority were light shrapnel shells and not high explosive and the enemy were thirty feet underground in dugouts. Mallory saw little of that first day; it was a battle of which 'we see, as it were, only the rim of a seething cauldron…'. He later added:

> We were profoundly depressed that night; though we had no certain news of operations elsewhere, our hope of moving forward immediately seemed to have vanished.

The battery did not move. Instead, it was called into action time and again over the next few days. On 5 July the guns fired all day and Mallory was on duty except when relieved for meals. The shelling 'seemed' successful and periodically groups of German prisoners were seen to pass the gun line. 'A mixed lot like us own,' a gunner remarked to Mallory, 'some fine soldiers and some that look as if they could hardly hold a rifle.'

The bitter reality of that opening day, the dashed hopes, led Mallory to the inevitable conclusion that the war would not be over any time soon. He did not waver from his belief that Germany must be forced to retire, but the significance of battlefield successes appeared somewhat muted in his letters. A rewarding night attack conducted on 14 July was 'good news', as he wrote to Ruth next morning.

> It really seems as though we have given the Hun something of a whacking and also that his reserves are pretty well used up. Shall we find suddenly one day that the war is over – finished as dramatically as it began? Not a very near day I fear – or rather I don't dare to hope.

A battle of attrition had set in.

* * *

In writing to Ruth, each or every other day, George Mallory went out of his way to stress that he was relatively safe, certainly in comparison with front line soldiers. To a certain extent, this was not a false reassurance. He could see that serving in a Siege Battery in the Royal Garrison Artillery meant he was less likely to be killed and wounded than in the infantry, and he regularly indicated to his wife how fortunate he was: 'The chance of survival in my branch of the services is very large.' He did reveal once, but only long after the event, that a bullet had passed between himself and another man walking feet in front of him.

Yet his own position at the guns, although it by no means assured safety, did make him aware of the responsibility he owed to soldiers in the trenches whose survival was more tenuous, infantrymen whose lives he could save or take by the correct or incorrect registration of the guns under his direction.

Mallory served in a number of roles within the battery but his favourite was as Forward Observation Officer, and he frequently made his way to the trenches, learning to live with the gruesome sights that he saw.

> The surroundings are indescribably desolate and dotted with small crosses. We haven't many dead in the trenches (at least only one decapitated unfortunate has so far been discovered below the surface) but those outside could well do with some loose earth over them and the general atmosphere of filth is an attraction to insects of every description – particularly to black beetles which swarm everywhere.

He spent hours observing the enemy, making notes before returning to the battery, and often exchanged duties with another officer to continue his work.

On 15 July, he wrote to Ruth:

> I rather enjoyed my three days at the OP. I could see nothing except in the early morning before dawn, when I saw an amazing sight – a long line of trenches apparently on fire and exploding with great flashes and clouds of sparks at intervals…
> The country over which we have been fighting so far is reduced to a state of complete desert, one would be surprised to meet with a tree that had leaves or even branches except a ragged remnant.

George Mallory was more suited to the demands of outdoor living than those officers who had lived sedentary office lives, and he acclimatised quickly, although the drudgery and repetition of much of his work often tested his patience. He also loved his own company and read as much as he could, including a collection of four Shakespeare plays, and books by George Eliot, Henry James and HG Wells. In his letters to Ruth he discussed literature, the progress of the war and religion. In August 1916, he began writing a novel, *The Book of Gregory*, which would explore aspects of life that interested him, including the purpose of education and morality. He believed that education was the only means by which civilization could be maintained and advanced.

He studied history at Cambridge University (where he knew Rupert Brooke) but he also had a deep interest in the rigours of mathematics. During his training he took to range finding with ease and enjoyed the complexities of the slide rule. He hated confusion and inexactitude.

> Nothing annoys me more than not to be efficient and yet I perceive a real opposition between what is casually meant by efficiency and the experience of thought as I understand it; it is no use any more pretending there is none.

By the very nature of his passion for climbing, he had to be precise, measured and accurate in everything he did. Lives were inextricably linked, mutual trust and interdependence vital to success, otherwise injury and even death would surely follow.

If the infantry kept the enemy from over-running the gun positions, the guns played just as important a role in protecting the infantry from attack, either by discouraging an assault in the first place or by quickly breaking one up when it began. Precision and loyalty: when target registration was inaccurate, a man like Mallory felt intense anxiety.

On 24 July 1916, he was in an observation post. A telephone wire had to be mended and enemy shelling was making life unpleasant. By mid-day, Mallory had a splitting headache from the noise and when in the afternoon he had the chance to sleep for half an hour, he grabbed the opportunity with relish. By 4.30pm he was back at work. The conditions for observation were difficult: smoke billowed across the battlefield as shells from other batteries exploded close to the position on which he was ranging. Nevertheless, he carried out what he believed was a successful registration of an enemy position, before returning to the battery for dinner and bed. He was exhausted.

> Before I went to sleep I heard distinctly from the murmur of voices in the tent some mention of our troops being shelled out of a trench by our own guns. [It was] my suspicion that this battery was accused of the mistake. I can't tell you what a miserable time I had after that. You see, if my registration had been untrue, it was my fault...I went over and over again in my mind all the circumstantial evidence that it was really our shells I had seen bursting and had horrid doubts and fears.

In the morning, he discovered that his battery could not have been responsible. Yet this was not the only time his accuracy was called into question: just six weeks later, he had to attend an inquiry by senior artillery officers into another case of mistaken registration. This time, several batteries were in the frame and it was up to each Forward Observation Officer to plead his innocence. It was, according to Mallory:

> A hateful business... hateful to feel the uncertainty and doubt which must be felt in the best conducted battery under the circumstances, hateful because every one was really there to save his own skin – or, to put it just a little higher, to save the credit of his battery – and hateful finally because it was such cold work waiting three hours before our evidence was taken.

Once again, Mallory's battery was exonerated.

To a driven man such as Mallory, inactivity was as bad as

inefficiency, though clearly not as bad as misdirected action.

29 October:
To-day has been so utterly disgusting that I have been quite demoralized – cold pitiless rain and by consequence no duties.

20 November:
The worst of these winter conditions is that the more vile they are, the less there is to do…I have been rather in a drifting state lately, and I can see I shall have to take life in hand. If only I could order my day so as to do fixed things at fixed times.

For a man so evidently thoughtful and intelligent, boredom was difficult to deal with.

I believe depression with me comes most often through a discontented attitude towards my activities. That is a great danger out here because nothing I am obliged to do seems, in a sense, worth doing; nothing calls into play more than a small fraction of my…what shall I say? My intellect? Rather I think myself.

The pressures on officers within the battery were often intense, relieved by occasional opportunities to leave the line and visit Amiens. This town, with its beautiful cathedral and shops, was beyond the risk of enemy shelling and a source of small luxuries for the battery mess. The officers themselves rubbed along together but personalities clashed and friendships in an all-male environment were frequently in a state of flux. Mallory had few close friends, with the exception of one officer, Lieutenant Osborne Bell, with whom he enjoyed long discussions and intellectual argument.

You say I don't mention the other officers [in the battery] much. That is natural because in the ordinary way I spend very little time with them. I don't like Bell any less well than I did – better if anything. The others I put up with quite well and with no sense of martyrdom – much better than they put up with each other. Wood is regarded as a freak by everybody and adds nothing to anybody's gaiety. Dunbar and Casey were at cross purposes the first time they met and haven't agreed about anything since. Bell and Casey, who were on rest together, were very good friends I thought but recently Bell reported that he disliked Casey for his coarseness and that Casey was fed up with him. Bell also talks of Lithgow [the CO] as being uncomfortable with him...He [Lithgow] is really a very difficult person to work under; he worries and fusses far too much.

It was clear that not all officers were as congenial as Osborne Bell, and once again Mallory's mountaineering experience helped. His method when dealing with other officers was 'to preserve an unruffled dignity which is above being hustled. I prefer to be polite, reassuring, imperturbable and cheerful'.

Mallory may not have dwelt in his letters on his passion for climbing, but the Western Front was still the great outdoors, 'great' especially in the summer, and he regularly refers to trees laden with fruit, and the plants and flowers that grew in and around the trenches and gun positions. He talks of the small animals and insects that frequented the dugouts or were shaken through the cracks in the wooden ceiling when a bombardment was under way, and the black beetles that swarmed around the dead.

Lice were an ever-present trial for men living in close proximity to each other, sleeping in barns out of the line or living for months outside in filthy conditions, with few opportunities to undress and attack the creatures that swarmed their way up and down the seams of shirts or nested their eggs in body hair. 'My dear, I do sincerely hope you won't get them, it would be too horrid for you,' wrote Ruth to her husband in mid-September. Too late.

But it was against vermin that Mallory happily led his own personal campaign. After a visit to the small town of Corbie, he returned newly-armed with traps to catch rats and mice, 'for personal use so to speak', and set about catching his prey.

> The two mice which were building a nest of paper which they used to tear noisily each night were victimised in the first hour, and there were two more victims, mere visitors I suspect, last night. Rats, happily, don't infest my dugout but as they swarm in the neighbourhood I thought it wise to guard the entrance. A more useful purpose, however, seemed to be served by lending it to the officers' cookhouse – six rats were caught in an hour – we shall have to dig a special grave for the numerous corpses.

George Mallory remained with the battery throughout the summer, autumn and into winter, and his highly articulate letters reflect his interest in everything around him. His descriptions could, at times, be almost poetic:

> It's now midday. I'm sitting in a nasty little hole where the telephonists do their work; one's head touches the roof almost, which is covered with flies. Outside, an occasional ammunition wagon drawn by three horses blocks out the light as it passes along the track, now a swamp, and I can see the humps of earth covering numerous dugouts and a few figures moving slowly around in the rain. Beyond, the ground slopes gently up to the grey sky; it is green with short grass and thistles but not green enough and sadly cut up by trenches, gun emplacements and shell holes.

On other occasions his descriptions are excited and picturesque as he watched events unfold from an observation post:

> In the afternoon I saw the infantry make an attack. It was

thrilling – irresistible – looking down the slope about 2,000 yards in front of me was Eaucourt L'Abbaye, a group of monastic buildings…When our bombardment began, this place was smothered with shellfire all along the line, there was an intense 'curtain' of shrapnel fire – more like an umbrella than a curtain. Our men passed out of a communication trench in three bodies one after the other and ran down the slope and then wheeled round and crossed in front of Eaucourt L'Abbaye. What amazed me was to see them stop when they caught up with the barrage like people sheltering from a storm and then when it lifted going forward again. …The whole scene was romantic – the sun was shining brightly and the white ruins of the abbey church showed up frequently through the smoke which was blowing across throwing queer dark shadows.

The date of this letter was 29 September, and the Somme autumn was well and truly setting in. Nights were appreciably colder. Rain and then snow would soon make the Somme a mud bath quite as bad as anything witnessed later at Passchendaele, according to many men who served at both. Mallory had always missed his wife but the longing to go back to England, away from the filth and turmoil, increased with each passing week. He could never predict when leave might come, but the prospect was held tantalisingly before him. His letters reflect his yearning for home and Ruth, and for a man so relatively inured to the extremes of weather, he appears increasingly tired and listless.

I'm sorry I wrote you such a gloomy little note yesterday. The war had the best of me with a vengeance…I suppose in common parlance I'm wanting leave and yet when I'm depressed even that vision is under a shadow.

The battery had been in France since the end of February, and Mallory only since early May, so he had to watch enviously as one officer after another returned to England. But with each departure, his leave came closer and in the end he was able to write to Ruth on 9 December:

> It looks as if I might be expected from ten days to three weeks before Christmas. I'm afraid you'll have to take me when you can get me – oh my darling, I do hope there'll be no delay this time. Good night, your loving George.

There was no delay. Lieutenant Mallory received his leave just over a week later and was home for Christmas.

George Mallory returned to France on 29 December reinvigorated and ready for the months ahead. Soon after he returned, he was transferred to brigade headquarters, three miles behind the line, where he was given the job of assisting a colonel who hated delegating work. Mallory was therefore free of all but menial tasks. He learnt to ride and went on long walks. In February, he was made a liaison officer to a French unit. When the Germans retreated from the Somme Battlefield at the end of the month, Mallory was able to walk across the desolate landscape and the sights filled him with 'unspeakable rage'. The enemy, as Mallory saw, had adopted a policy of scorched earth, laying waste to almost everything in their path, cutting down trees, blowing up houses and crossroads, polluting wells, destroying crops; all meant to slow the Allies' advance behind them.

At the end of March, he returned to his old battery, but an ankle injury had been bothering him since Christmas and by April the pain had become so bad that he found it difficult to walk. It was an old climbing injury and the fracture, which had not been set properly, was coming apart. In May, he returned to England for an operation. He remained in England far longer than he expected. In September, he was passed fit to return to France but was instead sent to Winchester to train on some new guns, and in the middle of that month his second daughter, Berry, was born.

As Mallory was waiting for his posting back to the Western Front, he borrowed a motorbike and, while riding too fast, came off and crushed his right boot against a gatepost. He was sidelined again until the end of the year, when, instead of returning to France, he was once more sent away to train, this time on a battery commander's course at Lydd. The army, it seemed, had all but forgotten him. He went climbing in Scotland and enjoyed family life until finally, in September 1918, he embarked for the Western Front and joined 515 Siege Battery RGA near Arras. His commanding officer was Major Gwilym Lloyd George, son of the Prime Minister. On the night before the Armistice, he was visiting a friend when they heard shouts that a ceasefire had been signed, but neither quite believed it until the morning when the fighting officially ceased. Nevertheless, it would be a further two months before Mallory could leave for Britain.

* * *

George Herbert Leigh Mallory was born on 18 June 1886 at Mobberley in Cheshire. He was the second of four siblings, the children of a clergyman, Revd Herbert Mallory. From an early age, George climbed anything and everything, including his father's church roof.

At the age of thirteen, he won a mathematics scholarship to Winchester College where he was later introduced to mountaineering by one of the masters, who annually took a group of boys to climb in the Alps. George, who was encouraged to climb as a corrective to a supposedly weak heart, had obvious natural talent and took to the sport.

Six years later, he went to Magdalene College, Cambridge, to read history. He excelled at sport – he had been an excellent gymnast at school – and he rowed in the college eight. He also became friends with members of the Bloomsbury Group, including the future economist John Maynard Keynes, and Lytton Strachey, the writer and critic.

After graduating and a brief sojourn in France, he returned to England to become a teacher at Charterhouse School, where he taught Robert Graves, encouraging his interest in poetry and literature and taking him climbing in Snowdonia during the vacations. Graves would later recall that Mallory never 'lost his almost foolhardy daring, yet he knew all there could be known about mountaineering technique.'

At school, Mallory was never a disciplinarian but chose instead to teach by example rather than fear, unlike the headmaster and many of his colleagues. Even some of the boys were perplexed. 'He [Mallory] was wasted at Charterhouse,' believed Graves. 'He tried to treat his class in a friendly way, which puzzled and offended them.'

While he worked as a teacher, Mallory met Ruth Turner at a dinner party; she was twenty-one and Mallory twenty-seven, and the attraction was immediate. At Easter, Ruth went to Italy on a family holiday, inviting Mallory to join them. After a whirlwind romance, they became engaged in May 1914 and they were married by George's father on 29 July 1914, just as the crisis in Europe was escalating dramatically.

On the outbreak of war, many of Mallory's friends, including Robert Graves, enlisted. Mallory's conscience troubled him greatly. At school he taught history, emphasising to the boys how international disputes could be solved by diplomacy and a shared morality; the outbreak of war threw into sharp relief the collapse of his world order. He blamed the war on Prussian rather than German militarism and argued that, if the former could be beaten, the real German spirit might still be set free.

In December 1914, Lord Kitchener, the Secretary of State for War, had instructed headmasters not to allow their staff to enlist if their absence would impair the school's capacity for learning; Mallory would need permission to join up. For much of the autumn, he and Ruth went climbing in the Lake District. He was uneasy; he hated the jingoism of the newspapers, but after Ruth began working at a war hospital, he started to visit wounded soldiers and listen to their stories.

Not only had many of Mallory's friends enlisted but, by 1915, they were also becoming casualties, among them Rupert Brooke. In June, news arrived that his own brother, Trafford, had been wounded at Ypres.

In September 1915, Ruth gave birth to Clare, and family life seemed idyllic. However, even Mallory's former pupils were now at the front and he resolved to enlist, finally receiving the necessary permission and joining the Royal Artillery. He began training at Weymouth in January 1916, and Ruth and the baby rented a cottage nearby so that he could return to his family at weekends. The following month, he was sent to the army's artillery school in Kent. Six weeks later, Second Lieutenant Mallory was off to France. He would remain in uniform for the best part of three years.

In January 1919, just prior to his return to Britain, Mallory wrote to his wife. 'The only possible jar to our happiness will be my personal ambition. You must be patient with me, my dearest one.'

Ruth had already been more than patient, but she enjoyed bringing up the two girls, Clare and Berry. In 1920 they would have a third child, John. Mallory returned to teaching at Charterhouse but he was also climbing again, reviving the group of friends who had mountaineered together before the war. Sadly, of the original sixty members, twenty-three had been killed and eleven more wounded.

In 1919, Mallory and his friends were again in the Alps, and after a short period of acclimatization, both physical and mental, Mallory was climbing as of old; his native ability had never deserted him and would lead inexorably to his greatest challenge, Everest.

In 1921, Mallory joined a reconnaissance expedition to Everest, charting several possible routes up the world's highest mountain. The following year he returned and was part of an attempt to reach the summit, but the group was forced back by bad weather after reaching a new world record altitude of just under 27,000 feet, a feat achieved without oxygen.

By the spring of 1924, Mallory was nearly thirty-eight and

reasonably believed that this would be his last opportunity to climb Everest. That June, two attempts to reach the summit failed before Mallory and a brilliant young climber, Andrew Irvine, made a third attempt. Using oxygen, they set off from the highest camp for the top on 8 June. Both climbers were reportedly seen through a telescope just above the Second Step, the final barrier to a successful ascent, but both were quickly lost in enveloping clouds. Neither was seen again. Once asked why he wished to climb Mount Everest, George Mallory simply replied 'Because it is there'. They remain the four most famous words in mountaineering history.

* * *

In 1975, a Chinese climber claimed to have seen the body of an English climber at 26,500 feet; it was believed at the time to be that of Irvine, but the story could not be verified as the climber was killed in an avalanche the following day. The sighting rekindled interest in finding the missing men. In 1999, a team of climbers finally discovered the body of George Mallory at 26,760 feet on the north face of the mountain. He was conclusively identified by a name tag sewn into his shirt. After his personal belongings were removed, an Anglican service was said over his body and his remains were buried. The camera, which Mallory was known to be carrying, was not found and so proof of whether he reached the top remains elusive.

Nevertheless, many believe that Mallory did reach the summit and died on the way down. Robert Graves, in his autobiography *Goodbye to All That*, wrote that 'anyone who has climbed with George is convinced that he got to the summit.' Clare, Mallory's daughter, also believed that he reached the summit, on the basis of a promise George had apparently made to his beloved wife Ruth, to leave a picture of her there. As no picture was found on Mallory's remains, Clare believes he kept his word.

CHAPTER THREE

Arnold Ridley

—⁄⁄⁄—

As it went, it wasn't a question of 'if I get killed', it was merely a question of 'when I get killed', because a battalion went over 800 strong, you lost 300 or 400, half the number, perhaps more. Now it wasn't a question of saying, 'I am one of the survivors, hurrah, hurrah', because you didn't go home... Out came another draft of 400 and you went over the top again.

Arnold Ridley, interviewed 1971

HE WAS UNASSUMING, mild-mannered and placid. He was a man beset with minor medical problems, chiefly a weak bladder for which he regularly needed 'to be excused'. He lived at Cherry Tree Cottage with his geriatric sisters Cissy and Dolly for whom he would bring back a bag of sprouts after a day patrolling the cliffs at Walmington on Sea. As a member of the Home Guard, he led the defence of Britain against the Nazi peril before returning home to his sisters and his hobby of beekeeping.

In the fictional programme, he had been a conscientious objector during the Great War but had volunteered to serve as a stretcher bearer. During the Battle of the Somme in 1916, he had helped save the wounded from under the enemy's nose, a daring task for which he was awarded the Military Medal, and a photograph of him wearing the award hung above his bed. He was Private Charles Godfrey, real name Arnold Ridley, and he was one of *Dad's Army's* front rank and one of the television series' immortal characters.

Fact was somewhat different from fiction, something that would not have been lost on the actor and erstwhile soldier. Ridley had indeed served on the Somme in 1916, and he was extremely brave, but, on the face of it, these were the only parallels between his actual life and that of his alter ego. Arnold Ridley was an infantryman and a marksman with a rifle. Wounded three times on the Somme, he was eventually clubbed over the head by a German rifle butt when bombing his way down an enemy trench, and bayoneted. Seriously injured, he was discharged from the army as medically unfit and returned to civilian life an angry man, who chose to shun many of the people he knew. 'I was a very, very bitter young man, I'm afraid…a very, very, very bitter young man indeed,' he recalled during an interview at the height of his television fame. Hardly the Arnold Ridley – or Charles Godfrey – who is loved and remembered by both young and old.

On the morning of 16 September 1916, the 6th Bn Somerset Light Infantry was in trenches east of the village of Flers, preparing to make an attack on the enemy trenches just 200 yards away. It was their turn to take part in the next stage of the Somme Battle that had already lasted two and a half months. Not that the battalion was a stranger to the fighting. The men had gone over the top the previous month at Delville Wood, Devil's Wood to the rank and file, such was its infamous reputation. There, they suffered nearly 50% casualties, leaving only a lucky rump of the original battalion. Lance Corporal Arnold Ridley was not one of those 'originals' but he had gone into the action and was one of those fortunate enough to have come out unscathed.

Just a month later, the battalion was back, close to where it had fought before. The front line had advanced little in the previous four weeks but that was about to change. On 15 September, a new stage of the Somme Battle would begin and the men from Somerset would be in close support. The 14th (Light) Division, to which it belonged, was about to play its part in breaking the main German defensive line in front of the village of Flers.

In the event, the fighting was hard but also of historic significance. For the first time in military history, the infantry had been accompanied by a new invention, the tank. These new weapons of war were few in number and prone to malfunction and break down. Nevertheless, their presence on the battlefield stunned the enemy and helped win the day for the Allies. Flers, a small, insignificant village, had fallen, and it became a household name to every Briton, for one tank was reported being seen to drive right up the main street with cheering soldiers close behind. In a wider battle that cost so many lives for so little territorial gain, this reported episode was the raw material that newspapers loved, and the press were whole hearted in their praise of the tank and of Tommy, who had so successfully given the Germans a bloody nose. Ridley recalled the occasion:

> We in the ranks had never heard of tanks. We were told that there was some sort of secret weapon and [then] we saw this thing go up the right hand corner of Delville Wood. I saw this strange and cumbersome machine emerge from the shattered shrubbery and proceed slowly down the slope towards Flers.

It was an amazing spectacle, but the war was not about to stop while they took stock. That night, the 6th Bn Somerset Light Infantry were ordered forward to take up positions in ground just won east of Flers and to the south of another village, Gueudecourt. It was 4am by the time the battalion reached the front line and the men were exhausted. Straightaway, sentries were posted, one of whom was Lance Corporal Arnold Ridley.

> If you've ever tried to keep awake when you haven't had any sleep for days, it's not a question of allowing yourself to go to sleep. I can remember lying in a sunken road behind Gueudecourt. The trenches were full of water and I can remember getting out of the trench and lying on the parapet

with the bullets flying around because sleep was such a necessity and death only meant sleep.

The men were not only tired but hungry, too. Rations for four companies failed to materialise at the allotted time and when they did eventually turn up, there was only enough for two companies; the rest of the men would have to make do with their iron rations, the emergency supply all men carried and ate only when specifically ordered to do so. Water was also scarce, even more scarce than the food, as the battalion diary noted. The situation was hardly encouraging for the Commanding Officer, Lieutenant Colonel Thomas Ritchie, was well aware that his men were due to go over the top in a matter of hours. He was only awaiting final orders.

The usual procedure, whenever a battalion was ordered to make an attack, was to reconnoitre the ground in front to make sure that the men knew as much as possible about the terrain they were about to cross. However, the arrival of dawn at around 5.30am precluded any attempt to enter No Man's Land. The Somerset Light Infantry simply had no time to undertake such reconnaissance and this omission was to prove very costly.

At 4.30am, Lieutenant Colonel Ritchie had received his final orders to make an attack towards two lines of German defences known as Gird and Gird Support Trenches. Zero hour would be at 9.25am, in full daylight. There was a problem. Running at right angles to the objective was an unfinished enemy trench. Ritchie was unaware of its existence, as it was not marked on his maps and remained concealed on top of a low rise in the ground.

The attack would consist of two waves from A, B and C Companies, with D Company in close support. The orders were that once the first objective, Gird Trench, was reached, the men were to sweep forward to Gird Support. Each company was to leave one bombing squad in Gird Trench to clear the line of any remaining Germans. Operational orders stated that each squad would be made up of two 'bombers' who would throw grenades down dugouts, and two bayonet men under the command of a junior NCO. Six infantrymen would also be left behind to help in the process.

At zero hour the attack went in under the cover of a short artillery barrage.

> We were told that there was a pocket [of resistance] left over and that two advances had left this pocket and we were told that we would attack. We would get a five minute barrage, which we got, but Jerry and the German machine guns were firing, saying 'we know you are coming over, come on, where are you?' Although the plans had gone wrong, the whistles blew and we went over the top just the same. At that time I was a bomber and we got down to the first trench.

This was not the intended Gird Trench but the unfinished trench, nevertheless occupied by the enemy who put up a withering fire as the Somerset Light Infantry advanced.

> I went round one of the traverses, as far as I remember, and somebody hit me on the head with a rifle butt. I was wearing a tin hat, fortunately, but it didn't do me much good. A chap came at me with a bayonet, aiming for a very critical part naturally and I managed to push it down, I got a bayonet wound in the groin. After that I was still very dizzy, from this blow on the head presumably. I remember wrestling with another German and the next thing I saw, it appeared to me that my left hand had gone. After that, I was unconscious.

A German's saw bayonet had cut deeply into his left hand, cutting or damaging the tendons to his fingers and rendering them weak for the rest of his life.

Six Germans were taken prisoner in the unfinished trench while

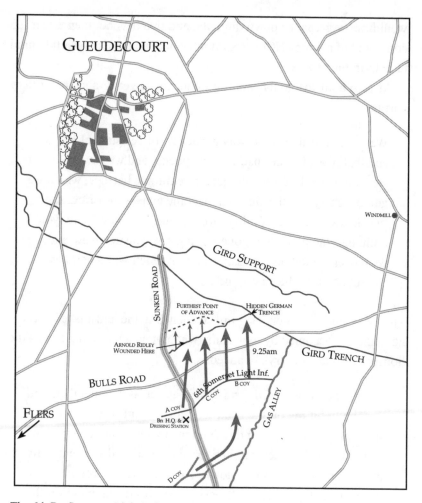

The 6th Bn Somerset Light Infantry's unsuccesful assault on Gird Support and Gird trenches, 16 September 1916.

another hundred or so were seen to run away. Believing they were in Grid Trench, the Somerset Light Infantry dug in, despite their original orders to advance further. Confusion then began. Within half an hour, runners were reporting back that B Company was being bombed from a trench to their right, Gird Trench, the original objective and now heavily defended. D Company was sent forward to support those in the unfinished trench but they too were unable to advance any further. Almost the entire battalion was now stuck in an untenable position. One company advanced fruitlessly a further fifty yards and dug in, only to be assailed by machine gun fire from the village of Gueudecourt and Grid Trench. There was deadlock.

By mid afternoon, Lieutenant Colonel Ritchie was informed that a neighbouring attack would be launched at 4pm and that he should help if at all possible, but Ritchie refused and maintained his position. At around 6.20pm, he received orders to attack once again at 6.55pm, supported by two companies of the 6th Bn King's Own Yorkshire Light Infantry [KOYLI] who would relieve his men who were stuck in the unfinished German trench. This gave him just 35 minutes to prepare. As a consequence, there was simply no time for runners to inform the men of the decision to advance and when the KOYLIs attacked at the specified time, they found the Somerset Light Infantry still in possession of the trench. As there was no room, the KOYLIs were forced to lie down behind the trench and were raked by machine gun fire for their efforts. When the Somerset Light Infantry did belatedly attack, they could make no headway against steadfast enemy fire and took to shell holes.

Back in the unfinished trench, Arnold Ridley came to. 'I was injured between my left thumb and finger. I remember thinking, "I'm all right now, I'm out of it."' Stuck out in No Man's Land, two hundred yards from the original front line trench, was hardly out of it and he would be trapped there under shell and machine gun fire for many hours to come.

> I always remember my disappointment the next morning when I found that my hand was still on because I thought, well, if I lost my hand I'm all right, I shall live, they can't send me out without a hand again. I was 20 then, it's not altogether a right thought for a young man to hope that he's been maimed for life.

The battle had been an unmitigated disaster, not only for the Somerset Light Infantry but for the entire Division. Every officer in the battalion that had taken part in the attack was killed or wounded, a casualty rate that made Ritchie comment that they had perhaps been singled out for special attention by snipers and machine gunners. There was no option for him but to withdraw any surviving men still lying in shell holes to the unfinished trench and hold the ground until early the following morning, when they could be relieved. His losses were 17 officers and 383 other ranks, not far short of two-thirds of those who took part in the fighting that day.

Arnold Ridley lay in the unfinished trench until darkness fell. Stretcher bearers were then able to work at finding and removing the men. At least Arnold was in a position now well known to all concerned. Those stuck out in shell holes forward of him had far less chance of being found. While waiting to be evacuated, he slipped in and out of consciousness, being fed and given water from the packs and bottles removed from the many dead around him. He would later recall:

> I'm all very hazy about this time because I didn't realise that I had a fractured skull, and that doesn't improve your memory. I eventually got back to Delville Wood, behind which was a dressing station.

The stretcher bearers worked incredibly hard and the remnants of the battalion only just managed to get clear of the unfinished trench and the crest of the hill by daybreak when they were relieved by the 13th Bn Northumberland Fusiliers. Arnold was patched up and taken to a dressing station at Ailly-sur-Somme. 'I was very lucky. I got mixed up with these Canadians and I was taken to a Canadian Hospital where I had the first of seven operations on my hand.' The wounds were treated although the fractured skull went undiagnosed for a further two years.

Arnold Ridley would never return to the front. In less than six months he had gone over the top twice and been wounded three times. His survival had been more than a little fortunate.

* * *

The outbreak of the Great War came at just the right time for school teacher Arnold Ridley, as he was to recall in his unpublished memoirs written in the late 1970s.

> In July 1914 when on loan to a Bristol elementary school for teaching practice, I succeeded in imperilling my scholastic career. A particularly irritating little headmaster so aroused my hot temper by doubting my word of honour and wagging a finger under my nose that I seized him by his scruff and seat and pitched him gaily out of the open window into his own playground, fortunately onto a part heavily grassed. Although I reported myself immediately to my university teacher who was sympathetic as to the provocation, I hate to think what might otherwise have resulted had not the declaration of war thrown life in general into a melting pot.

With the outbreak of war, Arnold Ridley sought to enlist first into the Royal Marines then into the 4th Bn Somerset Light Infantry, a territorial battalion, but was rejected on medical grounds. He had broken a toe playing rugby, and it had been badly set. At that date, recruiting offices were swamped with eager volunteers, and recruiting sergeants could afford to be fussy with those they took.

Arnold later admitted that he was not particularly patriotic but tried to enlist simply because his friends were going.

> The odd thing was that they all went out on garrison duty to India [with the 4th Battalion] and I didn't think any of them

fired a shot in the whole war and I was rejected medically unfit and ended up on the Western Front.

A year later, on 8 December 1915, he volunteered again, this time being accepted without difficulty. Belying his later image on television, he soon discovered that he was not only a good shot but a marksman, for which he was awarded the badge of crossed rifles, denoting his expertise.

There was a frightening amount of sadism. You would be lined up and they would say, 'I'll tell you lot o' perishers somethink! We sent out a draft of an 'undred from 'ere last week. Where are they now? I'll tell yer – all blinkin' dead! So don't get it into yer 'eads you're ever a-going to see your mothers again!' and that sort of thing. It wasn't very cheerful for a young man who had left home for the first time. I thought I was doing my duty for my country. I didn't know I was going to be treated like a convict. Did it make better soldiers of the callow youths we were then? I doubt it.

No. 20481 Lance Corporal Arnold Ridley embarked in heavy, sleeting weather for France around the middle of March 1916. As soon as he landed, he removed his marksman's badge because he did not want to be made a sniper. 'I didn't go to France to murder people,' he later recalled. He quickly joined his battalion in the field just south of Arras. He had been with his regiment only two or three days when he was wounded for the first time. It was a slight wound in the back from shrapnel, but serious enough to see his evacuation down the line to a base hospital at Etaples where he was treated and sent back. He had no sooner rejoined his regiment when he suffered a flesh wound in the thigh. Once again he was evacuated, all the way back to England.

It was the end of May before he had recovered sufficiently to return to his regiment's 3rd Battalion based at Devonport, near Plymouth. One evening, after he had been given a leave pass, he found himself walking up Union Street in Plymouth. The news had just broken that the naval Battle of Jutland had been fought. It seemed that even at home he could not escape the terrible and immediate effects of war, as he recalled.

> Not only did the first reports suggest a major defeat but most of the sunken ships were Devonport-commissioned. Union Street seemed full of women – some hysterical, some crying quietly and others, grey-faced with staring unseeing eyes and leading small children by the hand. They had no illusions, these women – they knew only too well that, when large ships were sunk in battle in the North Sea, there could be but few survivors.

During his time with the regiment, Ridley briefly became batman to a Lieutenant Edward MacBryan, brother of a famous amateur cricketer, who was due to be sent back to France to the Regiment's 1st Battalion and left soon afterwards. Arnold heard that he had been killed on the first day of the Battle of the Somme, just a week or two before his own embarkation for the Western Front. He must have been relieved to hear that his Division was not immediately earmarked for the battle. In fact it remained near Arras during July, making its way south to the town of Albert, just to the rear of the Somme battlefield, only on 7 August.

Eleven days later, the 14th (Light) Division with the 6th Bn Somerset Light Infantry was pitched into the fighting, Arnold going over the top on 18 August. 'I fought all the way through Delville Wood,' he later remarked, recalling that even before they set off for the attack, much of the preliminary British barrage had accidentally dropped on them and not on the enemy. Fifteen men were killed or injured.

The concept that surviving an attack was not the end but only a hiatus between actions was hard to accept, and seemed to come as a shock to many men once the enormous adrenalin rush of going over the top finally dissipated. Arnold Ridley came to accept that he would carry on until death; even injury appeared to be discounted. It was an individual prognosis that nevertheless appeared to define much of the generation of men who fought in that war.

As it went, it wasn't a question of 'if I get killed', it was merely a question of 'when I get killed', because a battalion went over 800 strong, you lost 300 or 400, half the number, perhaps more. Now it wasn't a question of saying, 'I am one of the survivors, hurrah, hurrah', because you didn't go home....Out came another draft of 400 and you went over the top again.

[There was] an awful feeling of a great black cloud on top of one the whole time, there seemed to be no future...I think one lost one's sensitivity. You lived like a worm and your horizon was very limited to 'shall I get back in time for the parcel to come? Shall I ever get back to eat that cake that I know mother has sent me?' You certainly lived one day at a time. I didn't dare think of tomorrow.....It was general abject misery. I think your imagination became dulled. I think in the end you just became a thing.

After he was wounded, he returned to England, arriving at Southampton, the port from which he had first left. He was in a bad way, especially as the wound in his hand had turned septic. He was sent to Woodcote Park Military Hospital, Epsom, where he recovered once again, only this time he was marked as unfit for further military service.

I returned to my depot for what had been termed final adjustment of discharge. All had seemed set fair when I was ordered to appear before a TMB [Travelling Medical Board] and after being kept stark naked for over an hour in a very well ventilated stone corridor on a bitter January morning I found myself in the presence of an excessively corpulent surgeon general. 'Well, what's the matter with you?' he demanded, anxious to get the matter settled with all speed. I held out my shattered left hand which was the most obvious of my injuries. He took it and twisted it in an agonising grip. 'How did you get this?' he demanded. 'Jack knife?' Probably this was only meant as a heavy joke but I was still suffering from shell shock, blue with cold and in considerable pain. 'Yes, sir,' I replied. 'My battalion is famous for self-inflicted wounds and just to make sure I cracked my skull with a rifle butt as well and ran a bayonet into my groin.'

The General's normally ruddy countenance changed to a deep shade of purple. He gave my hand a twist in the opposite direction. 'Treatment at Command Depot,' he barked, so instead of returning to civilian life, I was granted a further experience of military matters at No 2 Command Depot, County Cork.

Arnold would remain in Ireland for the best part of six months until he was eventually sent home to England in April 1917. On 10 May, he was transferred to the Army Reserve and was finally discharged on 27 August.

My pension was thirteen [shillings] and nine [pence] a week. But for my father and mother, I don't know what I should have done. I was in considerable pain because there was a nerve injury in my hand. I was in very bad physical health, I had lost weight terribly and I had been sent out to a command depot in Ireland where I had been for the winter. I had the feeling that they were trying to kill us off to save our pensions.

* * *

William Arnold Ridley was born on 7 January 1896 in Bath, the only child of William Robert and Rosa Ridley. The family owned a boot shop above which they all lived. His parents were nonconformists and his mother was a Sunday school teacher. Arnold's father was also a superb athlete who, in his spare time, taught boxing, fencing and gymnastics.

Arnold inherited his father's love of sports, although, as he said deprecatingly, he had also inherited his mother's total lack of ability to play them. This was not entirely true. When he was aged twelve, he joined the Bath (Rugby) Football Club and played a number of junior games, much later becoming president and a lifelong member of the club.

He was educated in Bath and was in his second year at Bristol University when the war broke out, interrupting his studies to become a schoolmaster. He had also developed an interest in acting and made his first professional appearance in a play called *Prunella* at the Theatre Royal, Bristol in 1913.

Five years later, Arnold had been utterly changed. From the young, healthy sports-loving boy, he had become a broken man. In his memoirs, he recalled in detail the terrible difficulties faced by an individual deeply traumatised by the war who was left to get on with his life:

> All my old friends were either dead or still in the services and I refused to make new ones, preferring to wander alone through the street and gardens of Bath in a state of Stygian gloom. Quite suddenly, self-preservation came to my rescue. I realised that unless I made a supreme effort to pull myself together, I stood a fair chance of being put quietly away in some convenient mental hospital. I had to do something about it and quickly too.

After a brief flirtation with the idea of teaching once more, Arnold returned to the stage at the Repertory Theatre, Birmingham. As a young actor, Arnold had been a leading light of the Bristol University Dramatic Society where he had met Sir Frank Benson. Sir Frank had admired the young actor and in 1917 he advised Arnold to try acting again.

By April 1919 *The Bath Chronicle* was trumpeting the success of one of their local boys on the front page of the newspaper:

> Mr Arnold Ridley, the only son of Mr and Mrs W R Ridley, of Manvers Street, Bath, we are pleased to hear is making gratifying progress in the histrionic art. This clever young actor's success is all the more pleasing as he suffers a considerable handicap by a wound received in the Somme fighting of 1916. As a lance corporal in the 6th Somersets he had a deadly hand-to-hand encounter with a German near Delville Wood, and the Hun bayonet pierced his left hand cutting a sinew, with the consequence that Mr Ridley's forearm is practically useless. But this defect he artistically camouflages in his stage make-up.

Arnold appeared in over forty productions in three years, but his health, both physically and mentally, deteriorated badly and he walked away from acting, returning home to work in his father's boot shop. It was while he was selling quality seconds to the people of Bath that Arnold turned his hand to writing plays. He would write over thirty in all, but it was his second, written in 1923, which brought him almost overnight recognition and also the greatest acclaim. The play, his first to be produced, was a comedy thriller called *The Ghost Train,* which had considerable success not only in the West End but across the world, being made into a film three times for both big and small screens and in time being translated into seventeen languages.

In the 1920s, and despite the turmoil in his life, Arnold married, but the marriage did not last and they parted without any children. In the 1930s he married again, but once more the relationship failed and they separated. Both divorces were amicable, and it says much about Arnold's character that he stayed on very good terms with both former wives. He continued to write in the 1930s and even set up his own film company, which, through no fault of his own, ran into financial difficulties and ceased production midway through its second feature. At about the same time, Arnold's father died. They had been exceptionally close, and once again Arnold sank into despair and took to whiskey, becoming a virtual alcoholic.

When war broke out again in 1939, he surprisingly returned to the army, joining the British Expeditionary Force in France, where he served as an intelligence officer until the evacuation of the BEF in the summer of 1940.

According to Nicolas Ridley, Arnold's son by his third marriage, 'His experiences in the Second World War were as bad and possibly worse than the First. We have no inkling of what happened because it was too appalling for words; there was nothing he could hint at. He shouldn't have been there; he had volunteered even though over age. However, his second marriage had broken up and he was in a bad way, and I think it was just an escape.'

In his memoirs, Arnold explained the reasons for his silence. He had set down very little about his Great War experiences, believing he could add little that others had not already written, but he chose to keep his silence about the Second World War for very different reasons:

> I shall write even less about my days with the BEF in France in the early months of World War Two but I have a very different reason: fear. Within hours of setting foot on the quay at Cherbourg in September 1939, I was suffering from acute shell shock again. It is quite possible that outwardly I showed little, if any, of it. It took the form of mental suffering that at best could be described as an inverted nightmare.

Back in Britain and demobilised from the army, he briefly joined the Local Defence Volunteers, the fore-runners of the Home Guard.

Discharged once again, he returned to writing and directing. In 1944, while he was at his cottage in Caterham, it was hit by a doodlebug. He woke up hours later and thought he was more or less all right, recalls his son. Except for bruised ribs, he appeared uninjured. However, shortly afterwards a delayed reaction caught him unawares. During a play rehearsal, he suddenly froze and could not speak or move and soon afterwards, he also began to suffer from blackouts. Arnold was fortunate. He met his third wife Althea, an actress, to whom he had been introduced during an ENSA tour of *The Ghost Train*. She would see him through his blackouts and private difficulties. They married and set up home in 1946. Arnold was already fifty years old, Althea being some fifteen years his junior. In 1947 their only son Nicolas was born.

The 1950s were a perennial financial struggle for Arnold, trying to keep his young family together, and the bailiffs were never far from the door. Plays such as his were seen as unfashionable, and the royalties dried up. Television was growing rapidly as the new and exciting medium in which to work. In the early 1960s, he took the part of Doughy Hood the baker in *The Archers*, later played a vicar in *Crossroads*, and also had two parts in *Coronation Street*. In 1973, he also appeared in *Carry on Girls* as the feeble Alderman Pratt. In 1971, aged seventy-five, he appeared in a production of *The Ghost Train* at Guildford. But it was his role in *Dad's Army* for which he is best remembered. He played Charles Godfrey between 1968 and 1977.

Curiously, whether by coincidence or design, Godfrey's character in some ways seemed to mirror Arnold's own. Arnold's mother had disapproved of his desire to become an actor and had always believed that he should have joined the Civil Service. In addition to this, given his love of sports and his father's career, it is interesting to note that Godfrey in *Dad's Army*, had served for thirty-five years in the Civil Service Stores in the sports department. He was also keen on amateur dramatics. In the series he is a bachelor, whose idyllic house is nevertheless quite isolated from the rest of the community. In one episode, he admits that he only realised his phone was cut off after two weeks, as hardly anybody ever phoned. He hates loud noises, which bring on headaches. In real life, although Arnold married three times, he had nevertheless, and for many years after the war, isolated himself from others. The rifle butt that fractured his skull also gave him headaches for the rest of his life.

In *Dad's Army*, Godfrey was a conscientious objector in the Great War. Fifty years after the war, Arnold Ridley expressed his respect for Siegfried Sassoon, who had made an outspoken statement against the continuation of the war, and for those who had refused to serve for reasons of conscience.

> I knew one man who was very badly treated as a Conscientious Objector because he wouldn't submit to a medical examination. Had he submitted, he would have been grade 99 and they would never have had him. He was half-blind and weedy but he just wouldn't on principle.

In the Great War, the fictional Godfrey had agreed to serve but only to save life with the Royal Army Medical Corps. Men who refused to serve commonly received the scorn of the general public and all too frequently a white feather, a mark of cowardice. Arnold Ridley returned from the war to civilian life and civilian clothes, and recalled receiving a white feather after all his courage and his wounds. He took it without comment. When asked why he, a returning soldier, should receive a white feather, he answered, 'I wasn't wearing my soldier's discharge badge. I didn't want to advertise the fact that I was a wounded soldier and I used to carry it in my pocket.' How very Godfrey. The unassuming nature of his *Dad's Army* character had its soul in Arnold Ridley.

Arnold Ridley received an OBE in 1982. He died on 12 March 1984, leaving his wife Althea, who died in 2001, and his son, Nicolas.

There has been some confusion over the years as to whether Arnold

Ridley won the Military Medal or not. In an episode of *Dad's Army*, a picture of Charles Godfrey wearing the MM is seen, but the actor himself never received one. He was, according to conversations between Arnold and his son Nicolas, recommended for the Distinguished Conduct Medal.

'A horrible irony is that my father was not the sort of man who was out for official recognition, yet all he had ever wanted was the Military Medal. He told me that when he came back from No Man's Land after an attack on the Somme, he was standing around with four or five other boys when an officer spoke to them. He said he was going to put them all up for the MM except for my father who, because he had a lance corporal stripe on, he would put up for the Distinguished Conduct Medal. All the other men got their MMs but he didn't get the DCM, and that did embitter him a little bit. It is exactly the sort of thing he would not have normally cared about, but I think he felt it was a badge of comradeship. When he was awarded an OBE for playing a small comedy part in a television series, I felt it was a poor reward for someone who had served in two world wars.'

CHAPTER FOUR

Ralph Vaughan Williams

—⚎—

It was no disrespect to our officers when he [Ralph Vaughan Williams] said goodbye to them using the words, and standing stiffly to attention: "My regret at leaving is that I shall cease to be a man and become an officer", a last jab at the military term 'officers and men.'

Private Harry Steggles,
lifelong friend of Ralph Vaughan Williams

RALPH VAUGHAN WILLIAMS was probably too set in his ways ever to make the transition from untidy visionary musician to smart professional soldier. He was certainly never graced with anything like military bearing or poise. Nevertheless, his service record remained unblemished except, that is, for an admonishment and two pence fine in October 1916 for neglecting to wear his cap badge. It was a minor offence but one which was gently symbolic of his four-year service in the army. The military authorities would no doubt have preferred a more professional soldier, but they did at least permit his rise from private to subaltern, although higher rank was always unlikely. When finally considered for further promotion, Vaughan Williams was turned down on the grounds that he was simply too unkempt.

Major Stanley Smith, Vaughan Williams' erstwhile Commanding Officer, described the problem as follow:

I beg to state that this officer was attached to the Battery under my command from February to August 1918. During this period

I found him a most reliable and energetic officer. His age, however, is very much against him, and therefore he is not as smart as might be expected. I also particularly noticed he was most untidy in his ways and dress. I cannot say that I can recommend him for promotion to higher rank.

Major Smith was not the only one to be aware of the composer's appearance. Over a year earlier, a fellow officer cadet had written that Vaughan Williams was 'not one to whom the proper arrangement of straps and buckles and all those things on which the sergeant major is so keen, came easily.' Throughout his life, people commented on his disregard of his appearance and clothes.

Vaughan Williams was always unconventional. Once on the battlefield, when he was ill, he continued to direct his section while lying flat on the ground and had to be ordered to rest, but then this composer, one of the greatest Britain has ever produced, was, by definition, not going to be run of the mill. Perhaps his attitude is best summed up by a friend, who wrote:

He was simply himself. He knew his own worth, but for other people's valuation of it, or for official recognition or worldly success, he couldn't have cared less.

When he was finally demobilised in 1919, he left the army an unusual legacy of nine choral societies, three musical classes, an orchestra and a band. The army had had an exceptional man in their midst, just not an exceptional soldier.

For a start, he need not have been in the army at all. By the time he was commissioned he was 45 years old, having served as a private in both France and Salonika. His untidiness was already well known; as a fellow officer cadet remembered, he needed help to get his equipment on correctly even for parades. Nevertheless, he left for France once more, newly commissioned, on 1 March 1918, and was almost at once part of the retreat in the face of the massive German advance of that spring. As he wrote to his friend and fellow composer Gustav Holst:

> The war has brought me some strange jobs – can you imagine me in charge of 200 horses! That's my job at present – I was dumped down on to it straight away, and before I had time to find out which were horses and which were wagons I found myself in the middle of a retreat…only one horse was killed so we were lucky.

Vaughan Williams had joined 86 Brigade of the Royal Garrison Artillery near Ecoivres, where he had been stationed with the 2/4th (London) Field Ambulance in 1916, and it was in August, when the fortunes of the Allies changed and the German army began to fall back, that his batman noted his officer's dedication to his job; they were following up retreating Germans and were in action in the open:

> Ralph was suffering from a temporary indisposition and feeling so ill that he could not stand, and so he was directing his section while lying on the ground. The OC Battery came along past where I was standing, about fifty yards behind the guns, took in the situation at a glance, turned to me and said, "Moore! Tell Mr Williams he is to go to bed." "Yes, sir. Mr Williams, sir, the OC says you are to go to bed."

It is easy to see why Vaughan Williams was a popular officer. His batman went on to say that when he himself had been ill, his Second Lieutenant had shown him great kindness. 'I think Lieut. Vaughan Williams had the respect of the whole battery,' he later wrote:

> In wartime, and with heavy guns, powerful horses and all the work of dealing with the equipment necessary to the Battery,

tempers can easily get frayed; with him this rarely happened.

In December 1918, Vaughan Williams wrote to his friend Holst that he was:

> slowly trekking towards Germany, not a job I relish, either the journey or its object…we usually march about 10km a day and rest every fourth day…then usually two or three wagons stick fast in the mud on the first start off and worry and delay ensues.

But the Armistice eventually brought a more restful and happy period: he was made Director of Music, First Army, as part of the authorities' desire to give the men recreation and educational opportunities before they were demobbed. He had always encouraged musical activity and during his time in France frequently organised concerts for the troops, even though a fellow officer recorded that:

> I saw him once or twice, drooping despondently over the keyboard of a ghastly wreck of a piano while drivers sang sentimental songs, execrably as a rule, to his accompaniment.

* * *

Ralph Vaughan Williams was born in 1872 in Down Ampney, Gloucestershire, where his father was the Rector. He was only three years old when his father died, and he was taken by his mother to live with her family on the North Downs. The family was intellectual and well to do (he was a direct descendant of the great pottery manufacturer Josiah Wedgwood, and Charles Darwin was his great-uncle), but Vaughan Williams himself believed strongly all his life in equality and made good friendships across the social divides which were so dominant in his lifetime.

He composed his first work at the age of six, and learnt the piano, organ and violin as a child. He went to Charterhouse School, where some of his work was performed and his Maths teacher said, 'Very good, Williams, you must go on,' which, the composer said later, was one of the few words of encouragement he ever received in his life. The Royal College of Music followed; he then read History and Music at Trinity College, Cambridge, before returning to the RCM to study composition. While at University, he made a close friend of his fellow composer, George Butterworth, and together they travelled round the British countryside collecting folk songs. Butterworth began a career in music but joined up at the outbreak of war. He was awarded the Military Cross during the Battle of the Somme, but was killed by a sniper; his body was never found and he is remembered on the Thiepval Memorial. His death deeply affected Vaughan Williams, who, with many others, saw it as a great loss to British music.

Another fellow student who was to influence him was Gustav Holst. Born 'von Holst', although of Swedish rather than German extraction, he dropped the 'von' in response to anti-German feeling early in the War. They corresponded while Vaughan Williams was on active service and remained lifelong friends, sharing an interest in the English choral tradition.

Vaughan Williams' musical development was slow, and he was thirty before he had his first work published, but time was well spent in Paris studying with the great French composer Maurice Ravel, who himself subsequently spent two years as a driver with the French artillery before his generally poor health deteriorated further from frostbite.

Between 1904 and 1906, Vaughan Williams collaborated with Percy Dearmer to edit *The English Hymnal*, contributing some well-known hymn tunes including one of the most famous, named after his birthplace, *Down Ampney*. In 1910, he had his first public successes, conducting the first performances of *A Sea Symphony* and *A London Symphony*.

He was over forty when war broke out, and could easily have avoided war service, but he enlisted as a private in the Royal Army

Medical Corps, signing up for four years or for duration of the war at the Duke of York's HQ in Chelsea. It is not clear why he chose the RAMC, but he may have been influenced by his age and by the fact that many older men volunteered to serve as medical orderlies. Initially, he lived at home, but in January 1915 he moved to Dorking for intensive training: squad drill, stretcher drill (which he particularly hated), first aid, kit inspections, and a march of fifteen miles a day. For Vaughan Williams, typically, the hardest part of the training was putting his puttees on straight and wearing his cap at the correct angle.

During his training, he became friends with Harry Steggles, with whom he was to serve in Greece as well as in France. Harry played the mouth organ, and they were fortunate enough to be billeted on a family that asked specifically for soldiers who were interested in music. They welcomed 'Mr Williams', as he introduced himself; it was some time before they learnt from other soldiers that he was in fact Dr Ralph Vaughan Williams, of whom they would certainly have heard. They had happy musical evenings together: Harry, accompanied by his friend, sang *When father papered the parlour*, a popular song of the day, which they subsequently performed together in France at Divisional Concerts and at reunions. His landlady also played the piano, and sometimes her illustrious visitor would come in quietly, wearing his carpet slippers, and listen or help her with her harmony. She was having lessons from the local church organist, and 'Dr VW' would play the organ for church parades. (In 1950, this lady went to a concert of his music in the Albert Hall; typically, he remembered her and asked after all the family.)

The training at Dorking was interrupted by a visit from the Secretary of State for War, Lord Kitchener. Ralph Vaughan Williams, with the rest of the unit, was warned that they would be part of a large gathering of regiments and that they should parade very early. The unit diarist wrote:

We shall never forget that inspection. We paraded at 4am in

pitch darkness, bitterly cold, and having our greatcoats on and boot brushes in our haversack to clean up with prior to the inspection. We marched and marched until we arrived at the parade venue, in Epsom Common. It was snowing slowly at first, but gathered strength so that in a few hours the troops were covered by a thick layer of snow which lay inches high on their caps and shoulders. The inspection actually took place at about 8.30am although we had been there about two hours. We felt we might as well have stayed in our billets because Lord Kitchener appeared to be more interested in the combatant troops than the RAMC who did not seem to get even a glance.

After the 'event' the CO took the men for a brisk walk on a nearby common to warm them up, a sensible decision, ensuring none contracted serious chills. Other regiments that had paraded in winter became so cold that men subsequently died of pneumonia. It would not be the last time the men of the RAMC felt ignored: a few months later, in France, the 2/4th (London) Field Ambulance's Main Dressing Station, patients included, turned out for His Majesty the King, and lined a bank above the road along which the King was expected. He had passed earlier in the day and would inspect the dressing station on his return, 'but he did not do so,' the War Diary noted with obvious disappointment.

In the spring, the Field Ambulance band was formed at Saffron Walden. The instruments were bought with funds raised from canteen profits and donations from friends in the town. The band practised when it could and 'made a small amount of progress', according to the unit history, a realistic assessment of the band members' mediocre abilities; music was inevitably considered a sideline when training for war was the priority. The band leader, Vaughan Williams, was not at fault, as the history was quick to note. When faced with one of the drummers, 'whose knowledge of printed music was nil,' Vaughan Williams persisted in helping him, sitting with him in his hut. It was recorded that 'the player, however, could not understand what he was told, in spite of great care and patience by the instructor.'

On 22 June 1916, mobilisation orders arrived and the unit embarked from Southampton for Le Havre, arriving the following morning. They marched briskly to the town centre, but their first impressions of France were not good. Thomas Lewis, a private in the unit, wrote:

> What we did happen to see was far from reassuring – sombre-miened French women [most wore black], decrepit-looking French sentries, and a gang of sturdy and defiant-looking German prisoners.

Within days, Vaughan Williams and the rest of the Field Ambulance found themselves heading for the village of Ecoivres, beneath Mont St Eloi on the slopes of Vimy Ridge. In the distance they could hear the heavy rumble of gunfire – the preliminary bombardment for the Somme offensive, twenty miles to the south.

Ecoivres was a dismal village, but sheltered by rising ground from hostile gunfire. The 2/4th (London) Field Ambulance War Diary records the men's first visit to the support trenches. As they walked up a mile-long communication trench, they heard footsteps stumbling along the duckboards. Towards them came some Scotsmen:

> ...covered in clay and mud from head to foot, over uniform, equipment, rifle and everything. Boots and puttees were indistinguishable. Their faces were white and strained...their eyes were red through lack of sleep. They greeted us cheerily as they passed, wishing us 'Good Luck' and went hobbling along their way. Their feet were inflamed by that condition we knew later as 'trench feet' due to standing in incessant wet.

It was a sobering sight for all concerned. Nevertheless, Vaughan

Williams, for one, was glad to be getting on with the war rather than training, not least as less attention was paid to the niceties of the soldiers' uniforms. Their billets were grim and his favourite description of them was 'barns infested, rats for the use of'. He was always entertained by the oddities of army cataloguing, in particular a medical equipment detail 'tapes, pieces of, two', which he loved quoting.

The task of the 2/4th (London) Field Ambulance was to evacuate the wounded from Regimental Aid Posts [RAP], positioned just to the rear of the front line, back to the Advanced Dressing Stations [ADS]. It was a long and difficult trudge, often in the dark, along duckboards that were frequently missing struts. In the trenches at Neuville St Vaast, the RAPs were in dugouts that offered reasonable protection, but the trenches by which they were reached were full of the dead, as Charles Chitty, a stretcher-bearer in the unit, described:

> One became painfully aware of the revolting stench of putrefaction. For earlier on, at fearful cost, the French...had shovelled their dead indiscriminately into the earth, so that here and there limbs protruded from the banks and parapets between which we wended our intricate way. Tortuous trenches truly, intersecting, bifurcating, crumbling here, and gaps restored with earth-filled bags there, shored up with planks and timbers, while those no longer in use were already overgrown with creeping plants.

On reaching their destination one of the stretcher bearers, relieved of his burden, sat down accidentally on a pair of shin bones, less the feet, which protruded from the earth. Inside a dugout where the men were to sleep, one soldier threw chlorate of lime on the floor to keep off the rats. 'The fumes given off,' recalled Chitty:

> became so unendurably oppressive to me, lying upon the ground, that at last, unable to bear any more, I climbed the

sloping steps, and laying my head outside, with a glimpse of stars above, sank in oblivion deep and dreamless, and as dead to the world and all its sorrows as those poor bones beside me.'

From these points, the Field Ambulance Stretcher Bearers brought the wounded to two Collecting Posts. Sometimes the trenches were narrow and stretchers had to be carried at head rather than at waist height, while the bearers slid and stumbled on the slippery and uneven duckboards. From the Collecting Posts, badly wounded men were transferred to the ADS at Aux Rietz, which was better protected, being in deep dugouts. Much of the evacuation of the seriously ill had to be by ambulance wagons at night.

The sight and smell of dead bodies was always present, as was the threat of shelling or sniper fire. The trenches were often water-logged. The stretcher bearers and transport men, including Vaughan Williams, groped their way along in almost total darkness, lit by occasional flares that rose into the night sky. Private Young described the scene:

Slowly we worked our way along the trenches, our only guide our feet, forcing ourselves through the black wall of night and helped occasionally by the flash of the torch in front. Soon our arms began to grow tired, the whole weight is thrown onto the slings, which begin to bite into our shoulders; our shoulders sag forward, the sling finds its way into the back of our necks; we feel half-suffocated, and with a gasp at one another the stretcher is slowly lowered to the duckboards. A twelve-stone man rolled up in several blankets on a stretcher is no mean load to carry when every step has to be carefully chosen and is merely a shuffle forward of a few inches only.

There were three stretcher bearers involved: at any time, two were carrying the wounded man and one walked ahead with a torch. They changed places at intervals, taking a few minutes to get their breath back, leaning up against the wet clay, too soaked themselves to notice the water streaming down the walls. In this way, it could take three hours to cover less than a mile. It is not surprising that the men frequently saw themselves as automatons, propelled only by the need to struggle forward.

Vaughan Williams took his turn at stretcher-bearing but owing to the very onerous nature of the work and the fact that he had flat feet, he was more often detailed to serve on the motor ambulances. This was no easy undertaking, especially at the crossroads between Aux Rietz and La Targette. Here, the road went through a wood and was pitch black, as the War Diary testifies. It was full of shell holes and scattered with debris; movement along it was slow and hazardous. And yet it was in this shell-pocked world that the contemplative Pastoral Symphony took shape in Vaughan Williams' head, as he later described:

> It's really wartime music – a great deal of it incubated when I used to go up night after night with the ambulance wagon at Ecoivres, and we went up a steep hill and there was a wonderful Corot-like landscape in the sunset. It's not really lambkins frisking at all, as most people take for granted.

Similarly, the sound of a bugler practising at Ecoivres inspired the long trumpet cadenza in the second movement of the symphony. The whole work has been described as an orchestral requiem.

In their spare time, the men played bridge or chess, wrote home or read, tried cooking on primus stoves or to get rid of the ever-present lice, which seemed to thrive on the various preparations intended to exterminate them, sent out by friends and relatives. The choir, formed and led by Ralph Vaughan Williams, provided more cultural entertainment. They had taken a box of music with them to France and practised whenever they had the chance, and, if enough of them were free at the same time, gave impromptu concerts. Singing gave them great pleasure, and there was much regret when the box of music was left behind when the unit later served in Salonika.

The assumption had been held by officers and men that any move they might make would be to another sector on the Western Front, but in November 1916 they received instructions to travel to southern France, and so after five months they marched away from Vimy Ridge. They had become so used to the sound of gunfire that they almost ceased to notice it and many slept badly for their first nights away from the trenches, so unused were they to silence. At Marseilles, they had a strong sense of joy at escaping from the trenches combined with excitement at the prospect of the voyage as they embarked on the HMT *Transylvania* for Salonika, in north-eastern Greece.

French and British troops had first arrived in Salonika in October 1915 to aid Serbia. When the 60th Division, including the 2/4th (London) Field Ambulance, arrived, the Front was relatively quiet, and continued to be so for the first few months that Vaughan Williams was in Greece. This was as well: the men had to refit all the ambulance equipment onto mules.

They had been only a few days in Salonika when they were introduced to 'those long-eared friends, the mules'. These provided unexpected entertainment. On one occasion, when the CO was giving a demonstration of how to load a mule, the animal suddenly reared up on its hind legs and dashed away, with its load dangling. It disappeared from sight, to the amusement of the troops.

The climate was very different from what they had been used to. It was very dry, and the ground was covered with dust and grit, blown into the men's sleeping quarters by even the slightest breeze. From time to time, there would be a whirlwind which dismantled the tents and hurled papers, books, towels, whatever was in its path, up into the air above their heads and out of sight. In exchange, it would deposit dust, fag ends and even manure from the horse lines onto the men and their kit.

From approximately 24 April to 22 May 1917, the Allies were involved in the Battle of Doiran against the Bulgarians; there were heavy losses, and the 60th Division had both Advanced and Main Dressing stations in the area. The 2/4 Field Ambulance was stationed about 35 miles south of Salonika, but some men were likely to have travelled closer to the Front. Railway trains made the transport of the wounded to hospitals much easier than it might otherwise have been, but the need for rescue was the same as always.

Vaughan Williams had carried a stretcher in France, and it is probable that he acted in the same capacity after the Battle of Doiran. The suspicion that he took part is confirmed by a letter to his wife Adeline, whom he had married in 1897: in order to let her know where he was, he included in it a musical scale in the Dorian mode. She would have recognised the significance of the name; it was an original way of outwitting the censor.

The area in which the 2/4 (London) Field Ambulance was stationed was described by its CO as very unsanitary, with flies everywhere and typhoid among the local population. Vaughan Williams shared a tent with his friend Harry Steggles and two empty pineapple tins which the pair named 'Isaiah' and 'Jeremiah'. In these tins the two men lit charcoal, whirled them round 'like the old fashioned winter warmer' to dispel as many flies as possible, and took them into their tent, sealing up any air intakes that they could find. They slept more, he wrote, from their rum ration plus carbon monoxide from Isaiah and Jeremiah than from exhaustion.

In the confined space of the tent, they were always losing things, but 'Bob' [Harry's name for Vaughan Williams: 'I couldn't call him Williams and RVW seemed impertinent' he later said] always gave up, declared that the missing item would turn up in the morning, and went to sleep. In this unlikely setting, 'Bob' introduced his companion to Palgrave's *Golden Treasury*, a poetry book Harry kept for the rest of his life.

One filthy night, recalled Harry Steggles, the two men sat with their knees drawn up in the bivvy, looking at a guttering candle, water creeping in along with snakes, scorpions and centipedes, and a few artillery shells flying overhead. Vaughan Williams suddenly said, 'Harry, when this war ends, we will (a) dine at Simpsons on saddle of mutton, and (b) see *Carmen*.' Many years later, Harry received a postcard inviting him to do both these things, and they had a wonderful evening together – Harry's introduction to opera, followed by a fine dinner with saddle of lamb. The composer had not changed his habit of odd dress, and wore a large straw hat; Harry was amazed at the deference with which he was met in spite of this unlikely garb, and reckoned that his friend had such a tremendous personality that he could wear whatever he liked and would always command respect.

Much of life in Greece proved to be fairly unpleasant and monotonous. Harry Steggles recorded that:

> RVW didn't mind what he did as long as we got on with the war. But Salonika was too dilatory for him. We went on mosquito squad work which consisted of filling in puddles to prevent mosquitoes breeding; he thought this useful in an abstract way. But what caused him the most anguish was to sit down and wash red bricks, which were laid on the ground to form a red cross, as protection from German planes; he swore one day, saying "I will do anything to contribute to the war, but this I will not do." I have never seen him so annoyed.

Music was and remained his one escape. 'It was in the shadow of Mount Olympus that RVW conducted our Christmas carols for what was to be the last time, in 1916,' recalled Steggles. 'The black velvet of the night, the moon lighting up part of Mt Olympus, we sang all the carols out in the open, a treasured memory.'

Standing in the fresh air, even to sing carols, would have been both invigorating and painful: by New Year, they were encamped in snow and at night their breath froze on their blankets. On another occasion, Harry remembered going out into a village and hearing singing and guitar music from a shop. They went to investigate, and found some armed Greeks, who were dancing. 'RVW was quite interested for he immediately bought more wine and wrote down the tune as they danced, much to my amazement.'

For the last three weeks that he was at Salonika, Vaughan Williams was on latrine fatigues all the time. He could have avoided this by taking part in a concert party or divisional theatre, but chose not to, on the grounds that they were doing very well without him and he might just have been useless.

In June 1917, he was transferred back to England to train for a commission. Harry recorded his words on leaving:

> It was no disrespect to our officers when he said goodbye to them using the words, and standing stiffly to attention: 'My regret at leaving is that I shall cease to be a man and become an officer,' a last jab at the military term 'officers and men'.

The following month Vaughan Williams reported to the War Office in London. He applied formally for training as an officer, specifically requesting to serve in the Royal Garrison Artillery. On the form, he listed his occupation as 'Doctor of Music.' He was admitted to the No.2 RGA Cadet School, Maresfield Park [in Sussex] with the rank of gunner on 1 August, and was commissioned as Second Lieutenant on 23 December 1917. He had turned 45 while at the School.

It was not an easy transition. He had to tackle unfamiliar subjects, and was determined to do well. His second wife, Ursula Vaughan Williams, whom he married in 1953 after the death of Adeline, noted that he and one or two others had to take a room in a cottage outside the grounds so that they could work in peace and quiet. This had to be done secretly, as they were not allowed outside the camp. They therefore made a large hole in the hedge and disguised it with removable branches, so that they could get in and out without the sentry noticing. Vaughan Williams, twenty years older than most of the other cadets, with dogged perseverance and hard work managed to pass out from the School successfully.

After he was demobbed, Vaughan Williams' life returned to what it had been before the War. He was invited to be Professor of Composition at the Royal College of Music, he worked with the Leith Hill Musical Festival and became Musical Director of the Bach Choir. He threw himself into work, partly as a way of dealing with the emotional aftermath of the War. Yet his music was inevitably affected by all that he had been through. The *Pastoral Symphony*, started in France and finished in 1921, has a loneliness and sadness that reflects the loss of so many men on the Western Front and in Greece. He had at times a more austere, restrained idiom, and set to music words about separation and death.

Vaughan Williams was a prolific composer, completing nine symphonies, six operas and a huge amount of vocal and choral music. At the beginning of the Second World War, he was frustrated by not being able to play a bigger part (he was seventy in 1942!), but wrote the scores for several films which were intended as propaganda. He also broadcast on the role of the composer in wartime, and was seen driving a horse and cart round Dorking, where he lived, collecting scrap metal. In 1948, he wrote his finest film score, for *Scott of the Antarctic,* which inspired his *Sinfonia Antartica* four years later. In same year he wrote his Sixth Symphony, of which the conductor Sir Malcolm Sargent said, 'I never conduct the Sixth without feeling that I am walking across bomb sites.'

The composer refused a title, but accepted the Order of Merit in 1935. He wrote that everyone should make their own music, however simple it might be, as long as it is truly their own.

Unfortunately, Vaughan Williams' time with the Royal Garrison Artillery had a lasting effect and in later years he gradually became deaf, a sad disability for one of the greatest of English composers. He died in August 1958 and his ashes are interred in Westminster Abbey. He would have been greatly touched by Harry Steggles' tribute, that he owed to this great man his love of music and poetry.

CHAPTER FIVE

John Reith

—ᗰ—

Damnation, look at the blood pouring down on to my new tunic. I've been hit in the head. Has it gone through and smashed up my teeth? No, they were all there. Was the bullet in my head? If so this was the end. Meantime I had better lie down. Apart from anything else, I was standing in exposed ground and if hit once could be hit again and there was no point in that.

John Reith, *Wearing Spurs*

IT WAS NOT ONLY ACCEPTABLE to detest the Germans in 1915, it was actively encouraged. After all, a war was on, Zeppelins were bombing civilians, civilian liners were being sunk, and to assert that the only good German was a dead one was seen as entirely appropriate by both the press and the Government. On the Western Front, both sides exchanged a daily bout of spite in the form of a short bombardment. It became known as the morning and evening 'hate', a trade-off in antagonism that let the other side know the fight was still very much 'on'.

Not all hate was reserved purely for the enemy. It could on occasion be fomented not just across trench lines but between men notionally fighting on the same side. Throughout 1915, a trivial spat grew into a private war fought between the 1/5th Cameronians' Transport Officer, Lieutenant John Reith, later the founding father of the BBC, and the Adjutant, Captain William Croft. For the best part of a year, neither man could or would find common ground on which to turn their mutual antagonism and direct it more usefully against the Germans. Such reciprocal dislike was hardly unique to the army, as it was no less common in civilian life. But this was not the shop floor or boardroom of a retail business, it was the Western Front, and injury and even death could be just around the corner for a man whose personal feelings about another happened to cloud his judgement or encourage him to rashness.

In a sense, it was a lifelong characteristic of John Reith that he could not get on with other men, especially those in authority, and when, in the Second World War, Winston Churchill dismissed him from his government post as being too difficult to work with, he was following in a long line of those with whom Reith had running feuds. He was a man not psychologically predisposed to playing a subservient role to anyone, particularly someone he disliked or considered his inferior. He was, as he described himself, 'intolerant, reserved and aloof'.

One morning in the summer of 1915, Reith found his conscience was troubling him. It was Sunday, after the morning church service, when he retired to a far corner of the field to try to persuade himself that his Christian duty was to forgive the Commanding Officer, Robert Douglas, with whom he was at loggerheads, and the Adjutant, William Croft. Either forgive or at least feel less animosity towards them. He did not succeed. 'Possibly,' he confessed, 'I did not want to. Life was dull now and a vendetta of this sort brightened things up a little – even though so one-sided in its results, all the tyrannical power being with them.'

Shortly afterwards, the vendetta got out of hand and might easily have cost Reith his life. In front of other company officers, he challenged the Adjutant to go out with him to a sap in No Man's Land. 'I had never put such concentrated venom into a question,' he recalled. Reith had been scathing about how rarely Adjutant or CO went into the front line, and he thought it might be a fitting end to their feud if they were both killed while out. 'I should love to,' the Adjutant replied, saving face.

There was a hole in the trench parapet through which to climb in order to enter the sap although most men chose to go over the top at speed instead. Reith declared 'We usually go this way.' He climbed up on the parapet and stood there full height. The Adjutant chose the other route. 'While he crawled along the sap to its head, I walked on the open ground above him.' He was well within sight of the German trenches and it was an act of self-confessed bravado. Reith was a perfect sniper's target but luckily none was active. He afterwards considered it the riskiest thing he ever did.

Reith's height, six feet six inches, was always inconvenient in the trenches, and on one occasion when he walked about with his head exposed, the second in command, Major Kennedy, asked if he wanted to get killed just to spite the Adjutant. 'I don't much mind if I do,' replied Reith, 'but I think I would like to kill him first.' Kennedy looked at him with mingled horror and sorrow. 'I wouldn't put it past you, Reith,' he said.

Personal relations between Reith on one side and the CO and Adjutant on the other had been strained even before the war. Reith was a pre-war Territorial serving with the 5th Bn The Cameronians (Scottish Rifles) but he had been somewhat reluctant to immerse himself fully in the social life of the officers' mess and was seen as something of an outsider for this reason. In 1914 he had moved to London and wrote to resign his commission, unable to attend functions or drill owing to the distance. He thought it strange that he had heard nothing in acknowledgement.

On the outbreak of war he was keen to serve immediately, got in touch with his old unit and was told, in a threatening tone, to return to Scotland. He was surprised and puzzled by a frosty reception from his CO and others, which was explained only when he found out that his resignation letter had never arrived and a mobilisation notice had not reached him in London. It had been assumed that he was trying to dodge his duty. His CO, perhaps with some insight into the difficulties the young man might present in the future, commented, 'Now you're here, Mr Reith, you will do your best with your brother officers to help the Regiment.'

Three months later the battalion crossed to France. Although acknowledged as an able officer – and, to his delight, made temporary Brigade Transport Officer in early 1915 – Reith's unconventional style and his aloof attitude soon caused friction. An early encounter involved a note from the Adjutant to Reith. Colonel Douglas had been round the transport lines and found two un-groomed horses. His message had been brought a long way by a cyclist, and it was pushed under the door when Reith was enjoying a hot bath. He had been told by a senior officer that he ran the best transport in the brigade, and this he firmly believed.

> No bath water boiled more vehemently that did my indignation. Till now CO and Adjutant had been at a comfortable distance from us. I could remember no occasion when either of them had come round our lines or had enquired if they could help in any way. I did not mind that at all; they had left me to my job…I hadn't the least idea why the horses weren't groomed, but there certainly would be some perfectly good reason…It was a good hot bath. I mustn't let the Adjutant spoil it. Run in more water. What a cad he was.

Reith settled back in his bath and sang loudly some of the fiercest Psalms he could remember, before writing a stiff reply to the Adjutant. 'It was a bit of a snorter,' Reith recalled.

Two un-groomed horses were not really the problem; other deep-seated issues existed. Reith had found himself a very comfortable billet when out of the line and the Adjutant believed that being On Active Service implied, as Reith noted, 'conditions of an astonishing austerity.' It was improper to accept exceptional comforts which either fate or friends had provided. The Adjutant lived a more puritanical existence out of the line, exchanging a good billet for one more monastic in style. He preferred to eat from his mess tin rather than off a plate. This was anathema to Reith, who enjoyed fully those pleasures he could obtain or to which he felt entitled.

The incident in the bath had come hot on the heels of other, smaller spats, and was a prelude to another. On 5 February 1915, in response to an order, Reith had turned his Transport men out remarkably quickly, eight minutes ahead of the infantry companies. The men were waiting and Reith moved to the head of the Transport column in search of news. The Adjutant suddenly appeared and demanded, in front of the men, 'Where the devil have you been, Reith, and why isn't the Transport out?' Reith, too surprised to be angry, replied that they had been on parade for eight minutes.

> There was no reply; no apology. I gradually got angry and felt something more should be said. "You've no right to talk to me like that and accuse me of not being on the job at the right time in the middle of a battle."

Having said this, he spun his horse round and rode off in a shower of sparks. Late that evening, there was a knock on the door of the billet. It was the Adjutant. "I've come to apologise to you, Reith: I was in the wrong tonight."

At that moment everything could have been so different, acknowledged Reith. He should, he believed, have said,

> 'Dashed good of you, sir. Won't you sit down and let's have a talk.' Cross-roads. How was I to know the tremendous personal issues which were at stake; and would I have acted differently even so? I was embarrassed, muttered vague thanks and lost control of the situation, which was a new one to me.

The Diary record [kept by Reith] of what happened next is brief but pretty clear.

> Then he gave me a jaw about my temper; said I went hunting
> around for trouble; putting people's back up and jumping down
> their throats.

Reith's hackles were up once more. He showed in his demeanour that
he was not interested in what Croft had to say and Croft made it clear
he knew Reith did not care. 'I certainly gave him credit for coming but
felt he spoilt it completely by the line he took.'

The result of this exchange was, if anything, the intensification of
the conflict between them. Reith worried about his own role for a long
time, feeling that he should have given the other man more credit for
coming and apologizing, and tried to build a better relationship with
him. But inevitably the two would clash again and their mutual dislike
came to a head the following month. Reith had asked the officer
commanding the Divisional Train if he could be relieved of a farrier
sergeant about whom there had been many complaints; he was
replaced by a man who was much more satisfactory. Reith's
authorization for this change of personnel had not gone through the
Adjutant, and after a sharp exchange of notes, Reith was called to the
Adjutant's office to be reprimanded for not going through the chain of
command. Assuming that this was an informal meeting, he made
matters worse by immediately sitting down.

> 'Don't you realize I'm givin' you a tellin' off? Stand up, will
> you?'… I should have ended by apologizing and promising not
> to offend again. That's what I should have done. But I didn't –
> silly fellow; oh no, nothing like it.

Reith refused to explain his action to the Adjutant, agreeing only to
give his reasons to the CO, if necessary.

Reith was summoned by the CO and told that he was being

transferred away from the Transport, 'returned for duty' as a company officer. It was as if there had been a privilege to being a transport officer, 'for good boys only.' smarted Reith. The job had been a privilege but only because he loved the work. It settled something in Reith's mind. He was going to seek his own transfer – out of the battalion, and out of the infantry altogether. He would become a Royal Engineer. In the meantime, he was sent to A Company in the trenches, 'There at any rate we should see very little of CO or Adjutant,' he wrote acidly. The job of Transport Officer was given to an officer new out from England; he could barely ride.

Reith's active service with the 5th Bn, Cameronians, was all but over, but it wasn't quite the end of his conflict with the CO. The following January, Reith was in Glasgow.

> I saw my late CO coming along by the edge of the pavement. About fifteen yards away he sighted me, smiled broadly and changed course to come alongside. I stared at him and gradually he realized that I had seen him and had, so to speak, no intention of seeing him. The smile faded from his face, was succeeded by a look of surprise and I suppose indignation as he sheered off and back on his original course.

Reith found it incomprehensible, after all the friction between them, that the CO should have tried to meet him as an old friend. 'Is memory so short?

Colonel Robert Douglas returned to the battalion and remained in command until shot through the head by a sniper on 3 July 1916. For all Reith's jibes about the CO being rarely in the front line, Douglas had been in a sap peering through a periscope when he was killed. He was 47 years old, unmarried and the sole partner in a sail-making company in Glasgow. He was taken to Bethune Town Cemetery the next day, his body carried by six senior NCO pallbearers as pipers played *Flowers of the Forest*. A number of senior officers paid their respects as he was laid to rest.

As for Reith's nemesis, Captain William Croft, little is known of his future service as his officer's papers no longer exist. However, unlike Colonel Douglas, Croft did survive the war.

* * *

For all John Reith's later success in civilian life, the army always held a particular appeal for him. At school he was a sergeant in the Officer Training Corps and a crack shot, but his dream was to be a cavalry officer, perhaps because this would allow him to indulge in his passion for wearing spurs (thus the title of his autobiography) at both appropriate and inappropriate moments. However, he couldn't ride a horse, and so in 1911 took a commission in the local Territorial Infantry unit. Disarmingly, he admitted that although he enjoyed the work, he was not a good mixer. When he was thirteen, his father told him that he would have to live on a desert island; certainly, he always preferred duties which left him to himself.

In August 1914, John Reith's first active service posting was to be sent with about sixty men to guard two 'vulnerable' points on the main railway line from Perth to the south: a railway bridge and an aqueduct. They took with them everything that might make for a comfortable life. Reith found billets in a farmhouse where he lived luxuriously for four weeks. They performed their duties with the utmost seriousness but if they were indeed serving their country, Reith thought, it was a most comfortable way of doing it.

In early September, orders were received to be ready for overseas service and Reith was offered the job of Transport Officer. He admitted to having no idea what this entailed but was keen to please and delighted that it meant wearing his cherished spurs. His inability to ride presented something of a difficulty, but he persuaded a fellow Transport Officer to give him secret lessons, so successfully that he was soon able to parade, mounted at the head of the Transport column in a brigade route march. Later, he confessed that this experience had been both anxious and embarrassing: he had been delayed by fifteen minutes 'owing to a difference of opinion with the animal' and he dare not dismount in case he could not get back on his horse without help.

Reith's next problem was that he had to set up the transport from scratch, the Territorial Army having no need for Transport in peace time. He used his initiative to hand-pick some of his men while others were foisted on him – usually men whom other officers were only too keen to try to get rid of, such as Bob Wallace, a difficult character, for whom Reith developed a high regard. His unit organized, the battalion went to France early in November via Le Havre, by train to Saint Omer and then by road 10 miles to billets where they got their first sight of an aeroplane and of the war – gun flashes on the horizon. It was both exciting and daunting.

Near Hazebrouck, they caught sight of the British Commander-in-Chief, Sir John French, and also the French General, Joffre, but Reith and his men were more impressed by the 350 battle-worn survivors of the London Scottish, who had recently fought their already legendary action on the Messines Ridge. These were fellow Territorials; they had shared peacetime manoeuvres together.

> There was an awe about this meeting with the London Scottish…some of them walked beside us and gave us bits of their story. We were tolerably smart; they were unshaven, weirdly clad and caked in mud.

The destination of Reith's unit was Armentières, which they found deserted. The front was close and not long stabilized, and there was real fear that the Germans would try to break through. They were now part of 19 Brigade – the only Territorials amongst the 6th Division's regulars. Reith found the Battalion Headquarters only eighty yards from the Germans. He had no nerves but was rather excited, indeed, he claimed to be happy and felt that this life was going to suit him, although from time to time he was pulled up short by the realization that the life might not last very long – the snag was a bullet or shell, 'or even a bayonet – but preferably not a bayonet.' As Transport Officer, his place was not in the trenches, which pleased him, as he thought it must be boring in a hole in the ground although perhaps safer, he felt, as the trenches gave some protection and the Transport was often targeted.

The initially frosty weather had turned to rain, and the Transport Park was very muddy. Reith wrote home for a pair of stout rubber boots with hobnailed leather soles, a source of great envy among his colleagues at the time. He managed to fix a pair of long spurs to them in such a way that one could get in and out of the boots without taking off the spurs. This, as Reith commented, was a novel approach but convenient and pleasing, if unmilitary. He was also unconventional in using an umbrella, to the general amusement to both officers and men.

Shortly before Christmas, Reith noticed a barber's shop open, decided that he needed a haircut, and went in. The barber had an odd way of operating, setting to work on one side and completing that before starting the other. Halfway through the process, he stood back to admire his handiwork; Reith's head looked distinctly strange, one side long and the other closely cropped. At that moment, a German shell landed in the square, just outside the shop, but failed to explode. With a loud cry, the barber dropped his tools and ran down the stairs at the back of the shop. Reith sat where he was, hoping that the barber would reappear. Unfortunately, before he could do so, a second shell landed, and no persuasion would make the barber come back. Reith had to go back to his billet with the weird appearance of half a haircut.

At Christmas, Reith decided he would give a dinner party. He had received useful presents a day or two earlier, cakes, oatcakes, sweets, biscuits and chocolate. He also managed to acquire six bottles of champagne. Christmas Day was bright and clear, everything appropriately white with frost. 'I did not propose,' Reith declared, 'to wage any war today.' Tablecloths, cutlery, flower vases and four massive candelabra were found, and four chickens cooked. There were nine at the party, all Transport men, including a sergeant, three corporals, two orderlies, a groom and a batman, and Reith, the only officer. In the middle of the feast, a messenger arrived. He could hardly believe his eyes, but was given a glass of champagne and some food, and almost forgot to deliver his message. The battalion relief was to take place at dawn and transport would be needed at 6am. They had enjoyed their Christmas: war could be resumed.

It was symptomatic of his time in France, indeed of his life in general, that he felt more comfortable in the presence of those whom he outranked. These were the men who would not threaten his authority and with whom he found it easy to get along. As a consequence he inspired a devotion amongst those he commanded in almost equal measure to the dislike he inspired in those under whose authority he came and in whose company he always felt awkward. It is noticeable that not only did his relationship with the CO and the Adjutant founder – conspicuously, neither is named in his autobiography – but he also had frequent disagreements with Major Kennedy, second in command, a man he neither 'disliked or liked'. Instead of meeting fellow officers at the mess, at his excellent billet in town (complete with bath and hot running water) Reith often found himself alone in the evenings, and invited Transport NCOs to dine with him. This was against regulations, but Reith maintained the practice for several months and enjoyed the company.

It was one of Reith's duties as an officer to read his men's letters home, a job which he hated, and he put them on trust to say only what they were allowed to say, and rarely looked at what they had written. He made an exception once in the case of Bob Wallace, by then acting as Transport Sergeant. Wallace, the man whom nobody else wanted, had a reputation for being surly. Reith was able to see behind this, and had come to respect Wallace greatly as a man and as a soldier. Wallace, in writing to his fiancée, had written of 'Mr Reith': 'Him and me is the best of friends.' Reith felt that he could have no higher tribute. When later in 1915 he was forced to hand over the Transport section to another officer, Reith's attitude to the new incumbent was typically cool.

> I told him how responsibility was divided among the NCOs, and advised him to take Wallace's opinion on everything. I was afraid he would not have enough confidence in himself to treat the NCOs as I had done, and they would not be happy with him; nor were they.

It is to his credit that his men took the news of Reith's departure badly. His servant refused Reith's offer to stay with the Transport, preferring to follow him into the trenches.

Leave came in mid-February, and John Reith saw his brother, who was a Chaplain in Boulogne, before crossing the Channel with his packages of enemy souvenirs, including a helmet and a drum. But in London he found himself irritated at seeing people apparently enjoying themselves so much, including many young men out of khaki and safe from the war. He was relieved to reach Scotland, where he fulfilled a long-held fantasy of attending church in his uniform with spurs jingling. The organist played *The Ride of the Valkyries* in his honour.

In March, after his return to France, Reith, his own horse lame, managed to acquire a new horse he named Sailaway. She was a thoroughbred, the sort of horse a general would ride, according to Reith, and named after a recent Ayr Gold Cup winner. She was a high-spirited blood mare and difficult to ride, but Reith calmed her and they became almost inseparable. When not on duty, he would take her for long rides in the countryside. She was much admired by everyone:

> She was very showy; delicate stepping, head tossing, long tail sweeping. The Adjutant came by; he did not stop or ask any question, but he took in the mare all right.

Within weeks, Reith's working relati onship with the Adjutant had broken down irreparably and Reith put in for his transfer. However, he was not about to hand over the horse to the Adjutant, who, Reith was sure, would want to take possession. The application process took a long time and meanwhile Reith continued with his new duties back in the trenches – but keeping his head down as much as possible from his superior officers and spending as much time as he could with his old Transport colleagues, and riding Sailaway. He also fell ill with trench fever and was signed off sick for ten days but he longed to get back to duty and even more for his transfer to come through. Meanwhile, he took action to prevent the Adjutant, whose own animal was lame, acquiring his beloved horse.

He wrote to a friend, a Veterinary Officer, explaining that he had applied for a transfer and asking that Sailaway should be kept for him until he could claim her. The VO took her as 'a sick horse' and agreed to add her to the strength of his own section, where she would be well looked after. Reith then said to his successor as Transport Officer, 'If the Adjutant asks for my mare, you won't be able to find her.' He did, and the mare couldn't be found.

In June, the Brigade was transferred to the 27th Division although it stayed in the same sector. While inspecting the lines one night, Reith found two men asleep in a sap. It was a very serious offence and regulations demanded that he should have reported them. But once again his sympathies lay with those he outranked. He rather admired the way that both of them could sleep in such obvious danger, so he stayed with them until they woke up. He himself never had the slightest problem sleeping in battle conditions and was famed for it in the unit.

After a month of waiting for news of his move to the REs, he got a missive from the War Office asking if he was willing to transfer. 'Why would I have applied in the first place if I did not want to go?' was his frustrated comment. Mid-July brought Reith's last spell of trench duty and on the 18th he and his men came out of the line, after almost nine months, and into rest. While in billets, he drank from the farm well and became violently ill. It was his twenty-sixth birthday. He was taken to a Field Ambulance and then a Casualty Clearing Station at Merville where he spent several days suffering from dysentery. He was then taken down country in a hospital train (still wearing his spurs) to No3 General Hospital at Le Treport and told there was every chance that he was going home. He had finally left the Cameronians: in nine months, his name had never been mentioned in the battalion's War Diary and neither was his departure.

Reith was worried, fearing his illness might scupper his posting to the REs. Despite his wishes, he was sent to London where he was once more annoyed by the perceived loafers and profiteers. Everything seemed so vulgar. On being pronounced fit again, he went straight to the War Office about his transfer. He was told that it had gone through three months earlier but the paperwork had been lost. Even worse, he was informed that he would have to start again and re-apply.

He headed for home and, while pleased to see his parents, brooded about returning to the 1/5th Bn Cameronians, but he soon heard that they had received notification of his transfer to the 2/2nd (Highland) Field Company RE.

After a month's leave, he attended a second Medical Board in September, and another month was suggested, but he pronounced himself perfectly well and happy to resume overseas duty. He had already got himself kitted out as an RE officer and wanted to avoid a posting to a home depot. 'I had war in the blood,' he declared, 'though where it came from was a mystery to all of us; certainly life at the front suited me as no other had.'

His wish was granted on 17 September when a telegram arrived telling him to report to the 1/2nd (Highland) Field Company near Béthune. He arrived at his new unit on 29 September 1915. Four days earlier, the offensive at Loos had been launched and quickly stalled. Troops were everywhere and Reith was keen to get up the line immediately. His arrival was a surprise to his new CO, and Reith found he had much more front line service than any of his new fellow officers, who seemed a little suspicious of him although they greeted him kindly. At the front, he watched through binoculars as an attack by a kilted regiment went in: heavy shelling was in progress and many of those going forward were shot down. The following evening, he was sent with a party of men to mark out a support trench seventy yards behind the new front line. In addition to the shells and bullets that flew about, he found all around him the detritus of battle:

> I had never witnessed such sights before; this was indeed a battlefield. I had seen dead men and dead horses but never in these numbers.

Next day, they were moved out of the line to Vermelles and then ordered to Cuinchy, which was notoriously hazardous. The chief danger came from the imposing brickstacks into which the Germans had tunnelled, making formidable positions, especially for snipers. Despite the danger, Reith settled well and was enjoying himself going out wiring and strengthening a damaged bridge to carry heavier traffic over the La Bassée Canal. This was real engineering work, and he had been an engineering apprentice before the war.

Another reason for happiness was his imminent reunion with his beloved Sailaway. On 7 October, he was about to fetch her from near Poperinge and had bathed and dressed in his best uniform when the CO said he was keen to go into the line to see some redoubts. There had also been a recent mine blown and Reith needed to see the damage with a view to putting it right, so they went together. Reith should have changed, as he was quite conspicuous, but he decided not to do so.

They departed, with Reith taking a short cut over the top as the communication trench was busy. The CO stayed down below and Reith soon hopped down again to join him. They had not gone far, with Reith in front, when he felt a smack against his head and his ears rang. It was similar to when he had been hit on the head by a cricket ball at full slog at school. But the Germans were unlikely to have cricket balls, he reasoned, and he soon saw, to his fury, blood all over his best tunic. Now he started to feel giddy and there were concerned men all around him. He felt he was dying, but there was little pain and as he lay on the trench floor looking up at the sky, he decided that he was content and at peace. 'In after years I have often wished that I could contemplate the blue of eternity with such equanimity as then.'

The sniper had been in one of the brickstacks just forty yards away, but Reith's luck held. Some of the bone in his face had been shot away, and he had lost a lot of blood but he was not badly wounded. Within the week he was in hospital in London, where there was talk of silver plates and skin grafts, but eventually the wound healed well. Two and a half years later, in March 1918, he applied for a wound gratuity, suffering, he claimed, from hearing loss owing to his wound. He was rejected. The medical board saw no reason to attribute his deafness, 'if any', to his facial wound. 'The disfigurement which you mention is said to be trifling and no wound gratuity is issued for disfigurement in itself.' It is interesting to note, however, that many years later Reith was awarded a small pension for physical injuries noted as a gunshot wound to his face and, perhaps more surprisingly, mental injuries. He had apparently suffered from neurasthenia, or shell shock.

John Reith would never return to France. After he was released from hospital he joined the staff of a munitions factory in Gretna before, in early March 1916, he was sent by the Ministry of Munitions to the United States as an Assistant Inspector in charge of a contract for one million rifles. He would remain there for nearly two years. On his return he transferred to the Royal Marine Engineers, with whom he saw out the war in Britain before transferring back to the Royal Engineers in 1919.

* * *

John Charles Walsham Reith was born on 20 July 1889, the youngest of the seven children of Revd Dr George Reith, a minister of the

United Free Church of Scotland, whose strong Presbyterian convictions the boy was to carry all his life. He went to the Glasgow Academy and then to school in Norfolk, but he was inclined to be lazy and, to his disappointment, his father apprenticed him as an engineer at the North British Locomotive Company. It was his enjoyment of his part-time soldiering in the 1/5th Bn Cameronians that helped him to tolerate his apprenticeship until he moved to London in 1914.

At the end of the war, Reith returned to Glasgow and the engineering profession, but in 1922 he moved once more to London, and became secretary to the London Conservative group of MPs in the General Election of that year; interestingly, the results of this election were the first to be broadcast on the radio. In the same year, he applied for the post of General Manager of the new British Broadcasting Company, typically commenting later that he felt that he had the credentials necessary to manage any company.

It was while he was in this post that the General Strike of 1926 brought Reith into conflict with the government, as he attempted to allow all parties the opportunity to comment on the radio; he had to bow to pressure from the Prime Minister, Stanley Baldwin, but he had achieved the singular success of giving the fledgling BBC a reputation for impartiality, and he had widespread public support.

Ten years later, in 1936, Reith personally oversaw the abdication broadcast of Edward VIII, but in 1938 he left the BBC and two years later became MP for Southampton and Minister of Information under Neville Chamberlain. Unfortunately, he never managed to work happily with Winston Churchill, who, when he was Prime Minister, sacked him from the government. Churchill later offered him the post of Lord High Commissioner to the General Assembly of the Church of Scotland, a position he greatly desired, but he would not accept it from the man he referred to as 'that bloody shit Churchill'. He did, however, take a naval commission, and by 1943 was Director of the Combined Operations Material Department at the Admiralty, a post he held until the end of the Second World War.

Through the forties and fifties, Reith held a number of public offices, and in 1948 the BBC's annual Reith lectures were established in his honour, but when he returned briefly to the Corporation for a broadcast interview in 1960, he admitted that since he ceased to be Director General, he had watched virtually no television and listened to scarcely any radio. 'When I leave a thing,' he declared, 'I leave it.'

He died in Edinburgh in 1971 at the age of 81.

CHAPTER SIX

Dennis Wheatley

—∿—

I saw nothing, but felt myself to be threatened by a spiritual force of overwhelming evil.

Dennis Wheatley, *Officer and Temporary Gentleman*

T HAT THE MASTER OF THE OCCULT should have been scared out of his wits by, as he called it, 'the most terrible occult manifestation that I have ever experienced,' is, perhaps, no more than an occupational hazard. However, the incident which he recorded in his memoirs, *Officer and Temporary Gentleman*, pre-dated anything he wrote on the occult, indeed it pre-dated any real interest in the dark side of life. It seemed that the occult had come to him, in a wood at night, in a place where man-made evil was about as tangible as it could be, the Western Front in 1917.

Lieutenant Dennis Wheatley had not long been in France, where he was serving with No.1 Section, Divisional Ammunition Column of the 36th (Ulster) Division, Royal Field Artillery. The location was the small village of Etricourt, near Amiens, where the officers were quartered in the walled garden of an old château which had been destroyed by the Germans a year earlier. As there was no more than a great heap of rubble left of the main building, the mess and sleeping quarters consisted of tents erected among the fruit trees.

Wheatley and the officer with whom he was sharing a tent decided that a winter under canvas was unattractive, and Wheatley set to work to build a house for the two of them, using the garden walls, which were solid. His fellow officer went on leave, and so he was left to do the job himself, in spite of having no building experience and little equipment, not even a spirit level. He got advice from professionals among the troops, and solved potential problems such as that of the chimney, which needed a baffle so that the smoke would not blow straight back into the room. He even managed a tank for hot water and a sunken bath. He later recalled that the bricks he had to use:

> ...were of different kinds and thicknesses, which was an additional handicap... and it was no wonder that before my house was one-third up my friends had christened it Crooked Villa.

In time, the unit's carpenters were persuaded to put a roof on Wheatley's house, and when the owner of the château, a French officer, came on a visit, he declared himself delighted, and said that he would live in the Crooked Villa while the château was being rebuilt.

Fortunately, the Front was quiet, and although Wheatley's duties kept him busy during the day, there was brilliant moonlight and he was able to work on his house until very late. All the other officers had long gone to bed, the lights in their tents being extinguished shortly after half-past nine, leaving Wheatley to work alone. He was feeling cheerful and actually humming to himself a well known ditty from a hit London musical comedy.

> I was busy mixing a new supply of mortar when a sudden change came over me. Without the least warning, I became aware that somebody was intently watching me from behind.

> I swung round expecting to see a figure, but there was nobody there. Nothing moved. It was a windless night and on all sides, except where the ruins of the château made a jagged heap, the garden was entirely surrounded by a high wall. Not a leaf stirred on the pear trees that could be seen as clearly by the

light of the full moon as by day.

I returned to my mortar-mixing. But only for a moment. I felt absolutely positive that some incredibly evil thing had its gaze riveted on the back of my neck.

Somehow, Wheatley managed to force himself to return to mixing the mortar. The walls of his little house were about three feet high and Wheatley, not a man to be put off, decided that two more courses of bricks should be laid before he turned in for bed.

How long I stuck it I have no idea. It may have been two or three minutes or only twenty seconds. I could feel that terrifying presence only a few yards behind me…Suddenly my nerve broke…Flinging down my spade, I dashed across the path to my tent, grabbed up my big torch and switched it on. As I sat on my camp-bed…I was shivering…sweat was pouring down my face.

Amazingly, Wheatley returned to his house-building the following night, and there was no repetition of his horrifying experience. Later, he discovered that the Germans had used the château as a field hospital and his men found blood-stained equipment there; he wondered if the sensation had been caused by the earth-bound spirit of a German soldier, who had spent his last agonizing hours in the château grounds, still burning with hatred towards the British for his death.

It was perhaps just as well that Wheatley spent only one night at his 'haunted' house; he was sent on a course, and by the time he returned, preparations for the attack on Cambrai were in full swing. He never saw his Crooked Villa again.

Life behind the lines was made more than tolerable by a friendship Wheatley developed with his 'house-mate', another officer in No.1 Section, Lieutenant William Pickett [Wheatley spelt the name Picquet in his memoirs]. Wheatley had travelled to Amiens on a night's leave, but although shops and hotels were open, there was little to do and he returned to his unit to pen a letter home.

> My only consolation, he wrote, is that I have with me in my
> section one Picquet, a subaltern of the old school for wit, a most
> amusing card, quite one of the best people, and when we are
> away in the evening to our house we wile away the time by a
> little "game of chance" or reading to each other books...

Thirty-three year old Pickett came from the village of Wargrave in
Berkshire. He had enlisted in December 1914 and had served in
France since the back end of 1915 with 154 Brigade RFA, joining 36
DAC in early July 1917. It was with Pickett that Wheatley had hoped
to share Crooked Villa. And it was because of Pickett that Wheatley,
in his autobiography, was able to recount one further strange
experience, albeit only second-hand. Lieutenant Pickett returned from
his leave, which had been brought forward because his sister was
dying. He had been present at her death, and said that just before she
died, she apparently greeted their father, who had died some time
previously. She then looked surprised and said, 'You here too,
Jacques?' Jacques was her brother in law, a Captain in the French
army, and, as far as anyone knew, alive and well. Next morning, they
received a telegram telling them that Jacques had been killed two days
earlier. There was no way that she could have known.

* * *

Dennis Wheatley had arrived in France in August 1917 and after a
couple of weeks was ordered to join his unit. Serving with the
Divisional Ammunition Column was a relatively safe job, Wheatley
believed. 'But there was really little to chose for relative safety in any
part of the Salient,' he also acknowledged; the Salient bent like a
horseshoe round the largely destroyed town of Ypres.

The Column's personnel were billeted in tents at Vlamertinghe, a
village that was menaced by occasional shellfire. On Wheatley's first

night there, his tent was cut by small pieces of shrapnel which passed through the fabric; he did not record whether he was in the tent at the time. Then, a few nights later, the Column was attacked again. The officers had dinner in an open-sided marquee and Wheatley retired to a tent but, unused to the distant shellfire, he could not sleep. At 11pm, several large explosions rocked the immediate vicinity, enemy aircraft dropped bombs near the horse lines, and Wheatley went to investigate. In a letter he wrote to a family neighbour, Wheatley described his first impressions.

> A Bosch dropped a bomb seventy yards from our mess (an erection of canvas and sticks) and when we ran out to see what had happened I was the first to discover a sentry not only dead but in bits, a most unpleasant sight.

What remained of the man was twisted beneath a wagon under which he had tried to take shelter.

By this time it may not have felt quite such a cushy job as Wheatley had once assumed. The first convoy of ammunition he took up to the batteries at St Julien was also hit, one of the horses in the leading team being physically blown under a wagon by a shell burst. Soon afterwards, while he was at the mess, the Germans again bombed the horse lines fifty yards away, killing 47 mules and horses outright, while another 52 had to be shot. Some 99 animals out of 150 were lost, excluding a further 20 that were wounded but were judged fit enough to carry on. There had been few human casualties but the sights and the sounds were as bad as any imaginable.

> There were dead ones lying all over the place and scores of others were floundering about screaming with broken legs, terrible neck wounds or their entrails hanging out. We went back for our pistols and spent the next hour putting the poor, seriously injured brutes out of their misery…To do it we had to

wade ankle deep through blood and guts.

A month in the Salient was a lesson, if any were needed, in the horrors of war. 'Things might certainly be described as lively,' wrote Wheatley to the neighbour, 'and I certainly experienced moments of acute fear.'

Those few weeks of intermittent fear were traded for an almost equal measure of relaxation and comfort when, much to the envy of the rest of the officers in the Column, Wheatley was sent to look after an ammunition dump well behind the lines. Two hours work in every twentyfour, on average, gave Wheatley more than enough time to begin a novel. He would manage 80,000 words before he was finally moved back to his Division, which was resting out of the line at Etricourt with its ruined château, garden wall, and malevolent ghost.

The Division left the village, and prepared for the Battle of Cambrai which began with spectacular results on 20 November, when a massed tank attack, coupled with the element of surprise, completely shattered the enemy's defences. Wheatley wote:

> I performed only my allotted and inglorious task of keeping some of our guns well supplied with ammunition. But I was there, and privileged to witness this glorious triumph of British arms.

He was, alas, also 'there' when the German counter attack pushed the British back, so that, by the end of the month, they were pretty much where they started.

After the battle, Wheatley was sent on a month's course at the Third Army's Artillery School at St Pol, where for three weeks he was laid up in bed with bronchitis. It was an inauspicious end to the year.

He returned to his unit, which was shivering in the severe winter near the then peaceful St Quentin. They were still there during the ferocious onslaught which began on 21 March 1918. Wheatley admitted being terrified and although not usually religious, he prayed fervently. Orders came to move back to a village called Aubigny, where Wheatley and his men had a narrow escape. He was ordered to take them to the village, which was considerably closer to the Front than where they had been. He was uneasy about the order, but mounted his horse and set off with his men. It was a difficult journey, but they were almost there when they were stopped by an infantry officer, who asked where they were going. On being told that the Germans were in Aubigny, Wheatley had the following conversation:

'Then where is the Front Line?'
'You've come through it.'
'I can't have.'
'Didn't you see some chaps digging about a mile back? That's the Front Line.'
'But there were no trenches.'
'This is No Man's Land, and I'm making a reconnaissance. For God's sake turn your people round while you've got the chance, or you'll be massacred.'

Clearly there was no alternative, although turning their long wagons, drawn by six horses, in the narrow road was no easy task. It was achieved as quietly as possible, and even the major, who was astounded to see them coming back, was persuaded, in a low voice, that the Germans were just ahead. Fortunately, as Wheatley wrote later, the enemy must have been so exhausted that they were asleep at their posts and heard nothing.

It was only twenty years later that Wheatley discovered that there were two villages called Aubigny in the area, and that he had chosen the wrong one. The other was five miles to the rear and so considerably safer.

Wheatley's section had become separated from the rest of the Divisional Ammunition Column, but in spite of the chaos, he kept his men together and even managed to supply some of the guns with ammunition. But the retreat was on, with only one discernable advantage: canteens, where possible, should not be over-run by the enemy; the contents were to be destroyed or given away free to retiring troops. Wheatley's section managed to acquire more than their fair share, to the point where he commandeered a farm wagon to carry additional stores. The owner, an angry farmer, did not want to relinquish his wagon, and produced to support his case a private in an odd-looking uniform, who spoke very good French but English with a heavy accent. Wheatley, believing he might be a German in disguise, arrested him and sent him under guard to the major. The guard returned to say that the man was on the major's staff and was a Brazilian who had volunteered to serve as a non-combatant for the Allies.

Gradually, his section was joined by stragglers of all ranks and regiments, and by the time Wheatley found his unit – ten days later and fifty miles away – he had command of over a thousand men. Despite this, he was berated for losing so much equipment and held personally responsible for losing the unit's money, which he had to pay back from his own pocket. He was not impressed.

The retreat took British troops right over and beyond the old Somme battlefield towards Amiens, a place that Wheatley was able to revisit. He found that most civilians had left and there were military police everywhere to prevent looting. Looking for food, he tried the Salon Godbert restaurant, which was well-known, and was invited to come inside and take a look. Amazingly, it was exactly as it had been when officers had been ordered to rejoin their units immediately, complete with half-empty plates, glasses of wine, and champagne – long since flat – in bottles bobbing about in buckets of long-melted ice. The kitchens were in the same state: clearly the chefs had seen no point in waiting and had gone home.

Orders arrived that the 36th Division was to be transferred to the Second Army and sent north. This involved the nightmarish job of entraining several hundred panic-stricken horses under shellfire at

Amiens. The horses screamed with fear and kicked out savagely; many were wounded and had to be shot. The train was hit, showering steam, red-hot coals and gore everywhere; 'the place', wrote Wheatley, 'stank of blood and guts and was scattered with carcasses and severed limbs.' Eventually they set off on their eleven-hour journey to the Mont des Cats, a little south of the Ypres Salient, just in time for the next stage of the German Spring offensive.

But Wheatley's war had almost ended. In early May, he started coughing badly and reported sick. He was first sent to Boulogne and then, on the 15th, evacuated home to England. He arrived at Charing Cross in sunshine and asked the ambulance driver not to close the curtains but to let him have a glimpse of London. At Piccadilly Circus, flower girls cheered him, blew kisses and threw blooms. He was laughing and crying at the same time. His luck held and he was placed in a private hospital for officers, complete with its own French chef. What Wheatley did not know was that his parents had been summoned and told he would not live. Although he was very ill for several days, his health improved and by early June he was allowed to get up and to have short visits.

His convalescence continued through the summer and autumn, with a stay by the Thames at Staines, complete with river trips. In September, he was pronounced fit for light tasks and was sent to Catterick, but his only duties were attending parades and lectures. He was bored, and finished the novel he had started writing while guarding an ammunition dump in 1917. He gambled that as the war ended, if he got himself boarded completely fit, he could have two weeks' leave to enjoy the celebrations in London, but he could not help worrying that he might be posted back overseas with the occupying troops.

It was an unnecessary anxiety; rather than return to his unit, he just let his leave end and waited to see what happened. Nothing ever did. The army must not have forgotten about him entirely, as he received a disability pension for a while afterwards, but he was never formally demobilised. He returned to work in the family business before turning to full-time writing.

* * *

Dennis Wheatley was born on 8 January 1897 in the London suburb of Streatham Hill into a successful middle-class family. His father ran a wine business with strong links to Germany. The young Wheatley was sent to Dulwich College, and, after he was expelled, spent four years as a officer cadet with HMS *Worcester*, a training ship for potential Merchant Navy officers. In 1913, aged sixteen, Wheatley was bundled off to Germany where he spent nine months studying the wine business. It was a time of independence and Wheatley matured quickly, being, he believed, mentally older than most of his contemporaries. It was hardly surprising that when war broke out, he felt more than ready to enlist.

On the Bank Holiday weekend in 1914 when the war crisis erupted, the seventeen-year-old Wheatley was watching the regimental sports day of the Westminster Dragoons, an élite London Territorial Yeomanry unit, on its annual summer camp at Goring-on-Thames. His two best friends were both serving and he was looking forward to seeing them. It was a lovely day, capped off with dinner at a hotel on the banks of the Thames, and drinks flowed freely.

Losing track of the time, Wheatley realised he was going to be home very late and would have to face his father's wrath. He decided to stay out all night and make some excuse in the morning. His friends suggested he came back to camp to sleep in their tent. They had not been long settled when the call went up that the whole unit should turn out and return to London. Mobilisation orders had just arrived from the War Office.

Despite being under age, Dennis wanted to enlist. Although his parents believed he was too young, he managed to persuade them that the Westminster Dragoons was a territorial unit and so would not be sent overseas. Reluctantly, permission was granted.

For most men, even those who were under age, enlistment was a relatively straightforward process; not so Dennis Wheatley, who began his own odyssey of enlistment that would take him round the military establishment. First stop the Westminster Dragoons. He joined the long queue at the drill hall but there were two problems. With so many volunteers and the likely speed of departure, only those with military training and who could ride were being accepted. His naval background saw him over the first hurdle but the second proved his downfall – literally. The only thing he had ever ridden was a donkey at Margate, and when he was put on a horse he was soon on his backside and out of the Dragoons.

Another opportunity arose. Dennis's father met a family friend, a doctor, now wearing the uniform of a major in the Royal Army Medical Corps. The doctor predicted that, contrary to popular opinion, the war was going to last a long time, and it was foolhardy for educated boys to enlist as privates when their skills and talents would be more readily needed as officers. He asked to speak to the boy. Wheatley was ecstatic. He had never even considered a commission, but he had seen from his time in Germany that officers were held in high esteem.

The doctor gave him a full bill of health along with a recommendation to see his colonel at the headquarters of the 1/4th (City of London) Bn (Royal Fusiliers) based at Hoxton. After a short interview with the colonel, it was agreed that Wheatley should become an officer in the unit. Yet there was one aspect of infantry life that young Wheatley had not considered – the amount of marching involved. He hated sport and was not fond of any great physical effort. His mistake was pointed out to him by his father's bank manager, who was a territorial officer. He promised to get Wheatley a commission into a cavalry unit, but the young man recalled his earlier shame and admitted that he could not ride. A compromise was reached: start riding lessons immediately and become an artillery officer.

Wheatley set off to see Colonel Nichols of the 1st (City of London)

Battery, Royal Field Artillery. A pleasant interview followed, and soon another form was produced and signed. Now came better news. While the first brigade was already full and in camp, permission had come through for the raising of a second one. There were already some two hundred recruits but only two officers and a quartermaster from the Regular Army. Wheatley said he could start as soon as his commission came through. The colonel, pointing out that that could take a week or two, needed help at once. Could he report for duty tomorrow? There was no need to worry about uniforms or drill, as it would simply be a case of keeping the men active by taking them off to play sports in Regent's Park. And so Dennis Wheatley became an artillery officer.

Wheatley revelled in the cheers of the crowds as he and his men marched off to drill in the park. Off-duty, he took his secret riding lessons and insisted on going through his paces wearing a sword. Nevertheless, his lack of experience was abundantly clear to all and he acquired a couple of nicknames from the men, which reflected his abilities: the Chocolate Soldier, and Puss in Boots from his splendid footwear. He took it in good stead, later writing: 'They did not regard me as a fine soldier but more of a pleasant sort of mascot.' Promotion to lieutenant soon came, owing to his seniority in the unit and the influx of new officers. This made his head even more swollen and he took to wearing a monocle. He was later to say that it helped him to look brave in action as it prevented ducking, which caused it to fall out.

Equipment was almost non-existent but a friendly carpenter made them a dummy gun and they trained with good spirits and, in Wheatley's case, an excess of zeal: while practising sword movements on horseback, he cut off his poor mount's ear. Around this time he also fell from his horse and sustained a knee injury, which resulted in three weeks in bed. In June he was back with his unit, now issued with its own horses and Boer War vintage guns. Still, they were better than dummies. The unit went to the coast for live firing and Wheatley did not cover himself in glory as his shells all burst too early owing to incorrectly set fuses. It all brought him to the conclusion that he did not really fancy being an artillery officer after all. He started to think about alternatives as he also developed pneumonia. In November he was sent to hospital and he was still convalescing when his unit set off for overseas duty without him, in January 1917.

When fit for light duty again, Wheatley reported to the 6th Reserve Brigade at Luton. It had no guns, few horses and consisted of about a hundred other officers and two hundred men, a mixture of wounded, recovering or those who had never been sent abroad. He knew no one, but made a friend who became important in his development as a writer – Gordon Eric Gordon-Tombe, who was a self-avowed hedonist but well read, and who spurred him into new and wide reading. There was plenty of time for books, as there was little army business and what there was could be interspersed with trips to London and gambling at cards. Once when he was losing badly, Wheatley later said, he called on the devil's help for a good hand and promptly got one, winning a lot of money. He was so shocked that he never invoked the devil again.

The good life ended on 8 August 1917 when Wheatley was sent to France equipped with an armoured tunic from his mother. His experiences left him under no illusion about how precarious life was, and he always tried to stack the odds as much as possible in his favour, galloping horses – against orders – up to the gun lines and making a den from ammunition cases to sleep in. And despite its weight, he wore his mother's armoured tunic. By his own admission, Wheatley was not a brave officer, nor even terribly efficient, doing just enough to get by.

After the war, Dennis Wheatley worked in the family business, and married his first wife in 1922. They had an extravagant lifestyle, which resulted in debts that had to be settled by Dennis's father. By 1927, he was again in debt, but his father died and he became the sole owner of the wine business. By 1931, the business itself was almost bankrupt, and he and his wife divorced; he married again later that same year.

About this time, encouraged by his second wife, he started to write, although he kept an interest in the wine trade for some years. His first book was not well received, but his second, *The Forbidden Territory*, published in 1933, was a great success, and from then on, his main occupation was writing. He wrote mainly adventure stories, covering topics such as Satanism and espionage, sometimes with historical settings, such as the French Revolution.

During the Second World War, Wheatley drew up a document of suggestions for dealing with a German invasion; he was the only civilian given a direct commission (in his case, as Wing Commander) onto the Joint Planning Staff of the War Cabinet. One of his responsibilities was taking part in the advance planning for the Normandy landings.

In 1947, Wheatley wrote a paper which he called 'A Letter to Posterity', and he buried it in an urn in his garden to be 'discovered' at some later date. This was largely a diatribe against what he saw as 'the false, pernicious doctrine that all men are equal', a 'warning' against socialist ideas; he seems to have been ready to engage in covert activity to destabilise a left-wing government, suggesting the 'formation of secret groups for free discussion' leading eventually to 'the boycotting or ambushing and killing of unjust tyrannous officials.'

In spite of the right-wing beliefs evident in his books, by the 1960s he was selling one million copies a year. Some of his books were made into films, notably *The Devil Rides Out* (the book was published in 1934 and the film was made in 1968 – a testimony to his continuing popularity). He also wrote non-fiction, including accounts of the Russian Revolution and the life of Charles II. He was widely seen as an authority on the occult.

Dennis Wheatley wrote over 70 books and sold over 50 million copies. He died on 11 November, 1977, aged 80.

CHAPTER SEVEN

John Christie

—ɯ—

*He had been gassed in the First World War, and he was dumb
for three and a half years, he was not physically dumb, but it
was psychological dumbness, something to do, you may think,
with the mind. He was dumb for three and a half years and
blind for six months, and you may think that is really the
beginning of this story...I do not suppose you will think that
did him much good.*

Mr Curtis Bennett, opening the defence for
John Christie, The Old Bailey, 21 June 1953

THE LIFE of John Reginald Halliday Christie was nothing if
not filled with twists, contortions, deceit and confusion. The
infamous murderer, who strangled seven women at his home,
10 Rillington Place, was eventually caught and hanged at Pentonville
Prison in July 1953. With his death, a particularly dark and unpleasant
chapter in British judicial history was closed.

More than three years earlier, in 1949, when the body of the first
victim was discovered, Christie successfully helped implicate a
neighbour, Timothy Evans, who was charged with the murder. At
Evans' trial, Christie was called to give evidence and was permitted to
make several allusions not only to the fact that he was gassed fighting
for King and Country in the First World War, but that he had served as
a Special Constable in the Second. Despite several convictions for
theft and violence in the 1920s and 30s, Christie painted himself as an
upstanding member of the community. Evans was found guilty and

hanged in 1950, allowing Christie to kill and kill again.

When Christie was finally arrested and charged with multiple counts of murder, a defence of insanity was pursued, an incapacity, so the defence claimed, that could be traced back to the traumatic moment when a mustard gas shell exploded close to him. This time his service counted for nothing in mitigation of his crimes, the jury found him guilty after just thirty-five minutes' deliberation and he was sentenced to death. Yet even then, the war years were not quite expunged from proceedings, for one old army friend remained faithful to Christie until the end. Ex-Private Dennis Hague, with whom the prisoner had trained in 1917, continued to visit his friend in prison, proving that the old bonds of army comradeship were never entirely severed.

Christie's service records survive at the National Archives in London and make for interesting and contradictory reading. There is some superficial confusion about his date of birth on enlistment, and even his length of service in France varies from three to six months. There is confusion too about when he was actually gassed. A contemporary misreading of his file led to notes that implied that Christie was gassed in May 1918 when it is clear he was gassed a month later. Nothing was ever simple when it came to John Christie.

In 1953, pre-trial reports on his service were requested for use at the Old Bailey as evidence in support of his plea of insanity. In the end, neither prosecution nor defence received a definitive explanation of what had happened to Christie thirty-five years earlier. Though it is true to say that none of these confusions or errors affected the outcome of his trial, interesting details remain elusive to this day.

That Christie fought on the Western Front was never doubted, in spite of his tendency to exaggerate aspects of his service. There is a reference in court documents to his serving in France from 1915, a claim easily dismissed. Interestingly, in a photograph of Christie taken during the Second World War, he appears to be wearing the ribbon of a medal to which he was not entitled, namely the 1914/15 Star.

Nevertheless, he was rightly issued with two other medals, the 1914-1918 War Medal and the Victory Medal, proving he had at the very least served overseas.

It was while he was in France, in June 1918, that Private John Christie was gassed, but precisely where and with which unit has never been established. Furthermore, the extent of his injuries, claimed by Christie to have left him temporarily blind and dumb, is also open to question. He claimed at his trial that he was serving with a battalion of the Duke of Wellington's (West Riding) Regiment but nothing in his service records or the medal rolls makes reference to any battalion other than a territorial unit with whom he served in late April 1918. The battalion was the 2/6th Sherwood Foresters and Christie, a signaller, served with D Company in the line close to Ypres.

John Christie was conscripted into the army in September 1916 aged eighteen and was placed on the army reserve until required. For seven months he remained in civilian clothes until he was mobilised in April 1917 and sent for training. It was at this time that he became close friends with Dennis Hague. Christie was to claim that he had refused promotion on three occasions to stay with his friend. He also boasted that he was a marksman and often won shooting competitions but there is no evidence to substantiate this.

For a year he underwent instruction, first in basic training and then, perhaps because of his higher than average IQ (some thirty-five years later it was assessed at 128) he was chosen for a course in signalling. He was careful and meticulous in all he did, to the extent that one of his training instructors asked him to leave his exercise book behind at the end of the course as a useful example to other recruits of what could be achieved.

At a time when conscripts were sometimes sent overseas with as little as six months' training, Christie was fortunate to remain so long in Britain. But then in March 1918 the Germans launched their all-out bid to win the war. This massive offensive had the explicit aim of driving a wedge between the allied armies, driving the French south and the British back onto their coastal ports and out of the war. The first onslaughts cost the Germans dear, but their tactics of rapid infiltration of the allied lines brought instant rewards, and by the end of March 1918 the British Army had suffered vast numbers of casualties in killed and wounded as well as an exceptionally large number of prisoners taken. For this reason, Christie's continued training was brought to a rapid halt and, along with tens of thousands of other teenage boys, he was rushed overseas to halt the German tide.

Christie landed in France on 2 April and after a brief halt at an infantry base camp he was posted to the Sherwood Foresters, joining his unit in the field one week later. Badly mauled in the first days of the German offensive, the battalion had been taken out of the line with just 18 officers and 364 other ranks left, far less than half its official fighting strength. Replenished with troops throughout the month, it returned to the line, only to suffer further losses on 17 April. Christie's draft was sent forward to make good these losses. For the next two weeks, the battalion undertook bouts of trench digging and training, suffering no reported casualties.

His sojourn at the front was brief. He joined the battalion in the field on April 20, but by May 7 he and the rest of his unit were back at Calais where the battalion was broken up as part of an urgent reorganisation of the army to make the best use of available resources. The vast majority of the men in Christie's battalion were sent to 'K' Infantry Base Depot where they would have been turned around and sent back up the line to units which required reinforcements.

In May 1918, the need for fresh troops was intense. The Germans were still in the last desperate throws of their attempt to break the Allies and men were required at the front. It is unlikely that any fit man with front line experience, however short, would have waited long at Calais before going back into the line. It stands to reason that if Christie was no longer with the Sherwood Foresters, he was serving with another unit and therefore his claim to be with the Duke of Wellington's Regiment is quite likely true, for there was no reason to lie. In his trial papers, it is clear that his service with this regiment went unquestioned and that the subject of his injury was more important than whom he was serving with.

The Duke of Wellington's Regiment was an average sized regiment of the British Army. By a process of elimination, it is possible to exclude nineteen of the twenty-two battalions, (at least seven never went abroad, others were disbanded or served elsewhere such as India or Italy), leaving three possible units with whom Christie might have served: the 1/7, the 1/5th and the 2/5th.

All three reported gas casualties in June, with the most likely contender being the 1/7th. The principal medical officer at Christie's trial, John Matheson, called to give evidence, wrote a detailed report on his subject, noting what Christie had said. 'While in the army,' Matheson wrote, 'he [Christie] was always employed as a signaller at Battalion Headquarters but was never in the firing line….' In the 1/7th Battalion War Diary, the adjutant notes that the unit was in the Ypres Salient when on the 29 May a draft of 112 other ranks joined the battalion, 'mostly youths of 18'. Even Christie had only just turned 20. On the 9 June, the diary states that three other ranks were gassed in the early morning, a gas shell bursting near the door of the Headquarters dugout. Was one of these men Christie? It is impossible to say for certain, but if he had retained his job as a signaller, the HQ dugout would have been a location with which he would have been very familiar.

Christie claimed that he had been overcome by mustard gas fumes, stating that he was unconscious and that when he came to, his eyes were bandaged. He also mentioned that he was slightly wounded in the right shoulder. If this was true, it must have been a very slight wound indeed, as no mention of treatment is made in his subsequent medical records. The effect of being gassed was undoubtedly traumatic. Mustard gas produced a particularly debilitating injury if inhaled in large doses. Gas masks had been improved since the first primitive examples were hurriedly introduced in 1915 after the Germans had been the first to use gas as an offensive weapon. Since then, both sides had used various noxious substances, mustard gas being one of the most common, alongside chlorine and tear gas. By 1918, masks had advanced to the point where they protected the wearer against most attacks, but if an individual was caught suddenly unawares then serious injury could still result.

Regardless of the precise circumstances in which Christie was gassed, by 18 June he was under treatment for mustard gas inhalation, being prescribed Mist Expectorant, and inhalation of menthol. By the 28th he was back in Calais at the 35th General Hospital, suffering from catarrhal laryngitis. He was so badly incapacitated that a month later he was returned to England and admitted to Stoke War Hospital before being transferred to a convalescent hospital in Blackpool, from where he was discharged to duty. He never went back to France.

In 1953, medical opinion stated that Christie, while sane, (there was no evidence of dementia, schizophrenia, or delusions) did suffer from an acute form of hysteria and this could be traced back to the war years. Christie always claimed that after he was gassed he suffered a loss of vision that did not return for five months and that he could not speak for three and a half years. 'He told me he could make people understand him by breathing out as he formed words with his lips and his tongue in a quiet room,' recalled Matheson, who argued that his loss of voice in particular was a hysterical manifestation. His medical notes, taken between 1918-1921, state that there is no mention of a loss of vision but that Christie had difficulty speaking. Notes written by army doctors in 1918 reveal that they believed Christie was suffering from 'Functional Aphonia', literally meaning that he had been struck dumb through fear, in other words he was suffering from a psychological rather than physical ailment.

It was almost a full year after the end of hostilities before Christie was demobbed. His discipline record during his service in the army had been good at a time when ill-discipline within the army was rife as men hankered after demobilisation. Christie's regimental conduct sheet notes only that on one occasion he was charged with being absent from 'lights out', having broken out of barracks with another soldier who was already under open arrest. Christie was reported absent until he was found in bed the next morning. He was charged and found guilty and awarded 10 days confined to barracks and 18 days loss of pay.

From August 1918 until the following March, he does not appear to have sought medical attention for his injuries until he was admitted to Lichfield Military Hospital. Whatever the nature of his complaint, he was discharged again after just four days, being once again diagnosed with Functional Aphonia. Physically, there was little wrong with him and certainly nothing that the military authorities felt they could do to help him further. He was returned to his unit where he remained in khaki for another seven months.

A month prior to his demobilisation, Christie was medically assessed again. The report noted:

> Gas Poisoning. Complains of cough in damp weather and sore
> throat with loss of voice. Heart normal. No physical symptoms
> in lungs. Speaks in a whisper, loss of voice.

Christie was awarded a 20% disability pension worth eight shillings a week for six months, and demobbed. Six months later he was back for a further assessment. A further report dated 6 March 1920 noted:

> Loss of voice and shooting pains down right side of chest
> lasting four days accompanied by red patch on back...Tremor
> eyelids, hands and tongue. Reflexes normal. Lungs and heart
> normal. Speaks in a whisper.

Christie's award was extended for another six months. The last assessment took place 1 February 1921 and was more optimistic. 'States he is much better. Voice very husky in wet weather.'

Disablement was assessed as 6-14% and he was granted seven shillings and six pence for another seventy weeks as a final settlement. Physically, Christie seemed better but his mental and emotional state was another question altogether. Tellingly, a note at the bottom of the doctor's assessment written shortly after the final award noted that the recipient was already in jail for theft.

* * *

John Reginald Halliday Christie was born on 4 April 1898, the second youngest of a family of seven children. Christie's father was a skilled carpet designer, a very strict man of whom all the children were very much afraid. He was a founder member of the Halifax Conservative Party, and an enthusiastic member of the Primrose League, a group promoting purity amongst the working classes. Christie recalled later that he could approach his father only through his mother, 'We almost had to ask if we could speak to him,' he recalled. John was his mother's favourite child, and in compensation for the rigidity of his father, his mother indulged him. A slightly built boy, John was dominated by his siblings, incapable of asserting himself, particularly with his four sisters who bossed him about. Throughout his early teenage years, John remained sexually naïve and, after one failed sexual encounter, he became the butt of local gossip and nicknamed "Reggie-no-dick" and "Can't-do-it Reggie", taunts that appeared to scar him deeply.

Christie was shy, introverted, sulky. He was also a child of well above average intelligence, and he performed well at school, being top of the class in arithmetic and algebra. However, as with most children of that generation, higher education was out of the question and he left to find work in 1913 when aged fifteen. He was a fan of the early silent movies, and an amateur photographer, and these interests led to a job as an assistant projectionist at Green's Picture Hall, a local cinema. At seventeen he was caught stealing and sacked from his job, his father banning him from the home. Christie became something of a drifter, working at different times as a clerk then a shoemaker, sometimes sleeping on his father's allotment where his mother would bring him food. It may have come as something of a relief when he was eventually called up to serve in the army. He had once been in the scouts, and later worked as a postman and a policeman: a smart army uniform conferred respectability, something he enjoyed, and perhaps even craved. Yet, at the same time, his early career in the army was punctuated by frequent visits to prostitutes who were easily found close to the military camps where he trained in Kent and later at Redmires near Sheffield.

Three years later, Christie was back in civilian life. His father, who had seemingly forgiven his son's earlier misdemeanours, helped him find a position as a clerk in a wool mill and it was here that he met twenty-one year old Ethel Waddington, a plain, placid, but pleasant girl whom Christie married in May 1920. For a short while all seemed well. Then, some months later, he left work to take a job as a postman and soon found himself in trouble. In April 1921 he was convicted of stealing postal orders and sent to Manchester Prison for three months. It was the beginning of a period in which he was charged with a number of offences, from obtaining money through false pretences, to being bound over for violent behaviour. Later, and perhaps most significantly, he was given six months' hard labour for malicious wounding: he struck a prostitute with whom he lived with a cricket bat. It was an assault that the judge, in his summation, described as 'a murderous attack'.

His life had declined into turmoil. His family disowned him, and he had difficulty in finding work. He was once again consorting with prostitutes. With his marriage in difficulties, he suggested that he and his wife start again, moving first to Sheffield in 1924. There was little change in his circumstances and he was soon on the move, this time alone, as he left his wife and moved to London. She was not to hear from him again for another seven years.

What little money Christie had to make a new life was reduced still further when his modest war pension ended in 1926. Not surprisingly, he was soon in trouble and was sent down for violent behaviour and for stealing money from a priest who had befriended him. In 1933, while in prison, he contacted Ethel and suggested a reconciliation. She was bored and lonely and seemingly jumped at the chance, joining him in London on his release. Christie's life settled down. He found work but the inner turmoil that plagued him continued. He became a patient of Dr Matthew Odess who was to see him Christie a staggering 173 times in the following few years. Among his patient's many complaints were nerves, stomach problems, sleeplessness and trouble with his eyes. Dr Odess noted his patient's quiet voice and prescribed a range of pills and sedatives to calm him until their next inevitable meeting often just a few weeks or even days later.

Throughout the 1920s and 30s, Christie's employment record was chequered. He worked for a few weeks in Barnes as an electrician, then two and a half years as a lorry driver in Fulham. He was a coach driver for a while, a job from which he was sacked. Two months later, he received another jail term for stealing a car. After his release he found new accommodation, a ground floor flat, 10 Rillington Place, and a job as a foreman at a cinema which he held until 1939 and the outbreak of the Second World War.

For the next four years Christie became a full-time Special Constable at Harrow Road. At his trial ten years later, his occupation was noted and the judge asked whether it was normal not to check into an applicant's background before he was given a job of such responsibility. 'Apparently not,' was the only reply.

This new job gave Christie respectability and power. He was dedicated and zealous, receiving two commendations for his work, as well as gaining two certificates for First Aid, which he took with the St John Ambulance. The nobody had become somebody.

All this new-found success came to a juddering halt in 1943 when an affair with an office worker at the police station ended with Christie receiving a beating from the woman's husband. In disgrace, he was told to resign from the force. His decline into the abyss would now be rapid. In less than ten years he would be dead, convicted of killing seven women, and becoming perhaps the most notorious and reviled serial killer since Jack the Ripper: 'the Ripper of Rillington Place' as one national newspaper called John Christie.

Within months of leaving the police force, he murdered for the first time. Ruth Fuerst, a munitions worker and prostitute, whom he had taken home while his wife was away in Sheffield, was strangled, her body buried first under the floorboards and then later in the garden. He later claimed to have been thrilled with the killing and felt at peace. His next victim was a woman he met at work in a radio factory. A friendship developed and when Muriel later complained of catarrh, Christie professed some medical knowledge and invited her to his house, again while his wife was away. Eerily, and with overtones of the Great War, Christie gassed Muriel, one of at least three such victims who were rendered unconscious before being strangled.

After the war, the Christies appeared a happily married couple, often spotted walking arm in arm while John was frequently seen pottering around the garden. Then in 1948 a young couple arrived at the house, Tim and Beryl Evans. Tim was a twenty-three year old illiterate. He worked hard but was fond of a pint and of telling tall stories. Small in stature, he had a sharp temper when crossed or when he felt himself belittled or confused. Beryl was nineteen and pregnant. Shortly afterwards they had a baby named Geraldine; they also began to have serious rows. Beryl became pregnant again and decided on an abortion: Christie, with his limited medical knowledge, offered to conduct the procedure which was still illegal in Britain. When Tim Evans was away, Christie murdered Beryl, telling her husband she had died during the abortion. He had disposed of the body and swore Evans to secrecy, saying that both could go to prison. As for baby Geraldine, Christie told him that he had devised a plan for the infant to go to a childless couple; in fact the baby had also been murdered.

Evans eventually went to the police but instead of telling the truth he continued with the story that his wife had died taking pills to induce an abortion and that her body was down a drain. A police investigation discovered nothing. Evans made a second confession, this time naming Christie. It was time for Christie to implicate Evans and he quickly told the police of rows and of an illegal abortion that he had advised against. He also mentioned his previous service in the police force, to win favour with the investigating authorities. Another visit was made to the house and this time bodies were found and Evans was arrested and charged. At the trial set for January 1950, Christie appeared as the key witness for the prosecution. Evans' feeble mind was no match for Christie's relative eloquence. Asked to speak up as his voice was so quiet, Christie apologised and said that he had been gassed in the Great War. It was the first allusion to his service, which was mentioned on at least three other occasions during the trial. Evans, for his part, had no service in the Second War to win comparable favour with the jury.

After the Evans case, Christie's health declined rapidly. His visits to the doctor increased and he complained of sleeplessness and stomach problems. His marriage once again ran into difficulties and his wife accused him of impotence: shades of "Reggie-no-dick" once again. Ethel herself became his next victim at the end of 1952, quickly followed by a further three women in rapid succession, all of whom were hidden in the flat. His life in freefall, Christie moved out of the house and, incredibly, sub-let the flat. Human remains were discovered almost immediately and a warrant issued for Christie's arrest.

Christie never left London. He walked aimlessly about looking ever more unkempt and thin. On 31 March a policeman close to Putney Bridge noticed a scruffy man wearing a hat, peering over the embankment into the river. Asked his name, the tramp replied 'John Waddington'. Told by the policeman to remove his hat, he did and was immediately recognised. For Christie the game was finally up. His last days were spent sitting in the same cell that Evans had occupied three years earlier.

CHAPTER EIGHT

CS Lewis

—⚡—

It was the first bullet I heard – so far from me that it
'whined' like a journalist's or a peace-time poet's bullet. At
that moment there was something not exactly like fear, much
less like indifference: a little quavering signal that said, 'This
is War. This is what Homer wrote about.'

CS Lewis, *Surprised By Joy*

IN THE WINTER OF 1916, Clive Staples Lewis travelled to Oxford University to sit the scholarship examinations. The Battle of the Somme had drawn to its muddy conclusion and Lewis, who had just turned eighteen, knew that, whatever the result of the exam, his participation in the war was likely and none too distant. If ever fighting had revealed to the British public the degree of sacrifice required to win the war, the conflict in Picardy left no one in any doubt as to the eventual cost.

Lewis felt somewhat ambivalent about the exams he was about to undertake, even though, as he said, there was 'hardly a position in the world save that of a don in which I was fitted to earn a living.' For that reason alone, the examinations were important and the competition by definition stiff. 'I was staking everything on a game in which few won and hundreds lost,' he wrote.

The examinations were foremost in his mind, but he could just as well have been referring to the 'greater game', as some called it, then being played out across the Channel. There existed the toughest of all examinations in the crucible of war.

> Whether I won a scholarship or not, I should next year go into the army; and even a temper more sanguine than mine could feel in 1916 that an infantry subaltern would be insane to waste anxiety on anything so hypothetical as his post-war life.

The news of the death on the Somme of Donald Hankey, the respected author of the apposite *A Student In Arms*, only reinforced Lewis' view that the longterm future of any subaltern in the war was, to say the least, tenuous.

Lewis had read Hankey's book only the previous summer holiday, but had failed miserably in his attempt to explain his confused feelings to his father:

> He replied at once with fatherly counsels about the necessity of hard work and concentration, the amount that he had already spent in educating me, the very moderate, nay negligible, assistance he would be able to give me in later life.

CS Lewis' relationship with his father was warm but also strained, and while he wrote to him often, all conversations foundered on one particular rock, his father's inability to listen to his son and accept ideas alien to his own, whether it was his younger son's readiness to enlist or his loss of faith.

Whatever the incompatibility between himself and his father, CS Lewis took the exams and was duly awarded a scholarship to University College. Shortly after the award, the Master of the College informed Lewis that, with the exception of one hopelessly unfit case, every scholar was also 'with the colours'. As an Irishman, Lewis could legally have avoided service, there being no conscription in Ireland, but the thought never entered his head: he would serve.

In September 1917, as a newly commissioned infantry officer, he was granted a month's leave. He chose to spend three-quarters of his free time in Bristol, not at the home of his family but at that of a close friend, Edward Moore, another recently commissioned army officer, less than two weeks older than Lewis. The two had met during officer training in June when Lewis had been sent to join a cadet battalion at Keble College, Oxford, where they had shared a room.

The battalion contained a mixed bunch of cadets. The majority, according to Lewis, were men from the ranks, experienced men, leaders who were given the opportunity to take a commission. 'These are mostly jolly good chaps: clean, honest, infinitely good natured.' The next group, about one third of the intake,

> Were cads and fools pure and simple…all vulgar and uninteresting. They drop their h's, spit on the stairs, and talk about what they're going to do when they get to the front – where of course none of them has been. Then comes the third lot, our own set, the public school men and varsity men with all their faults and merits 'already ascertained'.

Moore, a former pupil of Clifton College, Bristol, had his 'ascertained' faults. He and Lewis had become very close despite the latter's first impressions that Moore was 'a little too childish for real companionship'. There were other friends in the cadet battalion: Martin Sommerville, a former pupil of Eton, Lewis's then 'chief friend'; Alexander Sutton, the company humourist, Denis de Pass, both former pupils of Repton School, and Thomas Davy, formerly of Charterhouse.

Although they were all destined to be separated when they were sent to their respective regiments and battalions, the friends kept in touch and affectionately called themselves 'the old set.' There was a sub-set to this friendship. As room mates, Lewis and Moore had made a solemn pact. So many young subalterns were being killed in France (the majority of Oxford Colleges lost a quarter of their enlisted members during the war) that if only one outlived the war, he would promise to look after the surviving parent of the other.

By January 1918, the first of 'the old set', Alexander Sutton, had been killed. Edward Moore followed on 24 March, missing believed killed, then a few days later Thomas Davy died of wounds. When de Pass was reported wounded and missing a few days later, Lewis assumed that he too had died. Only Sommerville remained, but he would also not survive, being killed in Palestine in September. All were second lieutenants, all were born in 1898, none, or so it seemed to Lewis, had lived long enough to survive their teens. Only much later did the news filter through that de Pass had been taken prisoner of war. He alone from Lewis's friends would live to see post-war life.

As Edward Moore had been reported missing, presumed killed, there was little hope for his mother, Janie, to cling to. One report suggested his body had been seen lying in front of a dugout on a canal bank; another, a more reliable account, appeared definitive. It was given by John Howe, a rifleman in Moore's company, 2nd Rifle Brigade. Early in the morning of 24 March, the battalion was retiring from the line:

> We were coming rapidly down a road which the enemy had covered with a machine gun. I was about three yards behind Mr Moore when I saw him fall with a wound in his leg. I stopped and bound up the wound. While I was binding up his leg, he got another bullet right through the head, which killed him instantly. The enemy were very close and we could do nothing but leave his body.

Edward Moore was posthumously awarded the Military Cross and, as he had promised, CS Lewis took care of Edward's mother Jane until she died thirty-three years later. Quite what, if any, provisions were made for Moore's mother and Lewis' father had both young officers died, is unknown. For, less than three weeks after his friend was killed in action, Lewis went over the top in an attack which would cost the lives of many in his battalion, and very nearly his own.

CS Lewis received a temporary commission in late September 1917 and was given a month's leave before joining the regiment to which he had been gazetted, the Somerset Light Infantry. In October, he travelled to Devon to join the 3rd (Special Reserve) Battalion where he met another officer, Laurence Johnson, a classics scholar who would have taken up a scholarship to Oxford had the war not intervened. The two men had great intellectual discussions and arguments about literature and culture, both in England and later behind the lines in France, where they served in the same battalion. Johnson was a man of great conscience and morality, as Lewis asserted. 'I had hardly till now encountered principles in anyone so nearly of my own age and my own sort.'

On 17 November, Lewis left for Southampton to catch a boat for France. After a period at the base, he reached the front on his nineteenth birthday, and found his battalion, the 1st Bn Somerset Light Infantry, in training and providing working parties for the line.

Throughout December, the battalion was in a quiet sector although the weather was frequently stormy. Medals were awarded to men for gallantry in actions at Ypres in October. There was a continual frost throughout the month and by Christmas, snow had set in. The battalion was primarily engaged in pumping and clearing out the trenches.

Lewis had been in the line on a number of occasions but reported in a letter to his father that he was only in danger once, when a shell landed near the latrines as he was using them.

His father was worried about Lewis serving in the infantry and made preliminary representations to have him moved to the artillery but Lewis resisted any move to transfer him. He accepted battalion life and made friends quickly from the moment he first blinked his way into a candle lit dugout and saw Captain Percy Harris, his Company Commander and none other than one of his former schoolmasters. Lewis mentioned the fact but the officer, well known in the battalion as a tough and unflappable leader of men, preferred not to recall his former profession and the matter was dropped. Harris had joined up in

September 1914, had served abroad since 1916 and had been made the D (Light) Company's commanding officer the previous month. He would later win the Military Cross and Bar and was Mentioned in Despatches. Another friend was Lewis' platoon sergeant, a thirtytwo year old from Frome in Somerset, Acting Sergeant Harry Ayres. Most officers new to the line relied heavily on such men and Ayres soon taught his officer the culture of live and let live, an unofficial, unspoken pact of non-aggression that helped keep men on both sides of the line alive.

> I had suggested 'pooping' a rifle grenade into a German post where we had seen heads moving, recalled Lewis. 'Just as 'ee like, zir,' said the sergeant, scratching his head, 'but once 'ee start doing that kind of thing, 'ee'll get zummit back, zee!'

And then there was Laurence Johnson. The twenty year old had already been serving in France well before Lewis arrived but although both men were in different companies – Johnson was in B Company – they were able to resume their friendship and intellectual debates.

The weather turned in mid-January and a thaw with heavy rain caused the trenches to collapse and made living conditions almost impossible and illness rife, as Lewis recalled:

> Through the winter, weariness and water were our chief enemies. I have gone to sleep marching and woken again and found myself marching still. One walked in the trenches in thigh gumboots with water above the knee, [and] one remembers the icy stream welling up inside the boot when you punctured it on concealed barbed wire.

The peaceful trench warfare, as Lewis described it, continued until the end of January but the strain and the cold proved as dangerous as any enemy and he was sent down the line suffering from trench fever.

Lewis remained in hospital for nearly a month, greatly enjoying the experience: 'as an alternative to the trenches,' he wrote, 'a bed and a book were very heaven.' When he returned to duty, he found a different atmosphere altogether. A huge German offensive was expected and preparations to meet it were in full swing. Out of the line, training was intensive, for no fewer than nine different defence schemes were drawn up and various contingencies to meet an attack analysed. Letters from Lewis to family at home were few and brief 'We have just come back from a four days' tour in the front line during which I had about as many hours sleep,' he scribbled in early March. His letters remained infrequent during the weeks that followed.

The German March offensive, begun on the 21st of that month, had set out to smash the Allied lines before the war could be decisively tilted against the Germans with the arrival of American forces on the Allied side. The initial assaults had pressed the British forces back across the Somme battlefields but had not been decisive, so the Germans altered their direction of attack to the line further north near Armentières. It was here, the Germans hoped, that the offensive, launched on 9 April, would continue to a successful conclusion.

The 1st Bn Somerset Light Infantry were at Fampoux near Arras and were not directly attacked on the first day, although they were heavily shelled. Later in the month, the battalion was involved in minor actions until the German assault at Armentières, when the battalion was bussed north to help meet the emergency there. The situation was unclear; streams of refugees were seen leaving the forward area which had not been involved in any fighting since 1914. Few trenches survived from that time and as the battalion war record states, 'the countryside was green and untouched by war. The farms were standing and were full of furniture and livestock.' The British line had halted just south of the La Bassée Canal; north of the Canal, opposite the Somerset Light Infantry, in the village of Riez du Vinage, were the Germans. Effectively in No Man's Land was a tow path along which French civilians cycled or pulled carts, intent on retrieving treasured possessions from deserted houses and farms that would soon be destroyed.

It was decided that an attempt would be made to form a deep bridgehead across the river, in effect to protect the Canal, as this was the only real barrier between the enemy and the land behind, where important coalfields lay. The Somerset Light infantry would attack on 14 April and seize the village on the other side of the Canal in what turned out to be the only successful advance made by any British battalion in the First and Second Armies on the Western Front that day. As part of the Light Company, CS Lewis would play an important role.

The attack on the village of Riez du Vinage was characterised as a local enterprise, an attack on the German line where it bulged in a small salient. Final orders were distributed at 2pm to the company commanders who passed on the information to junior officers and in turn to NCOs and other ranks.

They were informed that at 6pm, just as light was failing, the heavy artillery would open up a barrage on the German-held village, followed half an hour later by a barrage from the light 18 pounder guns, concentrating on the western edge of the village. When the attack was launched, the men would follow behind the exploding shells which would creep forward at the rate of fifty yards per minute, halting on the far side of the village and so cutting off German reinforcements or supplies. A machine-gun barrage on the west side of a nearby enemy-held wood called the Bois de Pacaut would also begin at 6.30pm with the aim of suppressing machine gun and rifle fire which might enfilade the British attack.

Three of the four companies in the battalion would lead the attack, with the fourth, A Company, acting as support and preparing to repulse any counter attack. During the afternoon, all four companies crossed the La Bassée Canal to take up their allotted positions ready for the signal to advance. 'Dribbling will be employed,' stated the brigade diary, in other words the number of men who might been observed crossing over the Canal would be limited to three or four at any one time. The last thing commanding officers wished to do was alert the enemy to the counter attack. If the Germans got wind that the enemy were massing, they would call on artillery support and plaster the area with shrapnel.

There were two principal crossing points over the Canal, a footbridge and, a few hundred yards to the right, a drawbridge. Once over the Canal, the men took up positions in and around a number of houses close to the bank. B and C Companies moved towards a fork in a road that led from the Canal to a point close to the outskirts of the village. The Light Company with Second Lieutenant Lewis lined up to their right on a second road that led straight into the village. They would provide a defensive flank to B Company. The bombardment began and the battalion started to deploy to its forward positions.

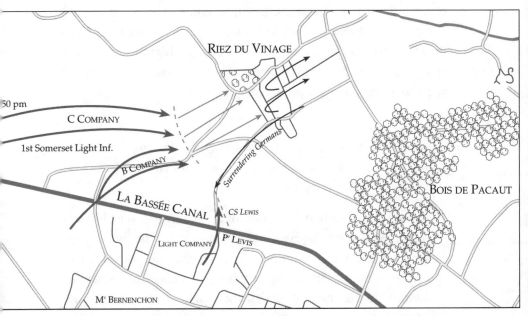

14 April 1918: the succesful evening attack made by the 1st Bn Somerset Light Infantry on the village of Riez du Vinage.

One sergeant, Arthur Cook, a professional soldier who had served with the battalion throughout the entire war, recalled that the preparation for the attack was:

> One of the most extraordinary advertisements of 'look out we're coming' I have witnessed in this war, in full view of the enemy; how they must have chuckled with glee. Just before 6pm we dwindled across our various footbridges in two or threes to our assembly points. The ground here was as flat as a pancake and every move must have been spotted, but not a shot was fired, why should they when a much larger target would present itself soon.

Twenty minutes later, they advanced. A German machine gun began sweeping the ground along the road and another began firing from the edge of the wood. The attack began to falter, so two platoons of A Company were sent forward, attacking in section rushes and leading the other two companies on. To the south, the Light Company came under heavy fire from the wood but this was silenced by the artillery and a machine-gun barrage. Sergeant Cook recalled:

> My company, B, was in the centre fully exposed. It was the opinion that the barrage moved too quick, leaving the enemy free to open up a devastating machine-gun fire on the target they had been waiting for.

> Captain LA Osborne, commanding A Company, took charge of the leading troops. He walked up and down the line urging the men on with no more ceremony than he would have displayed on the barrack square. It was a wonderful display of courage in the face of terrific fire... He soon had the line advancing in a succession of short rushes which captured the enemy outposts and several machine guns.

As the leading troops approached the village, some Germans ran out to surrender; those that did not were soon engaged in hand to hand fighting.

As the leading troops approached the eastern outskirts of the village, the Germans launched a counter attack but this was broken up by rifle and machine-gun fire inflicting, according the War Diary, 40% casualties. Half the remainder ran away, half surrendered to men of the Light Company and Lewis in particular.

> I took about 60 prisoners – that is, I discovered to my great relief that the crowd of field-grey figures who suddenly appeared from nowhere, all had their hands up.

Lewis was able to speak a little German and talked to their officer before directing the men back towards the British lines.

Within 45 minutes the whole objective had been gained and most of the night was spent consolidating the ground won. The Germans in retaliation shelled the village and the western approaches but caused few casualties.

One casualty suffered during the attack itself was Lewis' friend, Lieutenant Laurence Johnson. As an officer in B Company, he had been involved in some of the heaviest fighting inside the village. He had been seriously wounded and was evacuated to No. 4 Canadian Casualty Clearing Station where he died the following morning.

At dawn that day, the 15th, around two hundred Germans made another counter attack which was again beaten off, and for much of the rest of the day ownership of the village lay uncontested, allowing stretcher bearers to move about and collect the wounded.

Combat, however, was far from over. Lewis' Light Company, which had avoided most of the street fighting was ordered to cooperate with an attack that was to be made on the wood. Once again zero hour was set as the light was beginning to fade, but in the fighting that followed, the dark played havoc with the advancing troops. A battalion of the

Duke Of Wellington's Regiment attacked the wood from the west but came under sustained artillery fire and suffered heavy casualties before the two platoons of the Light Company were ready to go over. The Colonel wrote in the War Diary:

> The enemy put down a heavy barrage on our front line causing considerable casualties. Two platoons of the Light Company attacked and entered the wood alone and were fired on and forced to withdraw, suffering about 50% casualties, before the remainder dug in with the Duke of Wellington's.

Whether Lewis took part in this two-platoon attack is unclear. Nevertheless, it was during the fighting that he was wounded by a shell, which he believed to be not German but British. The explosion flung him to the ground, peppering him with shell splinters, cutting his face and his left hand. Splinters also wounded him behind his left leg and just below the knee while a piece of metal went into his chest from underneath his arm. A lot of earth was also spewed up into his face and left eye.

> Just after I was hit, I found (or thought I found) that I was not breathing and concluded that this was death. I felt no fear and certainly no courage. It did not seem to be an occasion for either. The proposition 'Here is a man dying' stood before my mind as dry, as factual, as unemotional as something in a text-book. It was not even interesting.

Lewis was able to crawl away and was picked up by a stretcher bearer. Whether he knew at that time or not, the news that Sergeant Harry Ayres had been killed next to him greatly upset the young subaltern.

> Dear Sergeant Ayres killed by the same shell that wounded me.
> I was a futile officer (they gave commissions too easily then), a

puppet moved about by him, and he turned this ridiculous and painful relation into something beautiful, became to me almost like a father.

Lewis was bundled off to a Casualty Clearing Station where his uniform was cut off and his wounds dressed. He was badly wounded, one of five officer casualties along with 210 other ranks in the two days of fighting. The Battalion had managed to recapture two batteries of British guns, sixteen light machine guns, and four heavy machine guns. In all, 135 prisoners were sent back and an estimated 260 casualties inflicted on the enemy.

News of Lewis's injuries caused consternation at home. These were not as serious as the family at first believed – they understood he had been hit in the face – and there was much relief when Lewis's brother, who was also serving in France, was able to visit him in hospital and ascertain the truth, as Lewis wrote in a letter:

The myth about being hit in the face arose, I imagine, from the fact that I got a lot of dirt in the left eye which was closed up for a few days, but is now all right, I still can't lie on my side (neither the bad one nor the other one) but otherwise I lead the life of an ordinary mortal and my temperature is all right.

The shrapnel was removed although one piece, which was diagnosed as 'nothing to worry about' remained in his chest for the rest of his life.

Lewis remained in hospital until late June, when he was transferred to a convalescent hospital in Bristol. In the short time he had been with the battalion, he had lost most of his friends and the effect on his morale was significant. In a melancholy letter to his father just after he had arrived, he wrote:

Nearly all my friends in the Battalion are gone. Did I ever

mention Johnson who was a scholar of Queen's? I had hoped to meet him at Oxford some day, and renew the endless talks that we had out there…I had had him so often in my thoughts, had so often hit on some new point in one of our arguments, and made a note of things in my reading to tell him when we met again, that I can hardly believe he is dead. Don't you find it particularly hard to realise the death of people whose strong personality makes them particularly alive?

Lewis remained in hospital until October. He never returned to France and was demobbed on Christmas Eve 1918.

There were few longterm effects of Lewis' wounds, except that he could not hold his left arm straight above his head, 'which I don't want to do anyway'. He complained of slight stoppages of breath, typical of a chest wound, and which would soon pass; he became tired easily and was prone to headaches. The other effect, not directly of wounds but of the war in general, was recurring nightmares:

On the nerves there are…effects which will probably go with quiet and rest…nightmares – or rather the same nightmare over and over again. Nearly everyone has it, and though very unpleasant, it is passing and will do not harm…

It was a war he could not forget, but interestingly a war from which he later felt strangely removed:

The War – the frights, the cold, the smell of H.E., [High Explosive] the horribly smashed men still moving like half-crushed beetles, the sitting or standing corpses, the landscape of sheer earth without a blade of grass, the boots worn day and night till they seemed to grow to your feet – all this shows rarely and faintly in memory. It is too cut off from the rest of my experience and often seems to have happened to someone else.

Lewis applied for a wound gratuity and pension, perhaps slightly over-egging the cake when he wrote claiming he was 'severely wounded.' The War Office replied that he was not entitled to any monies.

> I can hardly believe that they are trying to cheat me altogether, he wrote to his father, as it has been repeated time after time in every newspaper that we are all to have them – wounded or unwounded. I met a man from Keble the other day who had never been out, but who was demobilised with a pension of 10/- [shilling] a week on the strength of ill-health contracted while in the service….Certainly if we do get Bolshevism in England, the treacherous and dishonest bureaucracy has earned it.

In the end, owing to the efforts made on his behalf by his father, Lewis was awarded a small wound gratuity which helped pay his way through university, but he was not the first or the last soldier of the Great War to feel that the promised 'land fit for heroes' had been little more than a sham and that the years 1914-1918 had been wasted.

* * *

Clive Staples Lewis, known to his family and friends as Jack, was born in Belfast in 1898, the son of Albert Lewis, a solicitor, and his wife Flora, daughter of a Church of Ireland priest. His parents had very different backgrounds: his father came from a Welsh farming family while his mother had 'many generations of clergymen, lawyers, sailors and the like behind her' as CS Lewis wrote later, adding that he was aware from childhood of the contrast between her cheerful and tranquil affection and his father's constant emotional ups and downs, and that he himself had as a result a deep distrust of emotion. Both parents were widely read, and Lewis's mother was able to give her sons – Jack had an older brother, Warren, known as 'Warnie' – a good grounding in French and Latin.

In 1905, the family moved to a larger house, which they filled with books of all kinds. In the seemingly endless rainy afternoons, as Lewis wrote in his autobiographical work *Surprised by Joy*:

> I took volume after volume from the shelves. I had always the same certainty of finding a book that was new to me as a man who walks in a field has of finding a new blade of grass.

He had lessons from his mother and from an excellent governess, and his childhood was happy until the illness and death of his mother in 1908. His father never recovered from his loss, and Jack and his brother became very close in supporting one another. When Warnie went away to school, Jack took over an attic room as his 'study' and began to write, creating his own fantasy world of Animal-Land, where 'dressed animals' had chivalrous adventures; during Warnie's holidays, a whole history of this world was written, so that the older boy's love of trains and steamships could be incorporated.

The school to which both boys were sent, Wynyard School in Watford, exposed Jack to an England (flat and featureless, as it seemed to him) that he immediately disliked, and also to a vicious and sadistic headmaster. When Warnie moved on, the small group of boys who continued at the school survived by mutual support; the school finally closed and soon afterwards the headmaster was committed to an asylum.

Lewis's schooling took him from place to place, briefly – to his delight – back in Belfast, then to a preparatory school in Malvern, for a year at Malvern College, where he finally lost the Christian faith in which he had been brought up and which had for some time made him uncomfortable. He was unhappy at school, and eventually went to study privately with William Kirkpatrick, a fiercely intellectual Classics scholar in whose company the young Lewis flourished, reading widely in the Classics and also French (with Mrs Kirkpatrick) and German. He relished the endless questioning and intellectual rigour of his tutor, and developed a deep love of Greek literature in particular.

So in 1916, CS Lewis sat his examinations and won a scholarship to University College, Oxford, and in the following year was commissioned into the 3rd (SR) Bn Somerset Light Infantry.

In 1918, he was able to take up his scholarship to Oxford, becoming a Fellow of Magdalen College in 1924 and remaining there for thirty years, before his election to the Chair of Mediaeval and Renaissance English at Magdalene College, Cambridge. He was an inspiring lecturer and highly influential in the lives of many of his students, and a prolific author on literary topics; in particular, his 1936 publication *The Allegory of Love* being a landmark in mediaeval studies.

Three aspects of his personal life are outstanding: his care for Jane Moore, his re-conversion to Christianity, and his marriage and the death of his wife.

First, he kept his promise to his friend Edward Moore, who had been killed in 1918, and looked after Moore's mother Jane for the rest of her life. They became close friends and she was particularly important in helping him to recover from his wounds. In some ways, Jane Moore took the place of Lewis's mother who had died young, and she helped him to overcome his fear of the emotions: 'She was generous and taught me to be generous too,' he wrote of her. In 1930, Lewis and his brother Warnie, Jane Moore and her daughter, shared the purchase of a house in Oxford, where they all lived. Lewis visited Jane faithfully when she had to be cared for in a nursing home, until she died in 1951.

Secondly, while he was studying in Oxford after the war, Lewis was influenced by his own reading and also by his friendship with fellow writers Nevill Coghill and JRR Tolkien, to begin a return to Christian faith. It was a slow and painful process ('Really, a young Atheist cannot guard his faith too carefully. Dangers lie in wait for him on every side,' he wrote of himself at this time). In 1929, he at last accepted the faith he had earlier rejected, although he described himself as 'the most dejected and reluctant convert in all England'. Ironically, it is his religious writing, especially the Narnia books, for which Lewis is today most widely remembered.

In the early 1950s, Lewis began to correspond with an American writer, formally a Communist and atheist but by then also a committed Christian. Joy Gresham was separated from her husband, and came to England with her two sons. She was to Lewis an agreeable intellectual companion; his brother Warnie wrote that she was 'the only woman [his brother] had met who had a brain that matched his in suppleness, in width of interest and in analytical grasp, and above all in humour and a sense of fun.' It was on this basis that Lewis agreed to a civil marriage so that she could continue to live in England.

In 1956, Joy was diagnosed with terminal cancer. By this time, the couple were deeply in love, and wanted a Christian marriage; this was not easy because of Joy's divorce, but an Anglican friend performed the ceremony by Joy's bedside. Her cancer went into remission, and the two spent a few happy years together before her death from the disease in 1960. He wrote later in his anguished outpouring of pain *A Grief Observed* that it was incredible how much happiness, even how much gaiety, they had shared when all hope of her recovery had gone. Nothing prepared him for the agony of losing her, but he gradually came to realise that he remembered her most clearly when he was not actively mourning her loss. A film, *Shadowlands*, [1993] directed by Richard Attenborough, told the story of their relationship and Joy Gresham's death. CS Lewis himself died just three years after Joy, on 22 November 1963.

His literary and religious output was immense, as was its range, and much of it is still widely read today. But his series of children's fantasy novels with a Christian message, *The Chronicles of Narnia*, has been translated into many languages, sold over 100 million copies, and been adapted for radio, television, stage and cinema, and it is most of all for these books that he is remembered.

CHAPTER NINE

Basil Rathbone

—⚬—

Suddenly there were footsteps and a German soldier came into view behind the next traverse. He stopped suddenly, struck dumb, no doubt, by our strange appearance. Capturing him was out of the question; we were too far away from home. But before he could pull himself together and spread the alarm, I shot him twice with my revolver – he fell dead.

Basil Rathbone, *In and Out of Character*

SURELY THE MOST challenging part that Basil Rathbone undertook in his long acting career was that of impersonating a tree. The stage – No Man's Land – was overlooked on all sides, but for this show the actors hoped, for all they were worth, that the audience was looking elsewhere. It was a vital role, part of a larger performance, to obtain intelligence on the enemy – information which, when it was successfully obtained, was met with rousing approval by senior officers and officially recognised with the award of two Military Medals and a Military Cross.

In the early summer of 1918, the 1/10th Bn King's Liverpool Regiment (Liverpool Scottish) was in trenches near the northern French village of Festubert. This had a fearsome reputation, having been the scene of a short-lived but very bloody offensive three years earlier. Lieutenant Basil Rathbone was a battalion intelligence officer, a job which entailed sending out and frequently leading reconnaissance patrols into No Man's Land. Often twice a week he ventured over the top, usually with three hand-picked men, crawling out towards the German lines which were, at the time, just 200 yards away. His aim was to bring back useful information about enemy dispositions and intentions.

The soldiers under his command were, as he called them, 'old-timers', and knew all the tricks of the trade. They had little intention of getting into a fight with a German patrol and so frequently reported their 'suspicions' that the enemy were close by, halting the patrol when in fact none were about. On the patrol's return, it was Rathbone's job to write up a report.

> As I remember them now, many of them were masterpieces of invention; inconclusive, yet always suggesting that every effort had been made by our patrol to garner information and/or make contact with the enemy. Under such circumstances one's imagination was often sorely tried in supplying acceptable 'news items' that could be examined at Battalion H.Q. and then confidently filed away under the heading of 'Intelligence'.

By July 1918, the opposing trench lines on the Western Front had largely stabilised. Both sides were catching their breath after their exertions earlier in the year, when the Germans had launched repeated offensives in their attempt to drive a physical wedge between the British and French forces. These offensives had thrust several deep salients into the Allied lines but had failed to break through conclusively. That summer, rumours began to spread that the Germans were preparing to pull out of their forward positions. Distinctive noises at night indicated that enemy transport and guns were on the move, and Basil Rathbone was aware of the urgency of compiling genuinely accurate intelligence reports. With this in mind, he approached his Commanding Officer, Colonel Monro, with what appeared to be a hare-brained idea but which, on closer inspection, was less dangerous than it sounded and could provide vital information on German intentions.

'At night it was always most difficult to judge objects and distances. In daylight these difficulties would be obviated.' Rathbone suggested using camouflage, primarily tree foliage. 'The "ham" in me had suddenly become stronger than my sense of survival. Colonel Monro seemed intrigued and gave his consent.'

Rathbone's idea was to take a patrol into No Man's Land just before dawn and to undertake a number of patrols in full daylight. He proposed to take just two men with him: twenty-one year old Corporal Norman Tanner, a butcher by trade from Cheshire but, by 1918, a trusted scout who had served for two years in France; and Private Richard Burton, a former clerk from Preston who had lied about his age when he enlisted in May 1915. He was also twenty-one, a sniper with nearly 18 months' service on the Western Front. The next morning, Rathbone's batman woke his officer at 3.30am.

Camouflage suits had been made for us to resemble trees. On our heads we wore wreaths of freshly plucked foliage; our faces and hands were blackened with burnt cork. About 5.00am we crawled through our wire and lay up in No-Man's-Land. All sentries had been alerted to our movements.

For several days we tested our adventure, and it soon became evident that the enemy had no suspicions whatsoever of our presence. We were able accurately to locate German machine-gun positions, which were later phoned back to artillery and put out of action. We also noted a sparseness of enemy front line positions, supporting High Command's contention that something was up.

Close to the machine gun position, Rathbone had also discovered a number of enemy rifles and stick grenades, although what he did with them is not recorded.

It was in the light of this success that a more daring exploit was arranged: a raid on the enemy trenches to seize a prisoner or obtain other definite information about the enemy. The Colonel was willing to launch a much larger raid but first offered Rathbone the opportunity to go with a smaller party. To his great credit, Rathbone did not hesitate to accept the task.

The following day, he and his patrol wound their way into No Man's Land. Rathbone noted that as they lay there, a squadron of enemy aircraft dived to barely a hundred feet above the trenches. Each aircraft was painted a different colour and he deduced that they must have been part of Manfred von Richthofen's famous Flying Circus. Rathbone wrote later that he could see by the colours which plane was Richthofen's and which was flown by Hermann Goering, the Nazi Party's future deputy leader, who in the Great War was a fighter ace.

Richthofen was in fact already dead, killed in April 1918, but Hermann Goering was probably present. In July, he had taken over command of *Jagdesschwader 1*, Richthofen's former squadron, after the then commander, ace Wilhelm Reinhard, was killed.

As the aircraft passed overhead, they were engaged from the British trenches while, simultaneously, they were cheered from the German lines. Moments later the planes were gone but they left behind them an air of unreality, and as Rathbone lay between the opposing lines he could discern an almost festive atmosphere, with laughing and talking and 'casual movement' from behind the parapets of both friend and foe. It was the perfect moment to attack.

Crawling slowly forward, the raiding party reached the enemy line after almost an hour. Here they began to cut the barbed wire in front of the enemy's lightly held trench, then quietly the foliated three rolled over the parapet into the German line.

> The only sound now to be heard was a skylark climbing up into a cloudless blue sky, as the opposing armies took their midday siesta. We rose and proceeded slowly and with the utmost care along the German trench. We made our way around a traverse – then another stretch of empty trench – and proceeded further.

Suddenly there were footsteps and a German soldier came into view behind the next traverse. He stopped suddenly, struck dumb, no doubt, by our strange appearance. Capturing him was out of the question; we were too far away from home. But before he could pull himself together and spread the alarm, I shot him twice with my revolver – he fell dead. Tanner tore the identification tags off his uniform and I rifled his pockets, stuffing a diary and some papers into my camouflage suit. Now things happened fast. There were sounds of movement on both sides of us, so we scaled the parapet, forced our way through the barbed wire – I have the scars on my right leg to this day – and ran for the nearest shell hole. We had hardly reached it when two machine guns opened a crossfire on us. We lay on the near lip of the crater, which was so close to their lines that it gave us cover. The machine-gun bullets pitted the rear of the crater.

A quick decision was taken. Rathbone felt that their best chance of survival would be to split up and run from shell hole to shell hole in different directions. This, they hoped, would confuse the machine gunners and dissipate the concentration of fire as the Germans failed to decide whom to aim at. The plan worked and all three men made it back to the British front line, albeit 1½ miles apart. One man was recorded as having been slightly wounded.

The raid was deemed a success, but the excitement of the attack and escape had blotted out the inevitable angst at going in the first place. As Rathbone recovered his composure, an inescapable smell pervaded the atmosphere. 'Gosh, but you stink,' someone said. As Rathbone had dodged his way from shell hole to shell hole, he had trodden on a decomposing body and the sickly remains had engulfed his boot. The stench was so awful that Rathbone nearly fainted, and there and then he removed the offending footwear. Then, with the aid of someone's bayonet, it was impaled and hurled over the parapet into No Man's Land.

Up to that moment, I had felt no fear, sustained and driven by the bravura of the mission and with the image of Richthofen's bright circus dancing in my brain. With one shoe off and one shoe on, the reality and horror of war came rushing in on me.

The hot sunny day gave way to heavy rain. The next day, the 27th, the enemy wire and the machine gun post located during the previous day's patrol were heavily shelled. It is not recorded what Rathbone did and how long it took to recover from his exertions. Nevertheless, this was not his last attempted raid. On 7 August he tried again. Locating an enemy post north of Cailloux, he made an approach but was held up by barbed wire. Unable to get through, Private Burton shot one sentry before the party retired.

Basil Rathbone's bravery did not go unnoticed. At the end of August, the War Diary noted the following:

A conspicuous feature of the last two months has been the activity of the Battalion daylight patrols (snipers and scouts) under the able leadership of Lieutenant P St J B Rathbone. Highly appreciative comments on the invaluable information obtained, and the excellent work accomplished have several times been received from Corps, Divisional and Brigade commanders. As showing the dash and resource displayed on the execution of these exploits, two Military Medals were gained, one by 356372 Pte N. Tanner (scout) and the other by 356120 Pte R. Burton (sniper).

A few days later, on 9 September, news arrived that Basil Rathbone had been awarded the Military Cross, although he himself was away on leave. The Divisional citation in the *London Gazette* dated 7 November stated:

For conspicuous daring and resource near Festubert on 26 July

1918, and on three other occasions, viz – 5,7 and 14 August, when on patrol. Lieutenant Rathbone volunteered to go out on daylight patrol, and on each occasion brought back invaluable information regarding enemy's posts, and the exact position and condition of the wire. On 26 July, when on the enemy's side of the wire, he came face to face with a German. He shot the German, but this alarmed two neighbouring posts, and they at once opened a heavy fire with two machine guns. Despite the enemy fire, Lieutenant Rathbone got his three men and himself through the enemy wire and back to our lines. The result of his patrolling was to pin down exactly where the enemy posts were, and how they were held, while inflicting casualties on the enemy at no loss to his own men. Lieutenant Rathbone has always shown a great keenness in patrol work both by day and by night.

If there was a third man in the party, his name went unrecorded and his bravery unrecognised. Rathbone makes no mention of a third man in the patrol.

* * *

Both Tanner and Burton survived the war, which led to a curious incident. Eighteen years later, in the summer of 1934, Basil Rathbone was working in Toledo, Ohio, preparing for the opening of *Romeo and Juliet*. He was in his hotel room when the phone rang. His wife picked it up, handing it to her bemused husband, who knew no one in Toledo. On the other end of the phone was Corporal Tanner, a former 'Brigand'. The former Cheshire butcher had emigrated to the States where he had taken US citizenship, becoming a policeman. The two met up and had what Basil described as a 'somewhat emotional reunion.' They celebrated into the early hours of the morning. Basil later wrote, 'Some of the ghosts in my life have come back to haunt me, and some of them have been astonishingly real.'

Despite the subsequent evidence of his bravery, the prospect of conflict in August 1914 had not excited Basil Rathbone in the slightest. Aged twentytwo when war broke out, he was 'dreaming of prodigious accomplishments' in his chosen career of acting. He might have been brought up reading stories of the Empire by Rudyard Kipling; he may have been partly educated by the pictures on his nursery wall which carried stirring images of the Charge of the Light Brigade and the Guards Brigade at Waterloo, but when it came to the fight he was not keen to enlist.

> I felt physically sick to my stomach, as I saw or heard or read of the avalanche of brave young men rushing to join 'The Colours'...I was pondering how long I could delay joining up.

It was possible to escape military enlistment for a year or more, even if women, intent on humiliating those they saw as unpatriotic, handed out white feathers and slurs upon a man's honour. By late 1915, a move came to register all men in the country for service, ostensibly to provide industry with the manpower it needed, but with the longer term aim of supplying the armed forces with recruits when conscription became politically acceptable. Basil Rathbone duly attested under the Derby Scheme on the 13 November 1915 but he was not called up until 30 March 1916 when, as Private Rathbone, he began his training at Richmond Park, London with the 1/14th (County of London) Battalion (London Scottish).

He largely despised his basic instruction in weaponry and the unsubtle invitations to hate the enemy, and applied for a commission, undergoing officer training in Scotland. Notwithstanding considerable qualities of leadership, Rathbone, and a fellow officer with whom he was great friends, were informed that their classroom work was of 'an extremely poor calibre'. Both were at great risk of failing their exams, which would have meant an immediate return to the ranks and probable embarkation for France. Three weeks' dedicated study saw both men eventually pass, Rathbone being sent at his own request to the Liverpool Scottish. At the regimental depot he was given a platoon, but contracted measles in February 1917, and after a week in a military hospital he was sent home to 24 Hendrick Avenue, close to Wandsworth Common in London. Here he shared the house with his brother John, who was recuperating from a serious gunshot wound.

Basil and John were very close, although there was a full five years' difference in age. John was younger, and he had apparently had none of his brother's reservations about enlisting. In March 1915, he volunteered for service aged just seventeen and was commissioned into the Dorset Regiment. Curiously, although he was born in 1897, John wrote on his application for a commission that he was born in 1898 and was nearly thrown out as under age. The error was rectified with the presentation of a birth certificate and he was sent for training. In 1916 he embarked for France and in July he was shot through the chest and right lung during an attack on the Somme village of Guillemont. Eight months later his health was still delicate. In February, he had a bad attack of jaundice which confined him to bed and his brother's welcome company. It would be almost another year before he returned to the Western Front.

As soon as Basil was better, he returned to the depot and trained with the men under his command. He soon felt thoroughly adjusted to army life and, two months later, was finally sent abroad to join his battalion, the 2/10 Bn King's Liverpool Regiment, in the trenches near Bois Grenier. On 23 May 1917, the unit's War Diary refers to the battalion being in billets. It also notes that a 2nd Lt P St J Rathbone had reported for duty and was duly posted to B Company. Basil continued to serve with them until he was transferred to the 1/10th Battalion when the two battalions were amalgamated at the end of April 1918.

Other than a few partial memories of war service noted in Rathbone's memoir, *In and Out of Character*, published in 1956, not much more is known about his service. One incident worth mentioning is his departure for France. He left from Victoria Station where his parents came to see him off. His departure was nothing like as difficult as he'd expected. In fact, he felt oddly estranged from them. 'I could find in them no signs of any deep emotion, and for myself I can honestly say I disclosed none either. We had conditioned ourselves severely for this moment,' he later wrote, adding that his mother said to her husband. 'It's like seeing Basil off to school in the old days, isn't it?' Basil was not to see his mother again. She died just months later.

The other tragedy which was to overshadow much of Basil's life was the death of his younger brother, John. This is one of the few other stories of note to which he refers.

Shortly before John's death, Basil had met his brother in France. John's battalion had been in billets nearby, and so the brothers were given permission to meet. A 'glorious day' was spent together before John visited the Mess of the Liverpool Scottish:

> We retired late, full of good food and Scotch whiskey. We shared my bed and were soon sound asleep. It was still dark when I awakened from a nightmare. I had just seen John killed. I lit the candle beside my bed and held it to my brother's face – for some moments I could not persuade myself that he was not indeed dead. At last I heard his regular gentle breathing. I kissed him and blew out the candle and lay back on my pillow again. But further sleep was impossible. A tremulous premonition haunted me – a premonition which even the dawn failed to dispel.'

On 4 June 1918, John was killed in action. Basil recalled sitting in his dugout in the front line when 'for some inexplicable reason I wanted to cry, and did.' However, his memory is slightly at odds with the War Diary, which puts the battalion firmly behind the lines resting in the village of Vaudricourt. Wherever he was, Basil wrote a letter to his brother. No reply was received and in due course he received the dreaded news that John had indeed been killed.

The loss of John was a terrible blow. As Basil returned from the war in 1919, he recalled that while the recollections of fear and the filth were beginning to fade, the memories of those who had not returned remained forever vivid and, as the coast of England came into view, the men on board the troopship were silent. He was daunted by the prospect of adjusting to civilian life once again. At home he found his father considerably aged since the death of his wife and son, and his sister in mourning, a state that she never quite shook off. 'I was completely on my own for the first time in my life,' acknowledged Basil. Nevertheless, unlike his father and sister who 'had decided to live in the past,' he had a strong sense of moving on; his future firmly beckoned.

* * *

Philip St John Basil Rathbone was born in Johannesburg, South Africa, on 13 June 1892. His father, Edgar, was a mining engineer, while his mother, Anna, was a violinist. He had two siblings, Beatrice and John. His memories of South Africa would have been vague, for in 1896 the family was forced to flee to England after his father was accused of being a British spy. Whether he was or not, Basil never asked.

He may not have known the reasons for his family's rapid departure from South Africa, but Basil grew up knowing all about his esteemed forebears and he was aware of the great hopes placed on his young shoulders by the family. In his memoirs, he either implied or claimed family links with various people of note, including Major Henry Reed Rathbone. In May 1865, Henry Rathbone was sitting next to President Abraham Lincoln at the theatre when the assassin and actor James Wilkes Booth attacked, mortally wounding the President. In the family lineage there were also poets, the best known being Laurence Binyon, while an uncle was the Lord Mayor of Liverpool. A cousin, Eleanor Rathbone, was one of the first women MPs and championed the state payment of the family allowance, while another cousin was the accomplished actor Sir Frank Benson. In May 1916, he was knighted by King George V at the Drury Lane Theatre after a special Royal Command performance of *Julius Caesar*, Benson playing the title role. Sir Frank would play a crucial role in his younger cousin's acting career.

From 1906 to 1910, Basil attended Repton School. At just over six feet, he was tall for his generation and he excelled at sport, showing little interest in academic work. Basil also joined the school's OTC, learning the rudiments of military drill, but it was while at school that he showed a real aptitude for acting and a love for the profession quickly grew. His ambition to be an actor was briefly thwarted when his father persuaded his young son to work in an insurance company for one year in the hope that he might forget any dream of becoming an actor. After this year, Basil joined his cousin's theatre company. Frank Benson was one of the first men from the upper classes to choose acting as a profession and he had formed his own touring company as far back as 1883. He expected his cousin to earn his roles through ability, and cast him in his first professional role, in *The Taming of the Shrew* at Ipswich in 1912. Benson, seeing that Rathbone had genuine talent, took the young actor to America later that year when his company went on tour. It was while acting at Stratford upon Avon in August 1913 that he met his future wife Marion Foreman, and in October the following year they were married. A son, Rodion, was born the following July. He continued to act, despite inevitable pressures to enlist and in 1915 he appeared at the Lysander Theatre in *A Midsummer Night's Dream*. Shortly afterwards he joined the army.

Basil's marriage did not last. Within months of returning from the war, he left his wife and son for reasons he never disclosed, although feelings of guilt, particularly towards his son, wracked him for many years. In 1923 he went to the USA to act and soon met and fell in love with Ouida Bergere, a scriptwriter whom he later married.

Although much of his work remained in the theatre, his growing

December 1955: Professor JRR Tolkien, aged 63, Fellow of Merton College. Descriptions contained in his book *The Lord of the Rings* have an obvious resonance with his service on the Somme.

A medical return filled in by JRR Tolkien himself. It discloses the cause of his hospitalisation, noted as 'Trench Fever', and the route and date by which he returned home.

The graves of Rob Gilson, killed by a shell explosion, and Geoffrey Smith, who died of wounds in December 1916.

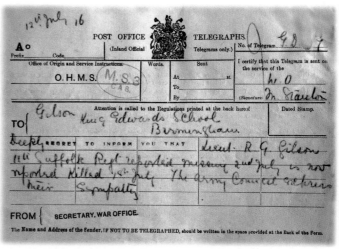

The dreaded Post Office telegram sent to Rob Gilson's family confirming his death in action on 1 July 1916. He had previously been reported missing.

A BATH ACTOR.

Mr. Arnold Ridley.

Mr. Arnold Ridley, the only son of Mr. and Mrs. W. R. Ridley, of Manvers Street, Bath, we are pleased to hear, is making gratifying progress in the histrionic art. He is doing excellently in Mr. John Drinkwater's company at the Birmingham Repertory Theatre. He acted admirably in a minor part in "Abraham Lincoln," which has attracted the King, the Archbishop of Canterbury, and "Society" generally to Hammersmith Theatre. Mr. Ridley has not gone to London, but remains at the Midland metropolis, where in "Gentlemen of the Press" he earned Press enconiums for his impersonation of "Vernal" (chief sub-editor of the "Daily Mercury").

Top left: Arnold Ridley, aka Charles Godfrey, relaxing between takes while filming the hit television comedy *Dad's Army*. Acting in the series gave Ridley a financial security he had never hitherto known.

Above: Arnold Ridley as a Lance Corporal in the 6th Somerset Light Infantry. He was wounded on three separate occasions. On 16 September 1916 he suffered bayonet wounds to his groin and hand. His skull was also badly fractured by a German rifle butt, although this injury was not diagnosed for two years.

Left: 'A Bath Actor': a newspaper cutting from the 1920s noting Ridley's stage success. It also paid tribute to his war service and the bayonet wound to his hand and wrist.

Gueudecourt

German trench hidden from view

Sunken road

6th Bn Somerset Light Infantry

The ground over which Arnold Ridley attacked on 16 September 1916. Just over the ridge, 200 yards away, was a trench hidden from view. Although this enemy position was seized, the actual objectives, Gird Trench and Gird Support, were not.

The hidden trench ran along the slight dip in the ground. In all, 150 officers and men of the 6th Bn Somerset Light Infantry were killed here, of whom just 24 have known graves. The rest are commemorated on the Thiepval Memorial.

6th Bn Somerset Light Infantry

German trench hidden from view

Second Lieutenant Harold Macmillan waiting in the village of Vermelles, just hours before taking part in the Loos offensive. As darkness fell that evening, he was shot through the right hand.

Guards Memorial   The Triangle   Serpentine Trench

Serpentine Trench, looking west towards The Triangle. Harold Macmillan left this position advance towards the German second line but was hit by machine gun fire.

Ginchy   Orchard

15 September 1916: Unsupported by artillery or tanks, the 2nd Grenadier Guards crossed a thousand yards to reach Serpentine Trench from the shattered remains of Ginchy, on the horizon.

Looking towards the British lines from the remains of the orchard, in the northeast corner of the Somme village of Ginchy. The apple tree (middle distance) stands close to the spot where Harold Macmillan supported a successful attack on a German machine gun post, 14 September 1916.

One of Britain's greatest mountaineers: George Mallory sits with his beloved wife Ruth shortly before he was drafted to France. They corresponded on a daily basis while George was serving with the artillery.

Mallory (left) and Irvine shortly before they left camp for the final assault on the summit of Everest. Mallory's body was discovered in May 1999, lying at a height of 26,760 ft. His belongings, including several handwritten letters, were found perfectly intact.

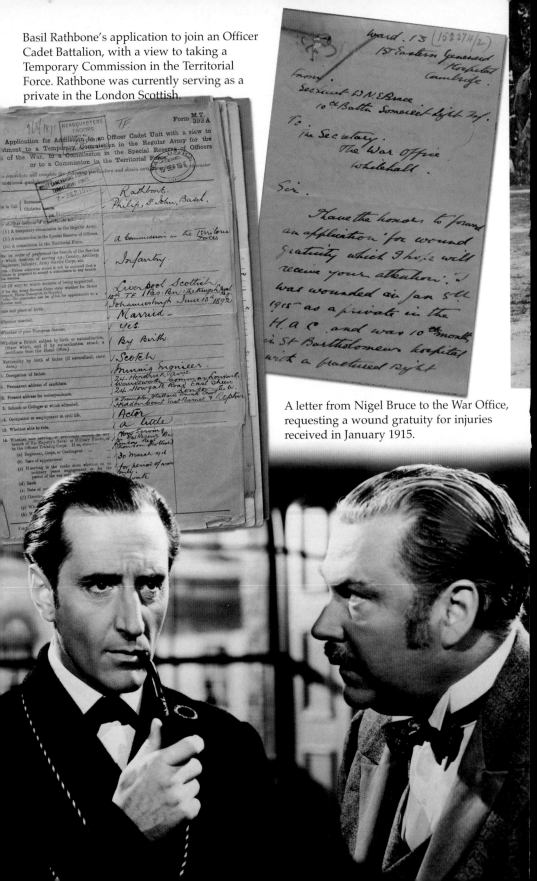

Basil Rathbone's application to join an Officer Cadet Battalion, with a view to taking a Temporary Commission in the Territorial Force. Rathbone was currently serving as a private in the London Scottish.

A letter from Nigel Bruce to the War Office, requesting a wound gratuity for injuries received in January 1915.

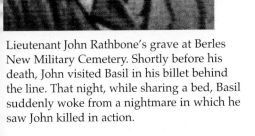

Basil Rathbone pictured with his platoon in France, May 1918, exactly a year after he had first embarked for the Western Front. In June 1918, Basil's brother John (left) was killed in action. After his death, Rathbone adopted an almost cavalier regard for his own safety, taking unnecessary risks but also winning the Military Cross.

Lieutenant John Rathbone's grave at Berles New Military Cemetery. Shortly before his death, John visited Basil in his billet behind the line. That night, while sharing a bed, Basil suddenly woke from a nightmare in which he saw John killed in action.

ft: The super-sleuth and his dependable side-
k: Basil Rathbone and Nigel Bruce during their
yday as Holmes and Watson. In their films
gether, Bruce was largely incapable of running as
chine gun bullets had ripped through both legs
d fractured his right thigh.

Winston Churchill in France. Closely associated with the failure of the Dardanelles Campaign, Churchill chose to resign his position in Government and serve in the trenches. He went overseas in November 1915, joining the 2nd Grenadier Guards, before being given command of the 6th Royal Scots Fusiliers in January 1916.

Laurence Farm, as painted by Winston Churchill in 1916. The farm served as Churchill's Battalion Headquarters. The heavily sandbagged exterior took the brunt of frequent enemy shellfire. The farm was eventually destroyed but the well (inset) can still be seen.

The plaque at Ploegsteert Town Hall unveiled by Winston Churchill's grandson on 11 November 1991, commemorating the time Churchill served in the area with the Royal Scots Fusiliers.

(Right) RC Sherriff in uniform.

RC Sherriff pictured at his home in the 1920s around the time his play *Journey's End* was becoming not only a national but an international phenomenon. He would later become embroiled in litigation, fighting off spurious claims from opportunists claiming copyright theft.

Bottom: Manancourt Château in the village of Etricourt. While in German hands, the 18th century château had been used as a field hospital. Later, on the edge of its grounds, Dennis Wheatley built a cottage he named Crooked Villa, where he had a frightening and macabre experience. (Inset) The Château at the end of the war. The owner promised Wheatley he would rebuild it, but he never returned.

Below: All that remains visible of the Château is a square of rough ground where the building once stood. In the trees and undergrowth on the edge of the grounds are a few bricks, worked stone slabs, and odd pieces of metalwork belonging to the once magnificent building.

Second Lieutenant Dennis Wheatley prior to his embarkation for France to join the 36th (Ulster) Division, Royal Field Artillery.

London 1930s: John Christie craved respectability, but he had a history of petty theft and was prone to outbursts of anger and violence.

An infamous address: 10 Rillington Place was part of a Victorian terrace built in the 1860s. It was here that the remains of six women, including Christie's wife Ethel, were found under the sitting room floorboards. In 1954, at the request of residents, the street was renamed Ruston Place. It was demolished in 1976 and the site redeveloped.

Christie, a man of above average intelligence, served as a signaller in France. In 1918 he was gassed and hospitalised. At his trial, he maintained that the effects were much more debilitating than the medical evidence would suggest.

Peter Llewelyn Davies MC, (front row, far right) during service with the King's Royal Rifle Corps. As one of JM Barrie's famous 'boys', Peter never escaped association with that 'terrible masterpiece', as he called *Peter Pan*. In 1960, suffering from depression, Peter Llewelyn Davies committed suicide.

Opposite top: One of the most memorable images of the 20th century: sixteen year old newspaper boy Ned Parfett, outside the White Star Line offices in London, announces the sinking of the RMS *Titanic*. The place where he stood on Cockspur Street is easily identifiable today.

Peter's brother George, pictured during pre-war training with Eton Officer Training Corps (far right). He was killed in March 1915 while attached to the 4th Rifle Brigade in Belgium, profoundly distressing both Peter and JM Barrie.

Opposite middle: Ned Parfett with his younger brother Thomas and sisters Kitty and Nellie. The picture is believed to have been taken when Ned was on leave.

Opposite far right: The letter from 2nd Lieutenant Percy Hunt confirming the circumstances of Ned's death to his elder brother George Parfett. Of the four Parfett brothers who served in the army, only Ned did not return.

Opposite: Ned Parfett's death plaque. He is buried in Verchain British Cemetery, eight miles south of Valenciennes. His nephew and other close relatives continue to visit his grave in France.

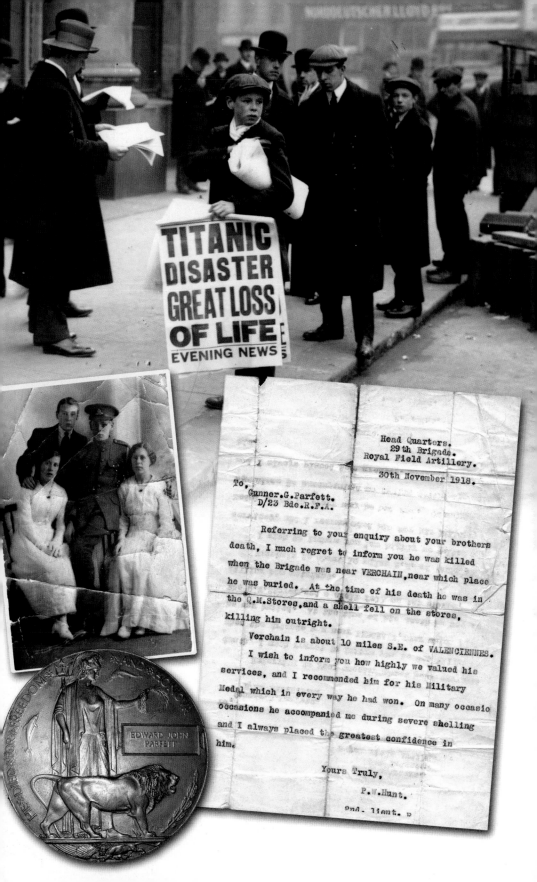

TITANIC
DISASTER
GREAT LOSS
OF LIFE
EVENING NEWS

EDWARD JOHN PARFETT

Head Quarters.
29th Brigade.
Royal Field Artillery.

30th November 1918.

To,
Gunner.G.Parfett.
D/23 Bde.R.F.A.

Referring to your enquiry about your brothers death, I much regret to inform you he was killed when the Brigade was near VERCHAIN, near which place he was buried. At the time of his death he was in the Q.M.Stores, and a shell fell on the stores, killing him outright.

Verchain is about 10 miles S.E. of VALENCIENNES.

I wish to inform you how highly we valued his services, and I recommended him for his Military Medal which in every way he had won. On many occasio occasions he accompanied me during severe shelling and I always placed the greatest confidence in him.

Yours Truly,

P.W.Hunt.

2nd. lieut. R

High Wood

Direction of attack 11th Warwicks

Intermediate Trench

The view north of the Somme village of Bazentin le Petit, looking east across Intermediate Trench with High Wood beyond. It was in this field that Milne (right) struggled in vain to maintain telephone communication during the battle.

AA Milne as a newly commissioned officer. He was 33 years old when he enlisted, later serving as a Signalling Officer with the 11th (Service) Bn Royal Warwickshire Regiment.

The summer of 1917. CS Lewis (left) punts down the Cherwell with his great friend, Edward Moore (right). Edward Moore's grave (centre) in France. After the death of his friend, Lewis looked after Moore's mother for the remainder of his life.

Sixty Germans surrender to CS Lewis from the direction of Riez du Vinage

Riez du Vinage

Looking across the La Bassée Canal towards the village of Riez du Vinage. Using a drawbridge, Light Company crossed the canal and formed up on the far side. Inset: Among the trees is one of the surviving Demarcation Stones, erected to show the furthest point west reached by the Germans during the spring offensive of 1918.

The road from the canal to Riez du ‑nage. CS Lewis took sixty prisoners here as they streamed out of the village to surrender. Inset: 'Dear Sergeant Ayres', CS Lewis' trusted friend, killed in the same shell explosion that wounded him. Harry Ayres' body was never identified and his name is on the Loos Memorial with the names of 20,000 other men who have no known grave.

SERJEANT
‑YRES H.C.
‑EARE W.J.
FOSTER H.B.
‑ART A.

Looking from a modern road bridge towards farmland to the west of the Riez du Vinage. It was across these fields that B and C Companies, 1st Bn Somerset Light Infantry, moved into position before the order was given to assault the village. When the attack stalled A Coy followed on in support driving the Germans back.

Riez du Vinage

C Coy

B Coy

Meteren today, looking up the ridge that the British attacked on 13 October 1914. Montgomery was shot through his back by a sniper. He was not expected to survive, and a grave was dug for him.

Bernard Law Montgomery back in France in 1916 after recovering from wounds. The medal ribbon denoting the award of the Distinguished Service Order can be seen above his left breast pocket.

The grave of D Company's Major William Christie. He had previously served in the Sudan in 1898 and the South African Campaign 1899-1902. His is one of the two conclusively identified graves.

Meteren Military Cemetery contains the remains of the officers and men killed fighting with the 1st Bn Royal Warwickshire Regiment. Only two are positively identified, the location of the others being in doubt after heavy fighting in April and June 1918 disturbed the ground. The graves face uphill, the direction of the attack in 1914.

reputation drew him to the cinema and from 1925 he made a number of films, playing opposite some of the great screen idols such Errol Flynn in *Captain Blood* and Tyrone Power in *The Mark of Zorro*. Rathbone also won two Academy Award nominations for best supporting actor in 1936 and 1938.

Nevertheless, it is for playing Sherlock Holmes that Basil Rathbone is best remembered. He starred in fourteen films between 1939 and 1946, the best known being *The Hound of the Baskervilles*. He played opposite Nigel Bruce, whose portrayal of the naive Dr Watson was the perfect foil for Rathbone's incisive Holme

> There is no question in my mind that Nigel Bruce was the ideal Dr Watson. There was an endearing quality to his performance that to a very large extent, I believe, humanised the relationship between Dr Watson and Mr Holmes. It has always seemed to me to be more than possible that our 'adventures' might have met with a less kindly public acceptance had they been recorded with a less lovable companion.

Basil's career in the cinema continued long after his role as Sherlock Holmes, and he also took to radio and television as well as returning frequently to the stage, always his first love.

Like his colleague Nigel Bruce, Basil died in America, both men suffering heart attacks. He was 75 years old when he died in New York on 21 July 1967 leaving a second wife and an adopted daughter. Of the many celebrities who have stars on the Hollywood Walk of Fame on Hollywood Boulevard, few have three to their name. Basil Rathbone's name is held in posterity on a star for motion pictures, another for his work in radio and one for his work in television.

CHAPTER TEN

Nigel Bruce

—␣—

In some places the parapet was only breast high and in order
to get cover during the daytime the men had to sit in the mud
on the floor of the trench, and very often a man would find
himself sitting on the chest of a mutely protesting Frenchman
who had been lying there for a month or six weeks.

The Honourable Artillery Company in The Great War, 1914 -1918

WHILE NOT ALL super sleuths need a sidekick to aid their detective work, it is hard to imagine Sherlock Holmes without Dr Watson, his affable, bumbling friend. The pair's success at solving crime disguised the fact that Watson's intellect was so immeasurably inferior to Holmes's that only a close personal friendship could explain why Watson was entertained without question by the genius detective. Off-screen, the two actors were the best of friends too, and that natural compatibility ensured that their partnership in front of the cameras worked so compellingly. It was just as well that the two were friends, for a convivial telegram that Rathbone sent to Bruce arrived just as the latter was contemplating a rather dramatic finale to his acting career.

The year was 1938 and William Nigel Bruce was at a low ebb. He had been involved in the failure of a Broadway production, *Knights of Song*, a short-lived musical about the lives of Gilbert and Sullivan. He was feeling morose, but then received two pieces of good news. The first was that his friend the film star Ronald Colman had married, and then came the second ray of sunshine during this depressing interim:

...a telegram I received the morning after the notice [of closure] of *Knights of Song* had been posted at the theatre. The telegram was from Basil Rathbone, and he said, 'Do come back to Hollywood, Willie, dear boy, and play Dr Watson to my Sherlock Holmes. We'll have great fun together'. Basil can never realise how much that telegram cheered me up, as when I received it, I was in the mood to put my head in the gas oven.

Within a year, the pair had made their first and perhaps greatest film, *The Hound of the Baskervilles*, one of many such films that would cement their fame and immortalise the pair to most people as the 'authentic' Holmes-Watson partnership. The preoccupation of film and television with the detective has spawned many other double acts who have tried to play Sir Arthur Conan Doyle's most famous characters, but few have begun to fill the shoes of Holmes and Watson left empty since the premature death of Nigel Bruce in October 1953, aged fifty-eight.

Nigel Bruce, along with so many of his British acting compatriots, including Colman and Rathbone, had served in the Great War, but unlike his friends he had been so seriously wounded that his injuries would plague him for the rest of his life. It is unlikely that Bruce's early death could in any way be attributed to these wounds, but like all those who served, he never entirely escaped the long shadow of the war.

On the morning of 5 January 1915, C Company of the 1st Battalion Honourable Artillery Company (Infantry) was in the front line near the Belgian village of Kemmel. The weather conditions were atrocious, much as they had been for the previous month, with the trenches, as far as they could be called trenches, a foot deep in glutinous mud. The one blessing was that the night had been quiet and as dawn broke, relative peace continued to reign. By first light, the battalion's commanding officer had already been out and reconnoitred the enemy trenches, carefully examining them from a rotting haystack east of Lindenhoek, about a thousand yards to the rear of the front line. The German parapet in front of Spanbroek Farm was clearly visible and the enemy appeared inactive.

Over half of C Company had gone sick in the previous week, leaving fewer than a hundred men left to hold the line. One of these 'survivors' was No.852 Private Nigel Bruce. He, along with his comrades, was lying low, shivering with cold and exhaustion. Indicative of the Company's plight was the absence through illness or injury of all their junior officers. One other officer, a Captain, was away on leave, which meant the company had just one Captain in command, thirtysix year old William Newton, well-liked and respected, cool under fire and known for his fearlessness. He was also the best shot in the regiment.

The conditions for the Germans, who stood between one and two hundred yards away, were hardly better, but they were at least on higher ground, enabling them to drain the water more effectively than their British foes below. With the advantage of elevation, the Germans could also see into the enemy lines, enabling snipers to pick off any careless men of the HAC who failed to keep down low down in the mud. By 9am, both sides had stood down from manning the parapet, such as it was. Breakfast was being served, and if there was a time when neither side had the other under too much observation, then this was it.

Despite outward appearances, the Germans were not idle. Shortly after 9am, there was a resounding clatter followed by the shouts of the injured. A German machine gun had opened up, firing down a section of British trench. In the dark, they had stealthily worked their way into a position where they could enfilade the line. When they ceased fire, five men lay dead or wounded. Captain Newton was among them, killed outright. Another man, Private Percy Ellis, was mortally wounded, while three others were seriously injured, including Nigel Bruce. He had suffered serious leg injuries that included a fractured right thigh. Stretcher bearers were called forward and Bruce and the rest of the men were evacuated out of the line and transferred to a base hospital. Bruce was soon on his way to England and St Bartholomew's Hospital in London. He was to stay there in a wheelchair for the next ten months undergoing operation after operation. Then, in December 1915, he was discharged from the army as no longer fit for service.

Although Bruce had been discharged, he felt, for reasons unknown, that he should re-enlist. He later wrote:

> I joined up again on October 14th 1916 in the 2nd Officer Cadet Battalion [in Cambridge] and was gazetted to the 10th Bn Somerset Light Infantry on 1 January 1917. I have since been in hospital with my old wounds and had three more operations, totalling eleven altogether.

His legs were very badly damaged. Seven operational scars were evident on his right knee and a scar on his left thigh. Indeed, his right leg was now slightly shorter than his left so that, instead of being with his unit, he tended to be more in than out of Cambridge's Eastern General Hospital. There was never any prospect of his returning to the front, although in August 1917 he became a very capable officer instructor. One year later, he suffered a further injury when he was hit by a cricket bat, presumably during a match, which fractured a bone and returned Bruce to hospital, a place of which he was no doubt weary.

There are, perhaps, not many people who might imagine that a serious injury would come as a blessed relief from the torture of front line life. Yet, so appalling were the conditions that winter of 1914/15, that for Nigel Bruce, being machined gunned in the legs might well have seemed a fair exchange for an honourable exit from the Belgian trenches he had served in for nearly a month with little rest.

The winter was harsh enough, but it had been compounded by the fact that the British Army was woefully unprepared for such conditions. It was a lesson they learnt quickly, but that was of little recompense for the men who shivered and shook in the front line during that first Christmas of the war. Only later in 1915 did the senior command pull back from positions that proved geologically nigh impossible to hold, where the line was not only overlooked by the enemy but was almost permanently flooded. That winter, there were few trench pumps to clear the water from the front line, and not enough manpower, and particularly engineers, to design and build habitable trenches so that men's feet were not submerged in the mucky morass below. Few men were lucky enough to receive a goatskin jerkin to withstand the cold, or trench waders to keep back the water. Desperately needed gloves or mittens were usually obtained not from the army but from families back home, along with extra socks, underwear, vests, castor oil for feet and Vaseline for sores and cuts. Food was also at a premium. 'Send me all the eatables you can,' wrote Christopher Fowler of C Company, in a letter home. 'Food is first and foremost. Even the scraps off your table would be welcome.' It was pure comradeship that held the men together, while letters from home cemented over any cracks in morale. Fortunately, the army's mail service was second to none.

They were the hardest living conditions imaginable, and Nigel Bruce stuck it for longer than most. It must have seemed a long way and a long time from the heady days at the outbreak of war when he had enlisted in the 1st Battalion of the Honourable Artillery Company. He left for France with the regiment on 18 September 1914, sailing from Southampton in the early morning and heading for the port of St Nazaire. It was not the most comfortable of journeys, stored like cattle in the hold, but when they arrived the next day, the weather was fine and warm as they marched into camp past fruit trees laden with rotten fruit left unpicked by a French nation that had mobilised millions of men to go to war.

For the next month, life for Nigel Bruce and the men of the HAC was easy. They moved to the town of Nantes, where they were used as police to turn soldiers out from the bars and cafés, escorting the difficult and truculent to a prison ship moored in the harbour. On a sadder note, the HAC also provided firing parties for the funerals of soldiers who had succumbed to their wounds in hospital.

Three weeks later, the battalion had still been nowhere near the firing line, the only Germans seen being prisoners and the wounded. To keep the men occupied and fit, long route marches were undertaken of between fifteen and twenty miles a day on hard cobbled roads, wearing out boots that were urgently repaired at local cobblers as no replacements were available. Then, six weeks after arriving in France, the 1st Bn HAC moved closer to the front line for the first time, undertook a night of trench digging and suffered their first fatality. Then, once again, the battalion was withdrawn. Only towards the end of November were individual companies sent to acclimatise to trench life. It was a harsh introduction. The weather had turned much colder and the way forward was difficult, with men becoming bogged down and stuck, three being held fast for seven hours until they were finally freed just before dawn.

In these early days of trench warfare, the lines were not set or interconnected, and strange sights were still commonplace, cats and dogs and farm animals roaming between the opposing lines. These could be disconcerting for men who were nervous of enemy attempts to raid the line. As they stared into the dark, any movement could be a German, though it often turned out to be a bush. 'A poor old cow that had been hit by a shell came and looked into our trench. I'm sure if it could have spoken it would have asked for a drop of rum,' wrote one private, Robert Harker of B Company.

Back out of the line, the men spent two days scraping mud that was half an inch thick from their clothes and equipment, shaving off beards and washing for the first time in four days.

On 3 December, the King reviewed the battalion, an unsatisfactory occasion as it turned out. The men paraded for an hour and a half before the King was due to arrive and when he did so, he motored past in his car. Nigel Bruce, along with his comrades, saw little more than a fleeting glimpse of the commander in chief, Sir John French, with the monarch, and the Prince of Wales sitting beside him.

Six days later, the whole battalion went into the trenches they were to occupy on and off for the next two months. "F" trenches, as they were called, were close to the Belgian village of Kemmel, facing almost the centre of the Wytschaete-Messines Ridge, and immediately opposite the spur of Spanbroekmolen. This was one of the strongest centres of resistance in the German line on the ridge and, unfortunately for the HAC, they dominated the "F" trenches completely.

These trenches had been built by the French, and their dead from the fighting in late October still lay close by. There was no wire in front of the parapet and no communication trench behind, making the only route to the front line across an open sea of mud, which was frequently swept by enemy bullets, from as little as a hundred yards away. Once in the line, things were no better, as one man recalled:

> In some places the parapet was only breast high and in order to get cover during the daytime the men had to sit in the mud on the floor of the trench, and very often a man would find himself sitting on the chest of a mutely protesting Frenchman who had been lying there for a month or six weeks.

Incredibly, that first tour of three days in the front line and three in reserve cost the battalion 12 officers and 250 men, most lost through exhaustion, exposure and frostbite. D Company alone lost 90 men laid out with exposure, three of whom subsequently died, while many others suffered from rheumatism, lumbago, bad feet, frostbite and piles as well as 'general breakdown,' as the unit diary describes it. The battalion, once 1,000 strong, now numbered not much over 400, and many of these were incapable of work.

There were few chances to get back at the enemy, although in mid-December Nigel Bruce's company was offered and took one opportunity. A company of Germans was spotted coming over the skyline, perfectly silhouetted by the light of a full moon. Every British soldier was ordered to man the parapet, and on a given order opened rapid fire, putting, as the war history states, many Germans 'hors de combat'.

The miserable weather did not let up, with intermittent snow and rain and a prolonged and whistling wind making life almost unbearable. 'The greatest writer of the day cannot describe the wretchedness of the trenches, we exist for letters only' wrote C Company's Christopher Fowler, on the very day that the men of the HAC were forbidden to write home, for there were too few officers left to censor the mail. Fortunately there was not such a ban on letters and parcels coming up the line and when the battalion finally came out of the trenches, there were 125 bags of letters and parcels waiting for them.

Even out of the line on rest, the accommodation was terrible. One village used for billets was regularly shelled, as Christopher Fowler recalled:

> We have had two days and nights in a village about 1½ miles from the actual lines, and the shells whistling and bursting about you is not an experience conducive to rest. One pitched into a house not 30 yards from us last time, killing three men and blowing the house to little bits. The force of the explosion rocks all the houses around, and unless they are pretty strongly built they also fall. When we come down we sleep on a cold stone floor and in our soaking clothes, but we are too tired to notice that. I have had a very deuce of a cold and cough for the last two weeks, but don't get an opportunity to throw it off.

Christmas Eve, and the battalion was back in the line. The next day there was no fraternization with the enemy, as elsewhere, but a little festive fun was still to be had. On the count of three, the men shouted

'Waiter' referring to the number of Germans who had served in London's cafés and bars before the war, and in reply the enemy sang their national anthem. The misery of lying low in the shallow trenches was also relieved when fog and a patch of dead ground behind the line allowed a few men to stretch their legs and walk around. The next day, war was resumed.

Throughout this period, the four companies in the battalion took it in turns to man the front line and support trenches. 'Marched off at 4 and relieved B Company – a very small trench with no cover to it and marshy and wet,' wrote Robert Harker.

> I was next to Kenneth [a friend] and we had an awful time – the snow came down and froze us – there were no dugouts here and no covering of any sort – our feet were in a foot of marsh all the time and we both very nearly cried of cold feet – I couldn't feel mine – the wind blew right on us – the enemy were about 200 yards away and as the trench had fallen in from the wet we had to lie nearly flat to get any cover at all – if we moved about we got bogged up to our knees – about 3.30pm I was so cold I couldn't stand it any longer so, risking bullets coming over, I started moving about to get warm and at once sank in up to my knees.

For Bruce, Harker and Fowler, the war was nearly over. Bruce was about to be wounded and three days later Harker was evacuated because of illness. Christopher Fowler died of wounds on 13 March. Robert Harker returned to front line duty as a newly commissioned subaltern and was killed in action one week later, while serving with another regiment.

As for the battalion, the difficulties continued throughout January. By the middle of the month, the numbers in the unit had dwindled to such an extent that men from the transport were ordered into the line, and even then the front could hardly be held adequately. Until a large draft was sent out, the unit would barely be fit for purpose. The 1st Battalion HAC continued to hold the "F" trenches until early February, a full two months after first taking them over. By then the battalion was hardly recognisable as the one that had left Southampton less than six months earlier.

* * *

William Erwle Nigel Bruce was born on 4 February 1895. He was the son of Sir William Waller Bruce, 10th Baronet of Stenhouse, Stirlingshire, while his mother was the daughter of a former general in the Royal Artillery. Bruce, like his elder brother Michael, was born in Mexico while his parents were on an extended stay in the country. How long they remained there is not clear. However, by 1901 both brothers were back in England, being raised, at least temporarily, by his aunt, Alice Selby, in the village of Crookham, Hampshire. Bruce later attended schools in Stevenage and Abingdon before pursuing his interest in acting prior to the outbreak of war.

After the war, in 1920, he made his first stage appearance in London's West End at the Comedy Theatre, but only six months later he left Britain to take a job as a stage manager at a theatre in Canada. He continued to act for the next eight years until he broke into films at the tail end of the silent movie era. In 1934 he moved to Hollywood and to an address in Beverley Hills. Over the next twenty years, he appeared in a total of seventy-eight films, including *Treasure Island*, The *Scarlet Pimpernel*, *Lassie Come Home* as well as two Alfred Hitchcock films, *Rebecca*, and *Suspicion*. However, it is for his role as Dr Watson, opposite Basil Rathbone's Sherlock Holmes, that he is best remembered. Although some purists argue that Bruce played Watson as too bumbling, more so than Conan Doyle had portrayed in his literary counterpart, most fans felt that Bruce's interpretation made him the quintessential Watson, making the part his own.

Together, he and Rathbone appeared in fourteen films, and Bruce also took part in over two hundred radio shows. In the end, Rathbone tired of playing Holmes and wanted to return to play other more varied parts, although Nigel Bruce would have been happy to continue in his most famous role.

Throughout his time in America, Bruce remained stolidly English and mixed mainly with British movie actors such as Ronald Colman. Unlike many, Bruce kept his British passport and never sought American citizenship. For the rest of his life, his war injuries caused him considerable discomfort; his 'groggy leg', as he referred to it, was operated on yet again in 1945, but otherwise he remained in what appeared to be excellent health.

It therefore came as a shock to everybody when on 8 October 1953, he had a heart attack and died at hospital in Santa Monica. He was cremated and his ashes interred in a chapel in Los Angeles. His last film, *World For Ransom*, was shot just before his death and released posthumously in 1954. An autobiography entitled *Games, Gossip, and Greasepaint*, which Bruce began in 1944, was never published. It was written periodically over several years between filming engagements and, much to his surprise, he thoroughly enjoyed writing it. However, apart from brief excerpts that are available on the internet, the current whereabouts of the original manuscript is unknown. He was married and had two daughters.

CHAPTER ELEVEN

Alexander Fleming

—∼ɯ—

'The picture I have of Captain Fleming,' wrote his sergeant, 'is that of a short RAMC officer carrying a tray loaded with pipettes, plasticine, platinum wire and a spirit lamp, standing on a cold winter's morning, with ice and snow everywhere, in a tent heated by a brazier, with me carrying out an autopsy on a table, while on another table another corpse lay awaiting its turn. We had six autopsies to do that morning! It was Christmas Day and from each of the bodies Captain Fleming took specimens.'

André Maurois, *The Life of Sir Alexander Fleming*

AS PART OF THE PREPARATION for the treatment of wounded soldiers, a laboratory and research centre was established at Boulogne in 1914 by Sir Almroth Wright, Professor of Pathology at St Mary's Hospital in London, and Head of the Inoculation Department. He took with him to France a young doctor, Lieutenant Alexander Fleming, Royal Army Medical Corps [RAMC], among whose many outstanding medical skills was an ability to conjure apparatus out of very little. This was a most useful gift, as their first laboratory had no running water, no benches and no gas supply. Fleming kept Bunsen burners going on methylated spirits, and blew glass, when it was needed, by using rubber tubes and a pair of bellows in a petrol tin. RAMC officers early in the war had to combine their medical skills with an impressive ability to improvise.

The RAMC had only a short history when Fleming joined its ranks, but it had already proved its worth. Founded on 1 July 1898, it received its baptism of fire in the Sudan the following year, and then, within a few months, sailed for South Africa, where 22,000 wounded soldiers, and a far greater number who suffered from enteric fever, dysentery and typhoid, were treated. Sir Almroth Wright and his colleagues were responsible for developing an anti-typhoid vaccine, and, against opposition from the medical hierarchy, made its use compulsory. This was so successful that whereas 8,000 men died of the disease in the Boer War, in the 1914-18 war it hardly appears in the statistics. At the beginning of the First World War, there were about 9,000 men in the RAMC; by 1918, there were 13,000 RAMC officers and 154,000 other ranks, serving in every sector of the conflict, and two of its officers, Arthur Martin-Leake and Noel Chavasse, had been awarded the Victoria Cross twice.

In 1914, most transport was horse-drawn, and the wounded passed through a 'chain of evacuation', in which they were seen at the Regimental Aid Post, the Advanced and Main Dressing Stations and the Casualty Clearing Station until, if they survived, they reached one of the main hospitals, such as the one at Boulogne in whose laboratories the quickly-promoted Captain Fleming was at work. Although the movement of casualties improved as the war progressed, Sir Almroth Wright argued that wounded men were often so exhausted by the travelling that they no longer had the strength to withstand operations. He was particularly opposed to evacuating men to England, for he knew that it was doctors in France who had experience of treating battlefield injuries. 'We accumulate surgeons in France and wounded men in England,' he commented.

The medical group in Boulogne soon gained experience of treating the injured, and the wounds they had to face were often horrendous. Wright, Fleming and their colleagues went to their laboratory every morning through the wards of the hospital, seeing the terrible effects of massive explosions and the infections resulting from open wounds. Every day, convoys of wounded men arrived, with splintered bones, torn muscles and severed blood vessels. Within a very short time, a patient's face would become ashen, his pulse would weaken and his breathing diminish; death followed quickly. Faced with septicaemia, tetanus and, most of all, gangrene, the doctors had few reserves of knowledge or equipment with which to help.

The standard recourse was to antiseptics, which, in Britain in peacetime, had been used successfully to fight infection. But by the time men wounded in battle reached hospital, their wounds were crawling with microbes. Fleming, inspecting odds and ends of uniform, found them infested with germs. He was aware that white blood corpuscles, left to themselves, killed an enormous number of microbes. In civilian life, bacteria passed from one individual to another, often with increased activity, but in war, the men were initially strong and healthy; the white blood corpuscles should have been able to do their work effectively, and yet the infections from war wounds were terrible. Fleming realised that part of the answer was that there was a great deal of dead tissue around the wound, providing a good culture in which microbes could flourish. From Boulogne, in September 1915, he wrote to the medical journal, the *Lancet*, advising surgeons to remove as much dead tissue as possible from the area of wounds.

There was still the problem of antiseptics, used as almost the only weapon against battlefield infection. Fleming could see that they were useless: men were dying in spite of the copious amount of antiseptics used. With his limited equipment, he was able to carry out a series of brilliant experiments which showed that not only did antiseptics do nothing to prevent gangrene, they actually encouraged it.

Antiseptics, he found, were useful in attacking superficial infections, but war wounds were rarely superficial. Scraps of underclothing and other dirty objects were driven by the force of an explosion deeply into the patient's tissues, where antiseptics were unable to reach. Fleming modelled a typical wound, 'as irregular and full of crannies as a Norwegian fjord', in glass, filled it with infected matter and left it to incubate. By the next morning, it was dirty and stinking. He then refilled the glass with antiseptic solution, and then with a sterile solution. By next day, this was as foul as the first lot; in other words, microbes were still lurking in the glass, in spite of the antiseptic solution. It was clearly impossible to sterilise a war wound in the traditional way. Fleming realised that supporting the natural resources of the body would be more effective, and he and Wright showed that a high concentration of saline solution would achieve this.

Wright visited London to lecture to the Royal Society of Medicine about his and Fleming's discoveries, but he was again fighting the traditionally minded and hidebound medical establishment, who felt that their methods were under attack, and who, critically, had little or no direct experience of war wounds. Frustrated, he returned to Boulogne and lectured there, trying to pass on his message about the treatment of wounds to doctors working in the battlefield – he realised that simply issuing orders (Colonel though he was) would have little effect unless the doctors themselves recognised the truth of what he was saying. He tried at the same time to persuade the War Office to set up a Medical Intelligence and Investigation Department to study a wide range of problems, such as trench fever, which were found in battlefield conditions. The Army Medical Service was appalled and told Wright to get back to his laboratory and not upset the *status quo*.

However, at a personal level, converts were made. One battalion Medical Officer, a Dr James, visited Boulogne on his way back from leave. When he saw the calm of the laboratory and the comfortable living conditions of the doctors, he was irritated: the contrast with the dirt and stench of front line aid posts was too great. But he talked to Fleming, and realised that here was a doctor who had become thin and worn out with constant work, day and night, a man who had an overwhelming desire to help the wounded men he tended. Dr James went back to his battalion with new and effective ideas about the treatment of wounds.

Even under these conditions, life was not all work. Visitors to the

Boulogne laboratory were frequent. Bernard Shaw came several times, and had long discussions with Wright about the relative importance of philosophy and medicine. One evening, they were so deep in conversation that they failed to notice that the chimney had caught fire and the room was filling with smoke. The other doctors took it in turns to check that the roof was still intact, while the discussion continued.

A visiting Canadian doctor remembered especially the scene at teatime:

> Boulogne being the great supply port for the BEF, there was always a crowd of guests, and the talk grew animated. Though Fleming said little, he did a great deal to keep the conversation at a practical level with his felicitous and opportune remarks…and his breadth of outlook. His views on the work done by the others, though penetrating, were always mixed with the milk of human kindness.

Whatever the challenge, then and throughout his army career, Fleming met it with quiet, undemonstrative efficiency.

> He never said more than he had to, recalled his sergeant, but carried on calmly and efficiently with his work. When I had to make a report to him, I got the feeling that he wasn't interested, though he was – much more than I thought. He took the whole thing in, solved the problem on the spot, and ended up with 'Right, Sergeant, carry on.'

In spite of their dedication, both to their work and to their discussions, the doctors made it a point of honour to relax from time to time; they swam and fished for trout. Sometimes their leisure activities were more boisterous: on one occasion, Fleming and one of the other doctors, feeling the need for exercise, had a wrestling match. They were rolling about on the floor when the door opened and a delegation of high-ranking French army doctors appeared. The wrestlers immediately jumped to their feet and started a learned discussion, but the expressions on the faces of the visitors suggested that they felt such lack of gravity was, to put it mildly, inappropriate to the medical profession.

On Sundays, Fleming and a couple of colleagues played golf on a course a couple of miles to the north of Boulogne. The links were situated on sand dunes along the Channel coast. Fleming himself was an indifferent player, but he would improvise a secondary game, adopting a range of non-regulation tactics, such as turning his back on the hole and putting the ball between his legs, or lying flat on the ground and apparently playing billiards with the ball. A rather self-important colonel sometimes joined them, and Fleming enjoyed getting out of sight behind a sand dune and dropping the colonel's ball into the hole; the colonel was elated at his 'success', and so, for different reasons, were the other players.

The scientists formed their own little group, good companions and somewhat careless of the demands of military discipline. Sir Almroth Wright was generally so unconcerned with his appearance that his orderly sergeant, Clayden, had to check him each morning to make sure he had his uniform on properly:

> One day I noticed that the seat of his trousers was torn and a piece of shirt was showing. I didn't quite like to mention it, so I told Captain Fleming and said that he really ought to draw the Colonel's attention to it. His reply was: 'Do it yourself.' So I went straight up to Sir Almroth, stood to attention, clicked my heels (which always earned me a mocking smile from the Colonel) and said, 'There's a hole in the seat of your pants, sir.' He looked at me. 'That's a nice way to talk, Sergeant, I must say! I suppose you think the nurses will be shocked. Well, what do you suggest I do about it?' 'I think, Sir, the best thing would

be for you to send your driver back to your billet for another pair.' 'What a brain!' he said. Captain Fleming and I had a good chuckle, and then everyone settled down to work.

In 1918, a new hospital was established at Wimereux, and it was decided that special studies of septicaemia and gas gangrene should be carried out there. Alexander Fleming went to be in charge of the laboratory, which was little more than a wooden shed. There he continued his work on antiseptics and the saline treatment of wounds. He also practised blood transfusion, improved the techniques and published his results in the *Lancet*. It was not at that date a widespread practice, and the blood donors were volunteers, encouraged by the promise of extra leave.

In order to keep fit, Fleming laid out two golf holes on a piece of grass behind the hut, and he and his friends played there at night, with candles in the holes, whenever wind and air raids allowed them to. But any leisure came to an abrupt end with the outbreak of the terrible Spanish flu epidemic. Sufferers, including the hospital orderlies, died at a heart-breaking rate, so that the doctors often had themselves to carry corpses to an improvised graveyard. Fleming studied the causes of the flu, wondering why a usually mild bacillus was causing so many deaths, and discovered that there were different forms of the bacillus, and that there was some other agent involved. His analysis was correct, but he was unable to find any way of stemming the epidemic. To make matters worse, gas gangrene was still prevalent, the stench was appalling, and flies were an additional menace, until he devised a method of spraying them down with xylene.

In spite of all his heroic efforts, Fleming felt despair at what he saw.

Surrounded by all these infected wounds, he wrote later, by men who were suffering and dying without our being able to do anything to help them, I was consumed by a desire to discover, after all this struggling and waiting, something which would kill those microbes.

He succeeded in the end, but not until many years after the war had ended and, in January 1919, he was demobbed.

* * *

Alexander Fleming was born at Lochfield Farm in Ayrshire, Scotland, on 6 August 1881. His father, Hugh Fleming, had married twice; his first marriage had resulted in five children one of whom died in infancy. After the death of his wife, he married Grace Morton, daughter of a neighbouring farmer, and they had four children, the third of whom was Alexander, known to his family as Alec. With his older brother John and his younger brother Bob, he roamed the countryside and developed keen powers of observation and quick reactions. He loved every aspect of country life, from helping to find sheep buried in snowdrifts to shearing them.

In due course, the boys went to the local school, walking across the valley in all weather conditions and, on fine days, barefoot. All his life, Fleming said that he could not have had a better start: his mother bound her large family together as an affectionate and mutually supportive band, and their early schooling taught him to study nature and to think through the implications of what he saw.

At the age of eight, young Alec moved to a bigger school in the nearest town; the daily walk of four miles each way gave him physical strength and endurance, invaluable later in his life. At twelve, he went to the Academy at Kilmarnock, which had a good reputation for examination success and, especially, science teaching. His oldest brother, Hugh, took over the running of the farm as their father had died when Alec was seven; Tom, the next son, decided to be a doctor, and moved to London; John trained as an optician, and, when he left school at thirteen and a half, Alec joined his brothers in London, where they lived together happily and were looked after by their sister Mary.

Alec found employment with a shipping company, hating the work but, as always, doing it well and conscientiously. In 1899, the South African War broke out, and in a wave of patriotism, John, Alec, and then Bob joined the London Scottish as privates. They were all good swimmers and good sportsmen, and Alec turned out also to be a first rate shot, and helped his battalion carry off the annual shooting trophy. He remained, in spite of this, indifferent to promotion and content to remain a private.

Just as he turned twenty, Alec was left a legacy by his uncle, and Tom, feeling that his younger brother had great gifts to offer which he would never be able to develop as a shipping clerk, suggested that he study for his own profession, medicine.

As he had no formal qualifications, Alec had to pass an examination before he was allowed to enter medical school. He had a few lessons, and then applied his prodigious memory and high intelligence to the task, passing top of all the candidates in the UK, in July 1901. He chose to study at St Mary's Hospital, on the sole basis that he had played water polo against the staff there.

Alec and his younger brother Bob remained members of H Company of the London Scottish, taking part in annual camps and rifle competitions. Alec loved the life. In 1949, after he was knighted and an internationally respected figure, he took the chair at a reunion dinner. In his speech he said:

This is probably the first occasion on which a humble private has presided... To be humble was a great advantage. There was no need for you to think: you just did as you were told... it is a wonderful thing in a Company to remain a private and to watch others do the climbing.

All his life, Fleming was modest and self-effacing about his achievements, and able, as then, to laugh gently at himself.

Fleming's choice of a career as a bacteriologist was the result, oddly enough, of his ability to shoot. St Mary's Hospital had a rifle club, and one of Sir Almroth Wright's assistants was anxious to get new blood into the team. He asked about the young doctor and was told that he won all the prizes, was inscrutable, and a first rate shot. He therefore tried to persuade Fleming to join Sir Almroth's laboratory in the Inoculation Department, and to persuade Wright to take him. Both agreed, and so Fleming became a bacteriologist; he remained on the staff for the rest of his working life.

In 1909, one of Wright's friends, a German doctor called Ehrlich, had discovered a compound, salvarsan, known as 606, that could treat syphilis in rabbits; he visited the laboratory, and Fleming soon became adept at using this new treatment on human beings; it had a rapid effect, and Fleming later wrote about it in the *Lancet*. He was able to use it on patients in the London Scottish, and there is a caricature of him, labelled 'Private 606' with a syringe in place of a rifle.

When war broke out, Fleming joined the RAMC, and went to Boulogne with Wright, now a Colonel, to found the laboratory and research centre there.

At the end of the war, Wright and his team came back to England, and in 1921 Fleming was made Assistant Director of the Inoculation Department. Personally, his life had become idyllic. On leave in 1915, he had married Sarah (known as 'Sareen') McElroy, an Irish nurse who ran a private nursing home in London. She was as exuberant and self-confident as her husband was quiet and self-effacing; it was a happy marriage of opposites. Sareen was one of twins, and not long after her wedding, her twin sister Elizabeth married her husband's brother John.

In 1924, their son Robert was born; his father doted on him, and gave up golf in order to have more time to play with him.

At work, Fleming continued to investigate ways of preventing infection apart from the use of antiseptics; in 1922, he discovered lysozyme, a natural antibacterial enzyme which he found initially in human tears (which he collected from all and sundry, with the use of lemons). Six years later, he was appointed Professor of Bacteriology in the University of London. In the same year, the general untidiness which characterised his working space ('Just put that aside: it may come in useful' was one of his catchphrases) proved invaluable. A visitor found him surrounded by dishes in which he grew his cultures; while they were talking, Fleming picked up several old dishes, removed their lids, and saw that the cultures were covered in mould. He prepared to throw them away. Then he commented, 'That's funny.' On one of the mouldy dishes, he noticed that, around the mould, the microbes had apparently been dissolved. He took a small sample of the mould and set it aside, later identifying it as of the penicillium family. He therefore named the anti-bacterial agent he had discovered 'penicillin'. He was to keep the dish for the rest of his life.

Fleming published his findings in 1929, but they made little stir in the medical community. Throughout the thirties, he continued to work at his discovery, but it was 1940 before the chemists Florey and Chain managed to isolate and concentrate penicillin. By 1945, the antibiotic could be mass produced and was widely used. In the same year, Fleming, Florey and Chain jointly received the Nobel Prize for Medicine. Fleming had been knighted the previous year.

In 1948, Fleming and his wife went to Spain, where he received many honours, but Sareen became ill and died the following year. Fleming was devastated; he worked even longer hours at the hospital, and, unusually, kept the door of his laboratory closed. His sister in law Elizabeth, widow of his brother John, spent much time with him, and his son Robert, now also a doctor, lived at home, but he was lonely and deeply distressed for a long time.

Gradually, he began contact with his colleagues again, and his old enthusiasm for research came back. He was helped greatly by his friendship with a young Greek bacteriologist with a growing reputation, Amalia Voureka. In 1951, she was offered the post of Head of the Laboratory in a large and important hospital in Athens, but before she went, she visited Fleming's country home and – the first person ever to attempt such a thing – cleaned the laboratory there. Fleming clearly missed her very much when she went to Greece, but his usual reticence prevented him from saying so clearly.

Then in 1952, he had the opportunity to go to Athens for a UNESCO conference, and he toured the country with Amalia. The evening before he left, they had dinner together, and Fleming at last summoned up the courage to propose. They were married in London in April 1953, and went off together to Cuba, where he was to lecture, and then New York, where, as usual, his programme was crowded with lectures, interviews and official engagements. Fleming's friends said that he seemed younger and happier than he had for years.

In October that year, the Flemings were in Nice when he developed a high fever, and diagnosed himself – correctly, of course – as having pneumonia. He was given an injection of penicillin, which had an almost immediate effect. 'I had no idea it was so good,' he commented.

Fleming retired early in 1955; soon afterwards, he became exhausted and clearly unwell, although he refused to 'bother' a doctor. On 11 March, he died suddenly of a heart attack. He was buried in the crypt of St Paul's Cathedral, but perhaps the honour that would have pleased him most was the inscription on a block of red granite at the entrance to Lochfield Farm, saying simply that Sir Alexander Fleming, discoverer of penicillin, had been born there.

It is impossible to know exactly how many lives have been saved by penicillin, but an estimate made by a Swedish magazine in the year 2000 was 200 million.

CHAPTER TWELVE

RC Sherriff

——~~——

The men marched like beasts of burden with heavy packs on their backs, rifles and bandoliers of ammunition slung across their shoulders. Sometimes they would break into a marching song to ease the misery, but now and then, as I marched at the head of my platoon, I would hear a clatter behind me and turn to see a man lying prostrate in the road.

RC Sherriff, *Promise of Greatness*

HAD ROBERT CEDRIC SHERRIFF returned to his old battalion a week after the German offensive in March 1918, he would have been struck by one inescapable fact. There was almost no one left with whom he had lived and worked. For the best part of a year, Sherriff had served as a lowly Second Lieutenant in the 9th (Service) Bn East Surrey Regiment until he was wounded in the summer of 1917. Of his friends and comrades, many had continued to fight until March, when, in the days following the offensive, the battalion's four companies existed in little more than name only. Of the thirty-eight officers Sherriff had known, just six were left to carry on. While the battalion survived, its skeleton companies replenished by new drafts of officers and men, its old guard had gone for good.

It was the lot of many subalterns to survive only a short time during major offensives. Killed, wounded, missing, or taken prisoner of war, the prognosis was not good for junior officers who, in particular, were often picked off by enemy snipers. Sherriff arrived in the autumn of 1916, one of several new officers sent to replace the thirteen lost during two days' fighting on the Somme. By comparison, the casualties in March 1918 were even more withering, and twenty-two new officers were immediately drafted to the battalion to help make good the losses.

After the war, Sherriff chose this eve of battle as the setting for his best known and critically acclaimed play *Journey's End*. It is the story of one company's officers, set in a dugout near the front line in the days and hours before the expected enemy advance near to the town of St Quentin in Northern France. It is not the story of the 9th East Surreys which was not even in the front line that fateful day although it was close by. Nevertheless, it was based on Sherriff's very recent experiences and was written partially as a result of examining letters he had sent to his mother from the front.

The storyline pulled few punches in evoking the tensions and intense pressures men felt when they were expecting an attack. Particularly interesting is the relationship between a company officer, Captain Stanhope, battle weary and exhausted, and a new idealistic young officer, Second Lieutenant Raleigh, who idolises the company commander he had once known at school. Who the originals of these officers were is not recorded, but Sherriff saw and served with similar men. The play ends with the start of the German offensive and the death of Raleigh as he is being comforted by Stanhope. The audience does not know what happens to Stanhope. However, Sherriff's own Company Commander, Godfrey Warre-Dymond, was one of the many officer casualties the battalion suffered in March. Like Stanhope, he was very experienced. He had survived almost two years in France and had been mentioned in Despatches. In the event, Warre-Dymond was fortunate. He was taken prisoner and survived the war.

The fact that Sherriff was not even in the trenches on 21 March is often forgotten. Even the critically acclaimed production of *Journey's End*, which played to packed houses again in the West End in 2004 and 2005, stated in its theatre programme that Sherriff had fought throughout March and April 1918. In fact, he was at home attending a musketry and Lewis gun course in Hythe, Kent, and did not set foot in

France that year. Like so many officers, Sherriff's overseas service had been ended by a burst of shrapnel as he made his way across the battlefield in appalling conditions. He was serving in C Company and was wounded when carrying out orders given to him by Captain Warre-Dymond. Sherriff received a number of relatively superficial injuries. His company commander's luck on this occasion held too, but another C Company officer with whom Sherriff was acquainted was less fortunate. Twenty-three year old Second Lieutenant William Sadler had been with the battalion only two months. He was badly wounded. Both he and Sherriff were evacuated almost certainly to the same (No 10) Casualty Clearing Station for treatment. Sherriff survived, Sadler did not.

* * *

Less than a week after the outbreak of war in August 1914, an advertisement appeared in the national press inviting young men between the ages of 17 and 30 to serve as oficers in the regular army until the conclusion of hostilities. Some 2,000 temporary commissions were being offered to unmarried men. University students, cadets or former cadets of a University Training Corps were urged to apply; otherwise the only stipulation was that applicants must be of a 'good general education'. Interested parties 'should apply in person to the Officer Commanding the nearest depot.' Within a week, eighteen year old Sherriff was on his way to the Depot of the East Surrey Regiment to make his application.

> I was excited, enthusiastic. It would be far more interesting to be an officer than a man in the ranks. An officer, I realised, had to be a bit above the others, but I had had a sound education at the grammar school and could speak good English. I had had some experience of responsibility. I had been Captain of games at school. I was fit and strong. I was surely one of the "suitable young men" they were calling for.

Wearing his best suit, he arrived at the headquarters and was shown into a room where a dozen similar young men were waiting to be interviewed.

> The Adjutant came in. He sorted out some papers on his table and called for the first applicant to come forward.
> 'School?' inquired the adjutant.
> 'Winchester,' replied the boy.
> 'Good,' said the adjutant. There was no more to say. Winchester was one of the most renowned schools in England. He filled in a few details on a form and told the boy to report to the medical officer for routine examination. He was practically an officer. In a few days his appointment would come through.

The next boy was from a similar established public school and he too 'sailed through triumphantly', recalled Sherriff.

> My turn came.
> 'School?' inquired the adjutant. I told him, and his face fell. He took up a printed list from his desk and searched through it.
> 'I'm sorry,' he said, 'but I'm afraid it isn't a public school.'

Sherriff tried to impress upon the officer that his school, while not famous, had been founded by Queen Elizabeth in 1567, but to no avail: his school was not on the list. The instructions in the national press were, seemingly, of little value.

> And that was that. I was told to go to another room where a sergeant major was enlisting recruits for the ranks.

Sherriff left the office without enlisting. Determined to be an officer, he returned to his job and worked for another fifteen months before, as he put it, the 'prodigious loss of officers in France forced the authorities to lower their sights and accept young men outside the exclusive circle of the public schools.' It was November 1915, and voluntary recruitment had fallen to levels that could not sustain the monthly manpower requirements of the army in the field. With conscription likely, Sherriff volunteered again, this time for the 28th Bn The London Regiment (Artist's Rifles). This battalion was an Officer Training unit, with whom he studied for his commission. This time he was successful. He was commissioned into the 9th (Service) Bn East Surrey Regiment and set sail for France on 28 September 1916, joining them in the field on 7 October.

Sherriff was not angry or embittered in any way at his initial rejection by the army. He understood, with time, that the rules were made for sound reasons.

> It was a rough method of selection, a demarcation line hewn out
> with a blunt axe; but it was the only way in the face of a
> desperate emergency, and as things turned out, it worked.

These young civilian officers may not have b come the Sandhurst-trained officers of old, integrated into close regimental life over many years of service abroad and at home, but they had the raw materials which senior commanders could identify with and trust.

Much of Sherriff's service abroad remains opaque, as he wrote and spoke little about his day to day life. The detailed battalion war diary makes few mentions of officers other than in a monthly roll call of those currently serving in the line. Only in a small number of cases are officers mentioned and usually only in circumstances where they performed an exceptional duty.

Nevertheless, the intuitive, visceral nature of Sherriff's *Journey's End* comes from the fact that it is written by a man who served and who, in the space of ten months at the front, saw most that there was to see. In his officer's records, Sherriff notes that he was present at Vimy, Hulloch, Loos, Lens, Ypres and Messines before being wounded. He suffered the fear common to all front line soldiers, he was bombed and shot at, and had to endure, as many have called it, the unendurable. When he did recall his life in France, it was often the extreme pressure under which all men lived that he remembered, and his anguish for the men under his command very real.

> Some of their feet were horrible to look at: raw skin and bleeding blisters and big, angry sores. Their army boots rarely fitted comfortably. They were made in a few standard sizes, and a man was lucky if he got a pair that was neither too big nor too small. To march all day in them with blistered feet must have been a torment....The men marched like beasts of burden with heavy packs on their backs, rifles and bandoliers of ammunition slung across their shoulders. Sometimes they would break into a marching song to ease the misery, but now and then, as I marched at the head of my platoon, I would hear a clatter behind me and turn to see a man lying prostrate in the road.

> The sergeants were instructed to prod them and order them to get up. There was always the possibility that the man had decided that he had taken as much as he could bear and had staged his collapse to get out of it. But most of them were genuine – down and out.

The intense pressure on officers may have been different but it was just as real. The enormous responsibility for the lives under their command took a toll on young lieutenants, as it did on their commanding officers. That pressure often found its release in drink, alcohol helping officers to deal with the ongoing tension and to quell anxieties that built up over an extended time in the line.

Neuralgia, typically violent pains in the head and neck, was one illness that afflicted many officers during the war. In *Journey's End*, Sherriff writes of an officer called Hibbert who complains of neuralgia and is accused by Stanhope of faking the symptoms to get out of the fighting. There is no evidence to show that Sherriff experienced any such accusation, but he knew how to write about the illness because he had also succumbed to it. At the time, he had survived four months in France, enduring all that life in the front line entailed, his suffering compounded by not only the heaviest winter of the war but the harshest in living memory. Among the other ranks, January's War Diary records four men suffering self-inflicted wounds, two noted as being deliberate.

Sherriff himself was admitted to 73rd Field Ambulance's Main Dressing Station at Braquemont on the 27 January, just two days after a fierce trench raid, in which a number of men were killed and wounded, and a day after a retaliatory bombardment by the enemy cut communication with the front line. For two weeks, Sherriff remained under observation until the Division moved to another part of the line at which point, as the dressing station was dismantled, Sherriff returned to his unit. No further such attacks of neuralgia are recorded in his officer's papers and he served for the next six months with the battalion, except for June and early July when he was sent on a sniping and intelligence course on a hill known as the Mont des Cats. After the course, he was sent to England on ten days' leave. He returned to the battalion as it began preparations for the new offensive at the end of the month. Fifty years later, Sherriff recalled:

> Secrecy appeared to be the watchword, and you just waited and did what you were told when the time arrived. I never knew a thing about the Battle of Passchendaele except that I was in it. I only discovered what it was about years later when I read a history of the war.

The 9th Bn East Surrey Regiment, part of the 24th Division, took part in the opening sequences of a battle that would become infamous for its terrible conditions and a byword for endurance and courage.

Sherriff's participation, as it turned out, was relatively brief but he had no such foresight when the battalion was ordered to ready itself for the coming onslaught.

> Our battalion was holding some trenches at the southern end of the British line when one night, without warning, we were replaced by another battalion and marched back to a village a few miles behind. This in itself was ominous. If they took you out for a rest, it usually meant that you were for it in the near future.

The battalion was brought up to strength with drafts from England and a march was undertaken north towards the battered town of Ypres. No one knew anything officially, but stories were rife. 'We depended on cookhouse rumours,' wrote Sherriff, 'which usually turned out to be right.'

By early July, the battalion was billeted in tin huts behind the line and had commenced training. There was the usual squad drill, musketry and route marches as well as platoon, then company, then full battalion training for offensive action. On 11 July, C Company was ordered to march to a training school six miles northwest of St Omer, where officers under instruction could drill the men. On the way, the company was bombed by a lone German aircraft, killing a twentynine year old married man, Edgar Phillips. On the 14th the battalion was together once more for a sports day. There were three-legged, wheelbarrow, sack and potato races, a tug of war, and the more orthodox sprints and long distance runs. On the 16th the officers were given two days' leave to Boulogne. It was, as Sherriff knew, the calm before the storm. On their return, the battalion marched back towards the line. More sobering gas mask drills were now undertaken in preparation for what was to come.

A week later, C and D Companies were sent into the front line under difficult conditions. The enemy were shelling the trenches for most of the day and night except for a lull between 4am and 8am. Aeroplanes were active overhead and the weather was fine. Patrols were sent out into No Man's Land. The two companies held the line but suffered a number of killed and wounded, including fifteen other ranks and a disproportionately high number of officer casualties. Four officers were killed, including the battalion's medical officer. A fifth officer, Second Lieutenant Sadler, was also lightly wounded but remained on duty. It was perhaps as a consequence of this onerous two day duty in the line that when the offensive began on 31 July, it would be A and B Companies that would lead the way, with C and D Companies in support. As Sherriff remembered:

The great preliminary bombardment had begun. We were surrounded by batteries of artillery, and for three nights it was bedlam. It had now begun to rain...Living conditions in our camp were sordid beyond belief. The cookhouse was flooded, and most of the food was uneatable. There was nothing but sodden biscuits and cold stew. The cooks tried to supply bacon for breakfast, but the men complained that it 'smelled like dead men'.

The latrines consisted of buckets with wet planks for the men to sit on, but there weren't enough of them. Something had given the men diarrhoea. They would grope out of their shelters, flounder helplessly in the mud, and relieve themselves anywhere. Some of the older men, worn out by the long marching and wretched food, were sick. They would come groping out of their shelters, lean their heads against the corrugated iron walls, and stand there retching and vomiting and groaning. Then they would go back to their huts and lie on the damp straw with their canvas packs for pillows. These were the men who were to break through the German lines, advance into Belgium and win the war.

In contrast with this human misery, there was something grand and awe-inspiring in that tremendous cannonade of guns. If you stood out there at night, you would see the whole surrounding country lit with thousands of red stabs of flame as salvo after salvo went screaming overhead.

Back out of the trenches, the war diary recorded that the men continued their instruction while the bombardment was under way. To help relieve the tension, an officer gave a gramophone concert which was well received before a number of gas shells landed in the camp forcing everyone to don their gas masks for two hours. The decision had been taken that A and B Companies were to go forward to support the other battalions in the brigade chosen to start the offensive in the early hours of the 31 July. C and D Companies would be held a little further back; their job would be to replace exhausted companies in the new front line, wherever that turned out to be. Sherriff later wrote:

At dawn on the morning of the attack, the battalion assembled in the mud outside the huts. I lined up my platoon and went through the necessary inspection. Some of the men looked terribly ill: grey, worn faces in the dawn, unshaved and dirty because there was no clean water. I saw the characteristic shrugging of their shoulders that I knew so well. They hadn't had their clothes off for weeks, and their shirts were full of lice.

Our progress to the battle area was slow and difficult. We had to move forward in single file along the duckboard tracks that were loose and slimy. If you slipped off, you went up to your knees in mud.

During the walk the great bombardment from the British guns fell silent. For days it had wracked our nerves and destroyed our sleep. The sudden silence was uncanny. A sort of stagnant emptiness surrounded us. Your ears still sang from the incessant uproar, but now your mouth went dry. An orchestral overture dies away in a theatre as the curtain rises, so the great bombardment faded into silence as the infantry went into the attack. We knew now that the first wave had left the British front-line trenches, that we were soon to follow.

The War Diary states that on the evening of 1 August, C and D Companies were ordered to move forward to an old trench where they sheltered overnight. It was a preparatory step to relieving two other battalions in the brigade that had gone over the top initially. Overall, the first day had been successful. All along the line, division after division had made substantial gains and the Germans were pushed back. The 24th Division had also done well. The first objective was taken, although the troops had not quite wrested the second from German hands and were forced to dig in and consolidate. Rain had come to the enemy's rescue. By mid-day a heavy drizzle had started and by the afternoon this had turned to pouring rain, making the battlefield a veritable quagmire. Sherriff again:

> All of us, I knew, had one despairing hope in mind: that we should be lucky enough to be wounded, not fatally, but severely enough to take us out of this loathsome ordeal and get us home. But when we looked across that awful slough ahead of us, even the thought of a wound was best forgotten. If you were badly hit, unable to move, what hope was there of being carried out of it? The stretcher bearers were valiant men, but there were far too few of them…
>
> The order came to advance. There was no dramatic leap out of the trenches. The sandbags on the parapet were so slimy with rain and rotten with age that they fell apart when you tried to grip them. You had to crawl out through a slough of mud. Some of the older men, less athletic than the others, had to be heaved out bodily.

From then on, the whole thing became a drawn-out nightmare. There were no tree stumps or ruined buildings ahead to help you keep direction. The shelling had destroyed everything. As far as you could see, it was like an ocean of thick brown porridge. The wire entanglements had sunk into the mud, and frequently, when you went in up to the knees, your legs would come out with strands of barbed wire clinging to them, and your hands torn and bleeding through the struggle to drag them off...

Reports filtered back that the men who were in shell holes or the captured enemy trenches were up to their waist in water. Any communication trenches were similarly found to be waterlogged, so the relieving troops were forced into the open, crossing over unprotected ground.

As C Company, including Lieutenant Sherriff, made its way forward, they were bombarded by German high explosive and shrapnel shells, causing at least twenty casualties amongst their ranks.

All this area had been desperately fought over in the earlier battles of Ypres. Many of the dead had been buried where they fell and the shells were unearthing and tossing up the decayed bodies. You would see them flying through the air and disintegrating...

In the old German trench we came upon a long line of men, some lolling on the fire step, some sprawled on the ground, some standing upright, leaning against the trench wall. They were British soldiers – all dead or dying. Their medical officer had set up a first-aid station here, and these wounded men had crawled to the trench for his help. But the doctor and his orderlies had been killed by a shell that had wrecked his station, and the wounded men could only sit or lie there and die. There was no conceivable hope of carrying them away.

We came at last to some of the survivors of the first wave. They had reached what had once been the German support line, still short of their objective. An officer said, 'I've got about fifteen men here. I started with a hundred. I don't know where the Germans are.' He pointed vaguely out across the land ahead. 'They're somewhere out there. They've got machine guns, and you can see those masses of unbroken barbed wire. It's useless to go on. The best you can do is to bring your men in and hold the line with us.'

We were completely isolated. The only communication with the rear was to scribble messages in notebooks and give them to orderlies to take back. But the orderlies wouldn't have the faintest idea where the nearest command post was, even if they survived.

We found an old German shelter and brought into it all our wounded that we could find. We carried pocket first-aid dressings, but the small pads and bandages were useless on great gaping wounds. You did what you could, but it was mainly a matter of watching them slowly bleed to death...

It came to an end for me sometime that afternoon. For an hour or more we waited in that old German trench. Sometimes a burst of machine-gun bullets whistles overhead, as if the Germans were saying, 'Come on if you dare'.

Our company commander had made his headquarters under a few sheets of twisted corrugated iron.

'I want you to explore along the trench,' he [Warre-Dymond] said to me, and see whether you can find B Company [it was in fact D Company]. They started off on our right flank, but I haven't seen anything of them since. If you can find them, we can link up together and get some sort of order into things.'

So I set off with my runner. It was like exploring the mountains of the moon. We followed the old trench as best we could.

As Sherriff looked around, he noticed a number of small enemy concrete blockhouses that had been captured during the fighting. He later recalled that as he was close to one he heard the report of an artillery gun being fired:

We heard the thin whistle of its approach, rising to a shriek. It landed on top of a concrete pillbox that we were passing, barely five yards away. A few yards further, and it would have been the end of us. The crash was deafening. My runner let out a yell of pain. I didn't yell so far as I know because I was half-stunned. I remember putting my hand to the right side of my face and feeling nothing; to my horror I thought that the whole side had been blown away.

Later, upon reflection in hospital, Sherriff realised how fortunate he had been. The light shell had hit the top of the pillbox, the majority of concrete splinters flying up and over the heads of the passing men, while small pieces of pulverised concrete were spat out laterally, hitting Sherriff and his runner.

How badly we were wounded we didn't know. We were covered with blood and mud. All that mattered was that we were still on our feet, with our wits about us, and we stumbled back the way we had come. The company commander took one look at us and said, 'Get back as best you can, and find a dressing station'.

We began the long trek back, floundering through the mud,

through the stench and black smoke of the coalboxes [howitzer shells] that were still coming over. Here and there were other walking wounded, mainly in pairs, supporting themselves pitifully with arms around each other's shoulders. Many were so badly wounded that they could barely drag themselves along, but to save themselves was their only hope. There was no one else to save them. How many survived I don't know. We saw some fall and lie prostrate in the mud. We could only hope that they went on again when they had rested.

It seemed hours before we reached a dressing station, then only by a lucky chance. It was a ramshackle tin shelter amid a dump of sandbags that once had been a gun emplacement. The doctor was treating anybody who managed to find his way there. A lot of men were lying around, and some stretcher-bearers were sorting out the living from the dead. The doctor swabbed the wounds on our hands and faces and tried to see through the holes in our uniforms where pieces had gone in. 'You don't seem to have got anything very deep,' he said. 'Can you go on?'

The evacuation of casualties was well nigh impossible from the terrible conditions in the front line. Sherriff was fortunate indeed to walk out of the battle. A large number of men had been brought forward from a reinforcement camp to help with stretcher bearing, but they were untrained and overwhelmed by the situation. The terrain was so difficult to cross that it took six or eight stretcher bearers to retrieve one casualty from the front line.

The dressing station Sherriff reached was almost certainly one belonging to the 73rd Field Ambulance who were dealing not only with the influx of wounded men, but a large number suffering from trench foot.

We were practically down-and-out, from exhaustion as much as from the wounds. But anything was better than staying in that dump of carnage. We said we could [go on], and he told us the way to the nearest field hospital – another mile or more beyond. It was nearly dark when we saw at last the subdued glimmer of lights in the tents where the wounded were receiving their first proper attention. It must have been six hours since we were hit. We had come on our feet at least five miles, but we were among the lucky ones.

Sherriff reached the 10th Casualty Clearing Station at Abeele. Here men received further medical attention and underwent operations if required before they were rapidly moved down the line to base hospitals so that new casualties could be accommodated. With the onset of the new offensive, a CCS could be overwhelmed with wounded soldiers. The 10th CCS had already received 2,015 officers and men in the two days since the offensive began, and over a hundred wounded Germans. On 2 and 3 August, another 713 were admitted, of whom two officers, one of them Second Lieutenant Sadler, died before he could be moved on. He was buried nearby. Sherriff was soon transferred by Ambulance Train down to the 14th Base Hospital at Wimereux.

Back at the Base Hospital, with the aid of probes and tweezers, a doctor took fifty-two pieces of concrete out of me – all about the size of beans or peas. 'Fifty-two pieces,' he said, 'one for every week of the year!' He wrapped them in a piece of lint and gave them to me as a souvenir.

Sherriff wrote that he needed no souvenirs from the fighting to remind him of how monstrous the Third Battle of Ypres was, and he remained critical for the rest of his life of the senior command which had conducted the campaign. His praise for the character of the young public school officers who led the men remained inviolate. Ironically, after he had written *Journey's End* there were people who criticised him for glorifying those officers too much, and others for discrediting them, which probably meant he had got the balance just about right.

Just how well Sherriff knew Second Lieutenant William Sadler is not known. He was not one of the young public school boys that Sherriff eulogised but he was typical of the new breed of officer, like Sherriff himself, who were not automatically considered officer material but who were offered commissions in the fullness of time. Sadler had lived in Hove, near Brighton, where he worked as a hosier. In his youth he had attended Croydon High School and, like Sherriff, he had attained the necessary 'good standard' of education. His death, and the poignancy of the subsequent letter from his father, underlines not only the extent of the losses on the Western Front but how random luck was.

William Douglas Sadler was twenty-three when he died but he had a great deal of front line experience. He had served as a private in France with the 16th Bn The London Regiment (Queens Westminster Rifles), a territorial battalion, since November 1914. In October 1915 he was in hospital with a septic thumb when news came through that he could return to England for a commission. He trained in England throughout 1916 and was eventually sent to France in April 1917, joining the 9th Bn East Surrey Regiment on 2nd May. He was mortally wounded on the evening of 2 August and died next day. He is now buried at Lijssenthoek Military Cemetery, seven miles west of Ypres. The news of his death reached his family soon afterwards, although from the following letter it seems that the young man's father held out some faint optimism that the truth might yet be otherwise. On 7 August, he wrote to the War Office seeking clarification. It is clear that he wished to shield his wife from the dreadful news until there was no hope, and asked if any reply could be sent not to his flat but to that of a neighbour.

Dear Sir, I should be most grateful if you would let me know at the earliest possible moment if it is true that my dearest son William Douglas Sadler, 2nd Lieutenant in the 9th Battalion East Surrey Regiment, has died of wounds which unfortunately I have just heard is so and we are most anxious to know at once the fullest possible particulars you can give so that we may be prepared to break the sad news (if it unfortunately should be true) to my wife, his poor mother [Agnes], who has worried for so long about him and our younger son that she is very run down and ill, so until we know the facts I do not wish to cause her un-necessary pain. I am quite aware that you must have a tremendous amount of correspondence to attend to but may be you will let me know as early as possible by wire or letter to E W Sadler, 19 Palmeris Avenue Mansions, Hove c/o Mrs L Godwin Hammack, 19 Palmeris Avenue Mansions, Flat 7.

So that my wife does not get a shock which might cause her death. Our only other son [Cecil M.] is an officer in the Royal Worcesters and he has also had a very rough experience and is also a great anxiety to us. Thanking you in anticipation of an early reply.

Yours truly
Ernest W Sadler
PS My eldest son WD joined up in August 1914 and has been at it ever since.

Ernest Sadler broke the news to his wife the following week.

By that time, Sherriff was back in England and in hospital. He had sailed to Dover from Boulogne with wounds to the right side of his face, right arm, hands and leg and was admitted into the Royal Victoria Hospital at Netley. The wounds, as the record shows, were indeed superficial, in fact Sherriff was lucky to have been sent home at all. By November he had been returned to duty, but he never returned to the Western Front. Instead he served in a Home Service battalion of the regiment until the end of the war; he was finally demobbed in March 1919.

* * *

Robert Sherriff was born at Hampton Wick on 6 June 1896, coincidentally the birth date of the oldest surviving Great War veteran, Henry Allingham. He attended Kingston on Thames Grammar School, where he edited the school magazine and was captain of the cricket and rowing teams. After leaving school in 1914, he joined the Sun Assurance Company in London.

After the war, he returned to insurance, this time as an adjuster. He took up his hobbies again and began to write plays, in part to help raise money for Kingston Rowing Club. The first play, *The Adventurers*, was sufficiently successful for an amateur dramatics group to be founded to perform annually the plays that he set himself to write.

He had discovered a talent, and although his first attempt at a novel foundered – he subsequently wrote several others – his main love was drama. It was during his recovery from scarlet fever that he started to write his seventh play, based on his wartime letters to his mother, and called *Journey's End*. It had a dugout for a setting and an all-male cast, a combination which did not at first inspire directors. But in 1928, it was given two performances, starring the youthful Laurence Olivier as Captain Stanhope; as a result, it transferred to the West End, where it ran for 594 performances; it was subsequently produced in many parts of the world and was later made into films both in England and in Germany.

When asked what he was going to write next, Sherriff declared that he was going to be a student and to take up rowing again; he entered New College, Oxford, in 1931 to read History. After leaving Oxford, he moved to Hollywood to work on film scripts; he adapted the story of *Goodbye Mr Chips* for the cinema and most notably wrote the screenplay for *The Dam Busters*.

Later in his life, Sherriff developed an interest in archaeology, and helped to excavate a Roman villa and part of Hadrian's Wall in Northumberland; he continued to write, and set one of his plays, *The Long Sunset*, in Roman Britain. Although his work was popular at the time, it is for *Journey's End* that he will be remembered; its highly successful revival in the early twenty-first century shows that this play has a lasting appeal.

RC Sherriff never married, and died in London on 13 November 1975.

CHAPTER THIRTEEN

Bernard Law Montgomery

———⟶———

*The doctors reckoned I could not live and, as the station was
shortly to move, a grave was dug for me. But when the time
came to move, I was still alive; so I was put in a motor
ambulance and sent back to hospital. I survived the journey
and recovered, I think, because I was very fit and healthy
after two months of active service in the field.*

Bernard Law Montgomery
The Memoirs of Field Marshal Montgomery

THE ROAD TO MILITARY DISTINCTION and fame is often paved with incidents of high drama and moments of great danger. These are times when life or death hangs in the balance, and fortune favours not just those who are brave but those who are lucky, too. Bernard Law Montgomery's journey to high command and acclaim began when his courage and nerve were noted on the battlefield, yet his subsequent survival came down to a piece of sheer good fortune. His valour, during an attack on a small French village, outstanding though it was, was no different from that of a number of other men, heroes and unsung heroes in their own right. A few, like Montgomery, were subsequently awarded gallantry medals; others, their names unknown, died unremarkable deaths, carrying out remarkable deeds.

The morning of 13 October 1914 was a typical autumnal day in northern France: a mist lay thick on the ground, and as the morning wore on, a steady drizzle turned to rain. Soon after British infantry reached the village of Fletre, reports began to arrive that German forces held the neighbouring village of Meteren, in considerable numbers. 10 Brigade, 4th Division, was sent forward to make contact with the enemy, with the 1st Bn Royal Warwickshire Regiment acting as vanguard.

Amongst their number was twenty-six year old Lieutenant Bernard Law Montgomery, then an unknown subaltern but destined, during the Second World War, to become perhaps the most famous of all Britain's military commanders. He had already excelled as a soldier, and even as a young lieutenant he quickly developed the ambition to rise to the top; the question was whether he would survive to realise that ambition.

Although the fighting on the Western Front was less than two months old, he had already narrowly escaped serious injury or worse when an unplanned attack on the enemy – without reconnaissance, planning or covering fire – cost a number of lives. Now he was to attack another German-occupied hill. This time, he was pleased to note, there were proper orders even if the plan itself remained somewhat ill-conceived.

The village of Meteren sat on the top of rising ground, protected by a steeper ridge to the north. Below, the land was made up of a series of farm enclosures, fields, wire fences and ditches. These ditches were half full of water; heavy rain made the land muddy and cloying. Meteren village was a perfect position to defend, and the Germans, as the British soldiers were to discover, had dug in, fortifying the buildings. They had placed Maxim machine guns in the roof tops as well as punching holes through the walls of farm buildings and houses that skirted the edge of the village, through which riflemen could shoot. They had an excellent field of fire, while a prominent church tower also gave them an unparalleled observation point over the whole landscape.

Any proposed advance would be fraught with danger, and there was a further complication. Unbeknown to the advancing Warwickshire infantry, a series of trenches had been dug on top of the rising ground as well as on the western edge of the village, in front of hedges, houses and walls. The enemy's positions could not automatically be seen from down below as there was no tell-tale parapet, for the excavated earth had been cleverly scattered.

At 11am, A and B Companies of the 1st Bn Royal Warwickshire Regiment were ordered to advance from Fletre and drive the enemy back on Meteren, the left hand company being directed towards a number of buildings that fringed the road leading from the village and from which enemy snipers could fire. As they advanced, they came across a barricade constructed across the main road. It was the first indication that an action was imminent. Within minutes they were under sporadic sniper fire but pressed on, coming to a small stream called the Meteren Becque, less than a mile from the village. Both companies forded the stream, but enemy action was now becoming intense and soon after, in rain and fog, the advance ground to a halt on the edge of the village. Major Poole, the officer commanding the Warwickshires, realising that these two companies required support, ordered his remaining C and D Companies forward to sweep up the slope and take any trenches at the point of the bayonet.

'Dash and spirit shown by all concerned,' recorded the war diarist later, but in reality the fighting was grim and difficult. The men were briefly supported by 88 Battery, Royal Field Artillery after Major Poole reported machine-gun fire from the village. However, the shelling was cut short, for visibility was deteriorating all the time, and as C and D Companies closed on the village, the British guns were as much a danger to them as to the enemy.

Lieutenant Bernard Montgomery was at the head of his platoon.

When zero hour arrived I drew my recently sharpened sword and shouted to my platoon to follow me, which it did. We charged forward towards the village; there was considerable fire directed at us and some of my men became casualties, but we continued on our way. As we neared the objective I suddenly saw in front of me a trench full of Germans, one of whom was aiming his rifle at me. In my training as a young officer I had received much instruction in how to kill my enemy with a bayonet fixed to a rifle...I had been taught how to put the left foot on the corpse and extract the bayonet, giving at the same time a loud grunt. Indeed, I had been considered good on the bayonet-fighting course against sacks filled with straw, and had won prizes in man-to-man contests in the gymnasium. But now I had no rifle and bayonet; I had only a sharp sword, and I was confronted by a large German who was about to shoot me. In all my short career in the Army, no one had taught me how to kill a German with a sword. The only sword exercise I knew was saluting drill, learnt under the sergeant-major on the barrack square. An immediate decision was clearly vital. I hurled myself through the air at the German and kicked him as hard as I could in the lower part of the stomach; the blow was well aimed at a tender spot. I had read much about the value of surprise in war. There is no doubt that the German was surprised and it must have seemed to him a new form of war; he fell to the ground in great pain and I took my first prisoner!

The assault was about to come to a grinding halt. At just after 1pm, Brigadier-General Haldane, the GOC 10 Brigade, sent a message to Major Poole ordering the regiment not to press the enemy but to halt and hold the ground won. An attack was to be made by other battalions in 10 and 12 Brigades as well as units of the neighbouring 6th Division: 10 Brigade was ordered to attack a line north of the Fletre-Meteren Road, while 12 Brigade would advance south of the road. The 6th Division would advance to the right of 12 Brigade. It would be the first formal British attack of the war.

Whether the message was relayed quickly enough is not clear. However, driven on in the belief that they could capture the higher ground on which the village stood, some of the 1st Bn Warwickshire Regiment, who had ventured south of the road, continued to push forwards, 'in a most gallant manner' noted Haldane, even if contrary to his orders. He then reissued the order to halt.

Given his close proximity to the village, it is quite likely that Montgomery was in this final advance before he halted. Either way, he ensured that his platoon took up defensive positions behind a ditch and hedge, and then went forward to see how his dispositions appeared from the enemy's point of view, 'in accordance with the book,' he wrote later. According to his memoirs, he was no more than a hundred yards from the village and while his move may have been encouraged by military manuals, it was also extremely risky. As he surveyed the scene, he was shot by a sniper, the bullet hitting him in his back and exiting from the front, passing as it did so through his right lung. He collapsed, bleeding profusely.

> My life was saved that day by a soldier of my platoon. I had fallen in the open and lay still, hoping to avoid further attention from the Germans. But a soldier ran to me and began to put a field dressing on my wound; he was shot through the head by a sniper and collapsed on top of me. The sniper continued to fire at us and I got a second wound in the [left] knee; the soldier received many bullets intended for me.

As he lay there, Montgomery shouted to his platoon that no one else was to attempt a rescue until it was dark. It was, Montgomery estimates, around 3pm, and he would be forced to lie there at least until after darkness fell at 5pm. In the event, he lay there in the pouring rain for three or four hours.

Shortly before Montgomery was shot, the large scale formal assault on Meteren began, with 10 and 12 Brigade launching a two-pronged attack against the village itself. At 3pm, the 2nd Bn Seaforth Highlanders attacked through A and B Companies of the 1st Bn Royal

Warwickshire Regiment, allowing the survivors to withdraw at dusk. C and D Companies, under two officers, Major Freeman and Major Christie, were unable to pull back until much later owing to their proximity to Meteren and the heavy fire, including artillery fire, that came from south of the village. Only at 8pm, when men of the King's Own Royal Lancaster Regiment advanced through them, could they pick up the wounded and withdraw. Soaking wet, seriously wounded, and lying underneath a dead man, Montgomery was still awaiting recovery from under the enemy's nose.

> No further attempt was made by my platoon to rescue us; indeed, it was presumed we were both dead. When it got dark, the stretcher-bearers came to carry us in; the soldier was dead and I was in a bad way.

Such was the number of casualties that the stretcher-bearers had no stretchers and Montgomery, lying on an overcoat, was carried by four soldiers until they were met by men from the Regimental Aid Post. Montgomery was barely conscious as he was placed in an ambulance before being taken to an Advanced Dressing Station.

> The doctors reckoned I could not live and, as the station was shortly to move, a grave was dug for me. But when the time came to move, I was still alive; so I was put in a motor ambulance and sent back to hospital. I survived the journey and recovered, I think, because I was very fit and healthy after two months of active service in the field.

Despite his general good health, Montgomery could recall nothing more until he found himself back in England and at the Herbert Hospital in Woolwich.

For his act of courage, Montgomery was awarded the Distinguished Service Order. As Brigadier General Haldane noted, he had 'led his men most gallantly and turned the Germans out of an entrenchment at the point of the bayonet. This officer set a striking example of gallantry under fire.' Another officer who set a similar example was Major Christie, who had led D Company from the very front. He had been mortally wounded and lay, like Montgomery, awaiting recovery. Despite the danger, two privates, James and Darrow, volunteered to find Christie, bringing him back shortly before he succumbed to his wounds. Officers such as Christie were frequently picked out by snipers who, by their actions, hoped to break the chain of command, and therefore the momentum of an attack. Officers would later take the precaution of dressing in other ranks' uniforms, wearing pips on their shoulder straps instead of their cuffs to denote rank. In 1914, they saw no reason to take such preventative measure; on the contrary, with their swords glinting in the sun, they stood out. Also killed that day was twentyseven year old Lieutenant Cecil Gilliat, who was shot through the head. Unlike Montgomery, he had made himself slightly less conspicuous when he had jettisoned his sword during the retreat from Mons in late August. Even so, despite the mist, the cut of his uniform may well have drawn the attention of a sniper. Like Christie, Gilliat was mortally wounded. He too was brought in and taken down to a casualty clearing station where he died soon afterwards.

Montgomery's gallantry award was one of a number given that day, a day when the men of the battalion were acknowledged by Haldane for their courage and resolve. Among those decorated were Privates James and Darlow, the men who had saved Major Christie. Haldane, the Brigade Commander, in recommending them for a gallantry award, noted that he did not normally put men forward for simply rescuing wounded comrades, but the 'extreme danger' into which these men voluntarily placed themselves, had been exceptional. They were awarded the DCM and both survived the war. Yet, for every hero recognised, another went unsung. Whoever the man was who died in his attempted rescue of Montgomery, he was performing as brave a task as that of James and Darlow. Unfortunately, no one other than the critically injured Montgomery witnessed the act, and he was in no fit state to be ascertaining identities. This man, forever unrecognised, saved Montgomery's life, his own lifeless body receiving all but one of the bullets meant for his officer.

As the casualties were being evacuated, a final effort was made to seize Meteren. On a pitch black night, the 2nd Bn Lancashire Fusiliers marched up a road on the southern side of the village, only to discover the place empty, except for a dozen or more enemy wounded left behind. The Germans suffered negligible losses but had held up an entire Corps of the British Army, inflicting 708 casualties which included 42 killed and 85 wounded belonging to the 1st Bn Royal Warwickshire Regiment.

Lieutenant Montgomery, now made a Captain after being promoted in the field, was admitted to Herbert Hospital on 18 October. His gunshot wound to the knee healed quickly, but the injury to his chest took much longer. Fortunately, the bullet had gone through his body without breaking any bones, and any internal bleeding had stopped quite quickly. The only indication of his injury was that he remained out of breath, a problem he found irksome for the rest of his life. By early December, he felt well enough to leave hospital and by the following February he was declared fit for service once again. However, he did not return to the front line.

> I had time for reflection in hospital and came to the conclusion that the old adage was probably correct: the pen was mightier than the sword. I joined the staff.

Despite the destruction, the civilians of Meteren never failed to remember those who had fallen liberating their town from the enemy. In 1918, Henry Russell, a private in the 10th Bn Worcester Regiment, was passing through the place and was moved by the care that inhabitants took over the graves of those who had died four years before. He wrote:

The villagers had not forgotten. Graves were scattered about in the most unexpected places; one was in a garden, another in the centre of a field of wheat, but wherever they lay they were kept supplied with fresh flowers by the people who lived near.

* * *

The bravery shown by the Warwickshires had gone some way to mending the battalion's reputation, damaged by an incident more than a month earlier, during the war's opening salvos.

The 1st Bn Royal Warwickshire Regiment had landed in France on 22 August 1914 as part of the 4th Division. After disembarking they entrained, arriving at the town of Le Cateau two days later. The town was in a state of confusion, with refugees clogging the main streets while in the distance the noise of fighting could be heard distinctly. As soon as practicable, the division was ordered towards the front line, only for one order to be countermanded by another as the men marched almost incessantly for much of the next twentyfour hours, unsure where they were going. On the 25th, already tired from walking, they received their only rations, the last they would be given for three days.

Such was the speed of the enemy advance and the relentless pressure being exerted on the retiring British Expeditionary Force that the decision was made that a stopping blow must be dealt against the enemy; a stand would be made at Le Cateau. The 4th Division were asked to cover the withdrawal of the 3rd Division and to protect the left flank of those who were about to stand and fight.

The German artillery opened up at 6am followed by small arms fire two hours later. As the morning wore on, the German infantry pressed forward, helped by a surface mist and dead ground. The British infantry fought back with great determination. On the extreme left of the line, the forward units of the 4th Division suffered heavy casualties. Two companies of the Warwickshires, including Montgomery's C Company, were sent to counter the enemy advance, helping to relieve the pressure on 1st Bn The King's Own (Royal Lancaster Regiment). Montgomery recalled that his CO, Colonel Elkington, 'galloped up and shouted to us to attack the enemy on the forward hill at once. This was the only order; there was no reconnaissance, plan or covering fire.' The men advanced uphill and into a 'perfect storm of shrapnel fire' with inevitable consequences, officers and men 'knocked down like ninepins.' Montgomery's own contribution was somewhat truncated.

> Waving my sword, I ran forward in front of my platoon, but unfortunately I had only gone six paces when I tripped over my scabbard, the sword fell from my hand and I fell flat on my face on very hard ground.

By the time he caught up with his platoon, many were already casualties, cut down by Maxim machine-gun fire on the ridge. The Warwickshires had no option but to withdraw and dig in. A full scale battle raged all along the line, which continued until early afternoon when fighting units were gradually withdrawn, often in confusion. Nevertheless the plan worked; the Germans had been dealt a stopping blow. The retreat could now continue although some battalions were badly broken up, with a number of men making their own way south in small groups, helping one another along. Lieutenant Colonel Elkington was last seen pulling back with just 60 men under his command. However, the two Warwickshire companies he had sent into action received no such order to withdraw and Montgomery and the other survivors remained in their positions until 10pm. Nobody knew what to do, Montgomery recalled, until they heard the distinctive sounds of the Germans advancing in great numbers. From then on the remnants of the Warwickshires' two companies marched south, sandwiched between the Germans' cavalry screen and the forward infantry units.

We had several very narrow escapes from being cut up and at times had to hide in woods to escape being seen by Uhlan patrols. We had no food and no sleep, and it rained most of the time. We were dead tired when we started so you can imagine what we were like when we finished it.

In the afternoon of 26 August, Lieutenant Colonel Elkington had begun a retreat towards the town of St Quentin, nearly twenty miles away. On 27 August, he met another officer, Lieutenant Colonel Mainwaring, Commanding Officer of what remained of the 2nd Bn Royal Dublin Fusiliers, and a decision was made to continue towards St Quentin. All the men were utterly exhausted but they drifted into the town and made their way towards the railway station where a train was promised for their evacuation. No train was there, indeed, on their arrival at the station, all the railway staff had disappeared.

At around this time the town mayor, who was highly agitated, arrived to say that the town was surrounded and that if the Warwickshires and Royal Dublin Fusiliers fought, the town would be destroyed. Both Lieutenant Colonels promised that if there was a way out of the town they would take it or, if surrounded, they would surrender. Both officers spoke to their men but they were too tired to listen, let alone make an escape, and so a document of unconditional surrender was signed. The exhausted men were eventually led away from St Quentin through the dynamic actions of a cavalry officer, Sir Tom Bridges. Sir Tom, helped by a trumpeter, marched round the square playing *The British Grenadiers* and *Tipperary* on a tin whistle and drum taken from a nearby toy-shop. The men began to cheer and, after a short exhortation from Bridges, they began to fall in and march away from the town although not before Bridges had pocketed the note of surrender. The words were damning, and both Elkington and Mainwaring were tried by a hastily-arranged General Courts Martial and cashiered from the army for 'behaving in a scandalous manner'.

It was late in the evening, on the day following the events at St

Quentin, that Montgomery and the other shattered men of the Warwickshire Regiment finally managed to rejoin the Division. As for the two Lieutenant Colonels, Mainwaring disappeared into obscurity, but despite the opprobrium that beset Elkington, he later joined the Foreign Legion as a legionnaire. In 1916, after being badly wounded in action and invalided home, he was reinstated to his rank and awarded the DSO.

* * *

Bernard Law Montgomery was born in 1887, in Kennington, London, the fourth child of nine. His father was an Anglo-Irish Anglican priest; the family came from County Donegal and maintained a house there. In 1889, Rev. Henry Montgomery became Bishop of Tasmania, and the family moved with him, coming back to London in 1901.

Montgomery felt that his childhood was unhappy, owing to a constant clash of wills with his somewhat fierce and overbearing mother. 'If I could not be seen anywhere,' he later wrote, 'she would say, "Go and find out what Bernard is doing and tell him to stop it."' His older brothers were more pliable than he was, and, in spite of help and support from his eldest sister, he felt that he bore the brunt of his mother's severity by himself. He was frequently beaten, and commented later that he had known fear from far too young an age.

Later, he began to understand the pressures on his mother, who had been married at just seventeen and who had five children before she was twentyfive, as well as having to look after distant cousins whose parents were in India. The only way in which she could cope with the duties of a vicar's, and then a Bishop's, wife was to be a strict disciplinarian. The young Bernard longed for more affection, and found it in his gentle father, who was himself bullied a great deal by his wife; in his memoirs, Montgomery pays tribute to him as 'an outstanding human being', and his death in 1932 came as a tremendous blow.

The young man's education had been patchy, especially during the years in Tasmania, when he was taught by a series of tutors imported from England. He had little learning and, as he said, no culture; he could swim like a fish and was very tough, but he had not even learnt to play cricket or football. It is a testimony to his own discipline and determination that within three years of starting, at fourteen years of age, at St Paul's School in London, he was captain of both the school's cricket and rugby teams. He had already decided that he wanted to go to Sandhurst, and was shaken to find out that he was considered backward for his age; again, typically, he worked until he made the grade, and entered the Military Academy in 1907, when he was nineteen. At that time, he decided that two attributes were essential for success: hard work and absolute integrity. About his future career, he had no doubts; later, he wrote that if he had his life over again, he would choose once more to be a soldier.

In spite of his undoubted qualities, Montgomery's Sandhurst career was not a smooth one. He was quickly selected to be a Lance-Corporal, an honour among the cadets, but his B Company started a feud with A Company, and violence ensued, with some cadets ending up in hospital. Finally, he outdid himself, setting fire to the shirt-tail of one of the 'enemy', who was badly burnt. Although this lad valiantly refused to say who had committed the outrage, it soon became clear, and Montgomery was reduced to the ranks and threatened with expulsion. Only one officer supported him, Major Forbes, who became his friend and guide; under his influence, the young cadet was allowed to stay at Sandhurst, and, appreciating his good fortune, he turned over a new leaf, worked hard and became successful.

There was, however, one problem: money. His parents, with many children and a small income, had never been able to allow him the amount of pocket money that other cadets received, and it was obvious that he could not serve in England, where his mess bills might well take up half of his monthly income. He therefore joined the Royal

Warwickshire Regiment, which was not known as an expensive regiment and which had a battalion stationed in India – where the pay of a junior officer was higher than in England. The plan worked, and in December 1908, at the age of twenty-one, Montgomery joined his regiment's 1st Battalion on the northwest frontier of India. He was there for more than four years, until, to his relief – he did not feel that he would have survived the conditions of life and the climate over a long tour of duty – he returned with his battalion to England in 1913.

By August 1914, Montgomery was a full lieutenant. As his battalion was mobilised, he was told to get his sword sharpened, although he had never used it for anything except saluting. He wondered at the order but obeyed it; when his CO demanded that he have his hair cut short as it would be easier to keep it clean, he had it properly cut by a good barber, having seen the work of the regimental barber on his CO's shaven head. The CO also declared that money was unnecessary as everything was provided for the soldiers; this was advice which Montgomery rejected, wisely, as he later discovered.

They crossed to France as part of the 4th Division, missing the battle of Mons by a few days, and by 26 August were bivouacked in the cornfields near Haucourt after a long night's march. They watched as a forward battalion was surprised by the Germans and withdrew in great disorder, and then rushed up the hill under heavy fire. 'If this was real war,' Montgomery wrote later, 'it did not seem to make any sense.' The battalion moved to the northern flank of the Allied front; on 13 October, the offensive began which led to Montgomery being awarded the DSO, and joining the staff.

By the time he returned to the Western Front in 1916, he was a Brigade-Major in 104 Infantry Brigade, and faced the battles of the Somme, Arras and Passchendaele; when the war ended, he was Chief of Staff of the 47th (London) Division with the temporary rank of Lieutenant-Colonel. He was thirtyone years old.

After the Armistice, Montgomery commanded the 17th (Service) Bn The Royal Fusiliers in the British Army of the Rhine, before entering the Staff College at Camberley; he wrote a series of training manuals, and was appointed Brigade-Major in 1920, serving in Ireland. He thought of himself as Irish because of his family connections and one of his cousins had been murdered by the IRA, but he eschewed the brutality of some of his contemporaries and an IRA officer was later to say that he 'behaved with great correctness'. He came to feel that such a conflict could not be won, and that the only solution was to give the Irish some form of self-government. The Irish Free State was established in 1923.

In 1927, while he was an instructor at the Staff College in Camberley, Montgomery went to Switzerland for a holiday, and there met Elizabeth Carver, the widow of a soldier who had been killed at Gallipoli in 1915, and her two sons. For the first and, he said, the only time in his life, he fell in love. He was thirty-eight, disliked social life and was, it was said, totally wedded to his military profession; he had never really entertained the idea of marriage. But his love was returned, and he and Betty Carver were married in July 1927. He wrote later that 'it had never before seemed possible that such love and affection could exist'. They went everywhere together, and she became the 'Colonel's lady' when her husband commanded the 1st Battalion of his regiment in Palestine and Egypt. Their son David was born in 1928.

When they returned to England, Montgomery was made a brigadier commanding 9 Infantry Brigade. After a family holiday in the Lake District, Betty and David were to enjoy the rest of the school holidays at Burnham on Sea, while Montgomery himself rejoined his brigade in camp on Salisbury Plain. Betty and David were on the beach when she was stung by some kind of insect; there was a violent reaction, and her husband was sent for. She died in his arms, from septicaemia, in October.

Montgomery spent time with David and then went home to Portsmouth, utterly distraught; all the spirit, he said, was knocked out of him. Gradually, he began to plunge himself in his work once again, spending time with the nine year old David whenever he could. He felt intense loneliness, and coped with it by equally intense work; in 1938 he was made Major-General, and went back to Palestine to defeat an Arab revolt before returning to England and taking command of the 3rd Division only a few days before the outbreak of war in 1939.

Montgomery's Division was deployed to Belgium as part of the British Expeditionary Force; the army was ill-prepared and ill-equipped; realising the seriousness of the situation, he spent time training his men for tactical retreat – a move which paid off in the withdrawal to Dunkirk.

Montgomery was always a man to speak his mind, and he antagonised the War Office with trenchant criticism of the command of the BEF. At the same time, he developed his ideas and trained his men, and in 1942 Churchill appointed him to lead the Eighth Army in the North African campaign. This decision brought resentment among the High Command, but the effect was immediate. Remembering the distance between senior officers and men that had horrified him in the 1914-18 war, he was determined that this should not happen again: he visited the units, talked to the men, arranged for cigarettes to be distributed – and took to wearing the black beret for which he became famous. The Battle of El Alamein began on 23 October 1942 and ended twelve days later with the first large-scale, decisive Allied land victory of the war. Montgomery had correctly predicted both the length of the battle and the number of casualties.

He was knighted and promoted to General. His tactics of raising morale, getting co-operation on a wide scale, with clear orders and excellent logistical backup, paid dividends.

After his outstanding success in North Africa, Montgomery commanded the Eighth Army during landings in Sicily and the mainland of Italy, before returning to Britain to lead the planning for the Normandy invasion. Politically, it was difficult for a British soldier to take charge of the ground forces in Europe – there was too great a preponderance of American troops – and General Eisenhower took over; Montgomery resented this, and was made Field Marshal as a form of compensation. His 21st Army Group advanced to the Rhine, and on 4 May 1945, on Lüneburg Heath, he accepted the surrender of the German forces.

After the war, Montgomery was created 1st Viscount Montgomery of Alamein, and became Chief of the Imperial General Staff from 1946 to 1948, and subsequently Chairman of the Western Union's Commanders-in-Chief Committee; he became Eisenhower's deputy in the creation of NATO. He was less happy with the political aspects of this work than with military command, and his difficult relationships with other men, including Eisenhower, made him also less successful.

After his retirement, Montgomery's right wing views caused controversy and a decline in his reputation. He was never an easy man. He was humane and capable of inspiring great loyalty among his troops, who defended him fiercely when he was criticised for his many conflicts with other high ranking officers. He found it difficult to get on with his contemporaries, and preferred to mix with junior officers. It was once said of him that he was 'great to serve under, difficult to serve alongside, hell to serve over'. He tended to belittle American generals, and Eisenhower had to be persuaded not to dismiss him. He was often vain and impatient with the views of other people, and found it difficult to admit when he was wrong.

But above all, he was a builder of morale, among both his soldiers and the general public. After his experiences in the Great War, he was determined never to waste soldiers' lives; he had a genuine concern for the wellbeing of his men, at one point even jeopardising his career by illegally hiring out land for a fair to raise funds for their welfare. He ensured that the men who made the Normandy landings were confident in their leader, their equipment, their plans and their cause. The British public was inspired to share this confidence.

Montgomery died in 1976 at his home in Alton, Hampshire, and after a state funeral was buried in the local cemetery.

CHAPTER FOURTEEN

Ned Parfett

—⁂—

Among the many records of fighting families must be included that of the four sons of Mr George Parfett, 50, Ethelm street whose four sons have served their country, one to the death, after being honoured by his grateful King.

The South London Press, 20 December 1918

HIS NAME REMAINS virtually unknown but his face is famous around the world. Ned (Edward) John Parfett appears on one of the most iconic images of the twentieth century. Caught in a moment of time by a professional photographer, he is the diminutive fifteen year old newspaper boy standing on the pavement on Cockspur Street, outside Oceanic House, the offices of the White Star Line. The photograph was taken on the morning of 16 April 1912, the day after the demise of the world's most famous liner, RMS *Titanic*. His bill-board broke the news to Londoners that the unsinkable had sunk beneath the north Atlantic waves, taking with it over 1,500 souls.

For many years the identity of the newspaper boy remained unknown and unheralded, except by his close-knit south London family. As with so many boys who, like Ned, were born at the end of the nineteenth century, their futures and their fates would lie in the hands not of a civilian employer but of a military commander and the luck afforded by war.

Ned Parfett was one of four brothers, all of whom served their country during the Great War. Two older brothers enlisted straightaway, twentyfive year old George in the Royal Field Artillery (RFA); he served in France from July 1915 until he was wounded and gassed in October 1917 at Ypres. He returned to France to fight again in 1918 and survived the war. The other brother, Richard, fought with The Prince of Wales's Leinster Regiment and landed in Gallipoli in May 1915. He later served in Salonika, the Middle East, and finally, France, also in 1918. He too survived. Ned, who was too young for overseas service in 1914, did not enlist straightaway but volunteered, probably under the Derby Scheme in 1915, which allowed him to be called up when required. By early 1916, he was undergoing training, first with the Royal Horse Artillery and then with the RFA as a gunner. He was almost certainly serving abroad by the end of the year. Little is known directly of his career overseas, no letters survive, and only a few photographs which were taken at home when he was on leave. One photo was taken on a camera owned by a close friend, Ernest Bufton, a corporal in the Royal Army Medical Corps [RAMC]. It shows Ned with a gunner named Baker, washing their hands in the snow near the village of Lupin, near Arras in November 1917. With them stands an RAMC officer named Captain Harris. In the background lie two bicycles, giving credence to the family's long-standing belief that Ned was a signaller under a forward observation officer.

In France, Ned served with 126 Battery, RFA. Six 18 pounder [pdr] guns constituted the Battery, which was one of four consecutively numbered that collectively formed part of the 29th Brigade RFA. This Brigade was in turn serving under the umbrella of the 4th Division. The 4th Division was a regular army division and had been abroad since August 1914 when the British Expeditionary Force set sail for France. Since then the Division, with the 29th Brigade RFA, had taken part in almost every significant engagement on the Western Front.

In March and April 1918, the Brigade's war diary shows that Ned was serving near Arras when 126 Battery was involved in an intense action on 28 March. The action helped to buy time for the retreating British forces and inflicted heavy casualties on the enemy. Ned was one of two signallers working under an officer, and was responsible for reeling out and maintaining a telephone wire from the officer back to the battery. Should communications break down, he would be responsible for repairing the wire, at which time the use of a bicycle could be vital to speed up the job.

Ever since the German offensive had begun a week earlier, the 29th Brigade had been involved on the periphery of events, as the weight of the German attack had fallen on units elsewhere in the line. However, at dawn on 28 March, the enemy heavily shelled the front and support lines around Arras, and the entire Brigade was called upon to open a counter barrage.

By early morning, news arrived that the enemy had cut the wire in front of the British trenches. There was a strong smell of gas around headquarters and the battery positions. By 7am, all telephone communication was broken with 126 Battery, and this was followed shortly afterwards by the sight of multiple SOS rockets fired by the infantry all along the section of the front. The Germans had broken into the trench system. They were shelled by all the batteries in the brigade, although most of the guns were hampered by the breakdown of communication with their observation posts, where Ned would have been working under shellfire. In the morning, 126 Battery lost one gun blown up by an enemy shell. However, of all the guns in the Brigade, 126 Battery was the only one with direct sight of the enemy and they were able to destroy two limbers, and kill or injure a large number of enemy troops before the remaining five guns were forced to withdraw. It had been an intense engagement. Ten days later, on 7 April, Ned Parfett was mentioned in Field Marshal Sir Douglas Haig's dispatches for work undertaken during exceptionally difficult circumstances in the first weeks of the German offensive in March 1918.

The citation read: 'The Devotion to duty and good work which has won you this honour does you great credit, and your example is of the greatest value, not only to your battery, but also to the whole of the Royal Artillery.'

The German offensive continued until June with diminishing results, for the enemy gradually dissipated their remaining offensive energies by switching the direction of their attacks in an increasingly desperate effort to break the front decisively. By July their attacks had petered out and in August the Allies dramatically turned the tables. From that time on there would only be one winner; it was just a question of how long the final victory would take.

Few soldiers could have foreseen that the fighting would end as quickly as it did. Most were taken by complete surprise when the news came that an Armistice had been signed and their initial reaction was frequently not one of jubilation but of shock and a sense of loss. What would they do now?

In London the reaction was altogether different. Jubilant civilians thronged the streets and celebrated the Armistice, singing and dancing on the pavements and in the roads. Ned Parfett's sister Nellie was working as a waitress at Spears and Ponds Catering Company when she got wind of the celebrations outside and left her work. She was one of those who made her way to the home of the Lord Mayor of London at Mansion House, in Queen Victoria Street. Crowds of people were awaiting the official announcement that an Armistice had come into force. Everyone was cheering, and in the spirit of the moment, Nellie's arm went into the air, waving, just as the Lord Mayor made his proclamation that the guns had finally fallen silent on the Western Front. It was only an Armistice but as far as the public was concerned, that was a technicality. The war as far as they were concerned was over. Yet, as the Mayor said his words, Nellie's arm inexplicably fell to her side. She recalled being surprised by the involuntary action, but at the time read nothing more into it.

While men in France and Belgium were caught off-guard by the sudden cessation of hostilities, they had known for a long time that the

German army was finally beginning to crumble. The expectation was that it would retreat to the Rhine and fight on, defending the fatherland for all it was worth. Victory might come, but not in 1918. Throughout September and October, the Germans had fought a rolling retreat, and once their last major line of defence, the formidable Hindenburg Line, had been broken, open warfare had largely been resumed and the trenches were left behind. German prisoners were frequently young, hungry and seemingly resigned to final defeat.

Three weeks before the Armistice, the 4th Division was advancing towards the small river of Ecaillon near the Belgian town of Valenciennes. The Germans were dug in on the far side of the river, dominating the high ground. They had dug a trench system known as the Hermann Stellung, protected by belts of barbed wire. But this was no Hindenburg Line, but rather a series of disconnected trenches and isolated posts protected by machine guns. Orders were given that the Division would attack in the early hours of 24 October. The artillery would soften up the forward areas before the troops went in.

Two of the battalions charged with crossing the river and taking the Stellung were the 2nd Bn Duke of Wellington's Regiment, and the 1st Bn Somerset Light Infantry. Both were in the 4th Division, serving in 10 and 11 Infantry Brigades respectively. The Duke of Wellington's were to take the village of Verchain, crossing the river, attacking the German defences and seizing the high ground. The Somerset Light Infantry were directed to cross the river slightly to the north, and break into the enemy's trench system. Other battalions in the Brigade would then continue the advance to a village two miles further on. In all, four objectives were set for the division, each coloured on a map, blue, yellow, red and green. It was an ambitious target.

At 4am, supported by a creeping barrage of shrapnel fired by six brigades of artillery, the Duke of Wellington's attacked in conjunction with the 1st Bn Royal Warwickshire Regiment. The Germans retaliated although their artillery proved weak and ineffectual. By daybreak, the village had been seized and the river reached. Rains had swollen what was often little more than a stream, and the water, although not more than four feet deep, was still twenty feet wide and fast running. Portable bridges had been constructed and carried to the river but most of the men simply dashed down the embankment and crossed with the water up to their armpits. The river was forded with little opposition and the men rushed the trenches of the Hermann Stellung.

A sunken road, still in enemy hands, held up the advance, and artillery was called upon to shell the road. Once again, Ned Parfett would have been heavily engaged, working with an observation officer, Lieutenant Percy Hunt, Ned maintaining the telephone or relaying ranges and trajectories back to the guns. In the late afternoon a second assault was made, once again under a shrapnel barrage and the attack was entirely successful. A second line of disconnected enemy trenches was taken on the high ground behind the Hermann Stellung, as well as 350 prisoners, 31 machine guns and two trench mortars. The enemy's resistance had collapsed, forcing them to withdraw over two thousand yards. As far as the 2nd Duke of Wellington's Regiment was concerned, the attack was one of the most successful operations it had ever been involved in.

The Somerset Light Infantry had fared just as well. They had crossed the river on pontoons under fire. A few casualties had been caused by the impetuosity of the men to get on, running into their own artillery barrage. The Germans held firm, but the Somerset Light Infantry began to outflank the enemy trenches and resistance suddenly gave way, the Germans surrendering in large numbers. As well as capturing machine guns and trench mortars, two field guns were also seized. By late afternoon, 11 Brigade had successfully made contact with 10 Brigade on their right and a line established well beyond the river. Only the furthest objective, the village of Querenaing, the green line on the maps, remained in enemy hands.

Ned Parfett's battery had been closely involved with the action on the 24th, and for the next few days they continued to support the rolling battle while the Commander in Chief sought to keep up the pressure on the Germans. On the 25th the village of Querenaing, became the next objective for the infantry. This also fell with little opposition and the guns of the Brigade were called to move forward to fresh positions, 126 Battery moving a mile north east of Verchain.

A pattern to the fighting had developed. The British kept up the pressure each day, not letting the enemy take stock. The Germans would fight a rearguard action, then fall back, mounting small counter-attacks to buy time for the main force to withdraw. The British paused only when they began to outrun their supplies. After the fighting on the 24th, other battalions in the brigade continued the rolling offensive and the Somerset Light Infantry and the Duke of Wellington's Regiment were withdrawn to billets in Verchain. In a week, the Division had advanced nearly five and a half miles, a remarkable achievement in the context of the Great War's drawn out battles of attrition.

Both battalions had a chance to rest, clean up and even bathe. In the meantime, the dead were collected and buried by their comrades and friends. The Duke of Wellington's Regiment and Somerset Light Infantry had fought side by side and now their dead were buried next to each other in a cemetery begun in the aftermath of the fighting. The rules of interment in the operational orders dictated that the men had to be buried a minimum stated distance away from the village and so they were, a mile to the northwest of Verchain. In all, twentynine men of the 1st Bn Somerset Light Infantry and fortytwo of the 2nd Bn Duke of Wellington's Regiment were intered in three rows, as well as a handful of men from other units in the Division.

On 26 October the attack was resumed, but by the next day reports were received that the Germans appeared to be preparing to counter-attack. 126 Battery, along with others in the brigade, swept the area to break up any concentrations of infantry.

By the 28th the front was quiet and no action of note was recorded. Another attack was proposed and the artillery of the Brigade was made ready. Meanwhile, new forward positions were reconnoitred for the guns. The Brigade's batteries continued to harass the enemy when news came through that any advance was to be postponed for twenty-four hours; this was later extended for a further day. On 29 October, the War Diary of the 29th Brigade recorded: 'No change in situation. Parties of enemy engaged by our fire and normal harassing fire during the night.'

It was almost the end of the month. 29 Brigade had suffered a number of casualties but most had been relatively light. Two men had been killed and one officer wounded as well as sixteen other ranks. A number had also been gassed, none seriously.

It was too early, perhaps too dangerous, for any man to believe he might actually survive the war, but for Ned Parfett there was reason to be optimistic. Ned was about to go on leave. He had had one other leave from the front in the two years he had served abroad, and now he was given instructions that he could return once more to England. He could not have known it, but his leave, and the time it would take him to return to his unit, would dovetail nicely with the Armistice; even by 29 October, a ceasefire was being mooted by the German military commanders to the Allied forces.

Ned was in the Quartermaster's store before leaving on a train for the coast and the ship that would take him home. It was late in the evening and enemy artillery had become a little heavier in the sector. In the stores, Ned waited with two other men from 126 Battery, Gunner William Scott, a lad from Manchester, and Saddler Corporal Henry Strachan, a twentynine year old married man with a home in Plumstead, London.

Whether any of the men heard the shell that hit the stores is unknown. A reconnaissance report of the 4th Division Artillery covering a twentyfour hour period, 29/30 October, noted that enemy howitzers were active in the early afternoon, while four German guns were recorded as having opened harassing fire during the night in the vicinity of Verchain. It is quite likely that it was a shell from one of these guns that hit the Quartermaster's store.

It was a fortunate strike by the enemy and exceptionally unfortunate for those inside, for the shell was not aimed but just part of the desultory gunfire that was a feature of much night firing. When the dust and the fire settled, all three men were found dead. Casualties were always a matter of great regret but expected in war. However, the circumstances surrounding these deaths were particularly heart-rending. Ned, as his family was soon to discover, was not only due to go on leave but had also been recommended for the Military Medal, an award he did not live to see. All three men had seen considerable action: Ned, with two years' service overseas, was by any measure a seasoned soldier, but Gunner William Scott had served even longer, having been in France since November 1915. In many ways, the most poignant death of all was that of Henry Strachan, a Scotsman from Edinburgh. He had sailed with the Brigade way back in August 1914, and had been involved in the retreat from Mons. For him to have survived the entire war to die just days before its end must have been the bitterest of blows to his family.

The three men were buried next to one another in Verchain British Military Cemetery. It already contained eighty-three casualties from the previous five days' fighting. Most, if not all, were men from the 4th Division. Ned and his comrades were added to a fourth row of dead, directly in front of the men his battery had helped to support in their attack five days earlier. Unlike so many other cemeteries on the Western Front, this one did not grow much larger. By the time the last of the casualties were buried on 1 November, the war had already moved on and peace reigned once again around the villages of Verchain and Querenaing. In all, just 110 men were buried in the cemetery.

In England, the immediate Armistice celebrations over, Nellie Parfett returned to the normality of work. In her spare time, as a member of the congregation of St Patrick's Church, she was often to be found in the church hall undertaking voluntary work. One day, as she was in the Sacristy, a friend of the family and fellow Congregationalist, Edward Long, came in to say that her parents had received an official letter from the army. Ned had been killed. Nellie fainted. In the years to come, she would look back on Armistice Day and the inexplicable incident. She was sure, she told her family, that her arm dropping to her side was an unconscious presentiment of her brother's death.

George Parfett's two eldest sons were still serving abroad when the news reached them. Richard was on his way to Germany and the Army of Occupation. His brother George, having recovered from the influenza pandemic that killed so many that summer, was still in Belgium when he wrote to the Headquarters of the 29th Brigade to inquire as to what had happened to his younger brother. On 30 November, he received a reply:

> Referring to your enquiry about your brother's death, I much regret to inform you he was killed when the Brigade was near VERCHAIN, near which place he was buried. At the time of his death he was in the Q.M. Stores, and a shell fell on the stores, killing him outright. Verchain is about 10 miles S.E. of Valenciennes.
>
> I wish to inform you how highly we valued his services, and I recommended him for his Military Medal which in every way he had won. On many occasions he accompanied me during severe shelling and I always placed the greatest confidence in him.
>
> Yours Truly
> P[ercy] W[alford] Hunt
> 2nd Lieutenant

Three weeks later, on 20 December 1918, *The South London Press* commemorated the service of all four Parfett brothers inside its pages.

South London's Roll of Honour, Four Fighting Brothers. North

Lambeth Family's Notable Record. It wrote: Among the many records of fighting families must be included that of the four sons of Mr George Parfett, 50, Ethelmst, Cornwall rd, Waterloo rd, whose four sons have served their country, one to the death, after being honoured by his grateful King.

Pictures of the four brothers appeared; three, the paper explained, had seen active service, while the fourth, Thomas Parfett, aged eighteen, had also joined the Royal Field Artillery but was still in training when the war ended.

Of Ned Parfett, the paper wrote that he had won his Military Medal shortly before his death [*The London Gazette Supplement* 13 March 1919].

In October, in a specially severe tussle, he acquitted himself so well as to earn the coveted distinction of a Military Medal, and it was hard when near the end of the fighting he fell near Verchain.

A letter congratulating Ned on his mention in despatches was also quoted. It was, according to the paper, signed by General Allenby, although the General was then serving in the Middle East. Whoever it was signed by, Ned's devotion to his service was clear.

The following year a letter arrived. It was Ernest Bufton, the friend on whose camera the picture in the snow at Lupin had been taken back in November 1917:

September 3rd 1919
Mr E. H. Bufton presents his compliments to Mr G Parfett....
I was a friend of Gunner E Parfett att HQ 29th Bde being then a Corporal in the Royal Army Medical Corps. I was very fond of Parfett and everyone else was and very sorry indeed to have to part with him being one of the best of friends one could

ever wish for and liked and trusted by all officers, NCOs and men in the Brigade....perhaps sometime when you have time you would come over and see me or I would meet you some where as I would very much like to see some one who belonged to him.

Please accept my very deepest sympathy and my very best wishes and hope I am not troubling you.

I remain

Yours sincerely

E. H. Bufton

Ned's belongings were returned to England, including a small devotional Catholic prayer book which he had kept with him and had worn presumably in a breast pocket. The book had taken some of the impact of the shell: its cover was torn and there was an indentation where shrapnel had hit it. A bandolier, left on his last leave home, was also kept by his parents, his mother hanging it in an alcove in the sitting room next to a crucifix and a large framed picture of Ned, with pictures of Ned's brothers and sisters. It became a shrine to the memory of her dead son. Long after her own death, the leather dried and the stitching split and it was eventually, and reluctantly, thrown away. The prayer book survived and in time was given to Ned's nephew, also called Ned. Ned Walsh, born in 1924, was named in his uncle's honour. He was also the first in the family to visit his uncle's grave.

In 1950, he went on a bicycle tour, passing through towns such as Béthune before he reached the village of Verchain and the cemetery where his uncle was buried. In the visitor's book kept behind a small metal door in the cemetery wall, Ned found the name of the man employed by the then Imperial [now Commonwealth] War Graves Commission to care for the cemetery. He lived in Solesmes, a neighbouring village, and Ned went to visit him. The gardener was named Archie Mowat, a former infantryman in the Scottish Rifles.

After the Great War he had married a French woman and had settled down; his son had recently been killed in the Second World War. Archie was the original gardener who had tended the cemetery since the early 1920s when the stone walls and the Portland stone headstones had been erected. He had looked after Ned Parfett for over thirty years, and he and his wife looked after his nephew too, for two days, until the bicycle tour was resumed. Five years later, Ned Parfett's then 63 year old sister Nellie made her only visit to her brother's grave. Family members have continued to visit ever since.

* * *

Ned Parfett was born on 21 July 1896 near Waterloo Station, one of six children and the third of four brothers. The family were devout Catholics with strong Irish connections, although most had lived in Lambeth, South London, or the London area, since the 1850s.

Ned was baptized on 30 August 1896 at St George's Chapel, Southwark, and along with his siblings he attended St Patrick's Chapel and School. By all accounts Ned was an able and diligent boy, being awarded a book, *Uncle Boo*, as a reward for school attendance in December 1909.

The following year Ned left school and quickly followed in his father's footsteps. George Parfett, a one-time scaffolder, had helped construct Westminster Cathedral in the 1890s. He was said to have been a good outdoor speaker and a prominent member of the building trades workers' union. He was subsequently injured in a building accident that left him lame and he walked with the aid of a stick. Unable to work on the building sites, he turned to selling newspapers with a pitch just at the end of Waterloo Bridge.

After Ned's death, the Parfett family remained in close proximity to each other. All of the children lived and worked near to their place of birth, with homes in Waterloo and North Lambeth. The eldest boys worked at Maples Furnishers, and the youngest, Tom, at Covent

Garden market. Ned's mother died in 1934 after which his father and his eldest daughter Kitty moved into a newly built block of flats in Lambeth just prior to the outbreak of the Second World War. The flats took a direct hit from a bomb in September 1940. Badly shocked, father and daughter were evacuated and taken in by other members of the Parfett family until they could find alternative accommodation.

Kitty's father died in 1942 to be followed in 1945 by his eldest son. Thomas died in 1963, and Richard a year later; none of the boys had lived very long. When Kit died in 1977 the last of the Parfett family left Waterloo. Nellie, the last of the six siblings, died in 1978.

CHAPTER FIFTEEN

Tom Denning

—ɯ—

Often I am asked: 'What were they like? Your father and mother, I mean. To have brought up such a family. One a General, another an Admiral, and you a Judge. What were they like?' To which I say: 'You forget. We were five brothers. Two were lost in the First World War. They were the best of us.'

Tom Denning, *The Family Story*

NINE DAYS AFTER the abortive attack by Arnold Ridley's battalion on Gird Trench and Gird Support Trench, another division arrived in the line to have a go at prising the enemy out of their heavily defended positions in front of the village of Gueudecourt. 64 Brigade, 21st Division, was to attack over precisely the same ground as the Somerset Light Infantry earlier, and, as it turned out, with similar results. In the attack would be Jack Denning, eldest brother of Tom, the future Master of the Rolls. He was an Acting Captain in the 1st Bn Lincolnshire Regiment, a battalion in 62 Brigade which, for the purposes of this assault, was seconded to help 64 Brigade.

Jack was a respected officer and would take C Company over the parapet. A pre-war territorial, he had been abroad since early August 1915. In June 1916 he had been wounded in the head by shrapnel, but, after basic treatment, had insisted on returning to the line. His front line experience had recently been recognised and he had been given command of the battalion's C Company.

In the attack, two battalions in 64 Brigade, the 1st Bn East Yorkshire

Regiment and the 10th (Service) King's Own Yorkshire Light Infantry [KOYLI] would lead the way, leaving the assault trenches and advancing to take the first objective, Gird Trench and Gird Support. They were then to halt. Jack Denning's company would start from well behind the British front line in a supporting trench. They would advance over open ground and push through to the second objective, a road on the outskirts of Gueudecourt. Finally, the first two battalions would regroup and attack again, taking a third objective, another road, leap-frogging the Lincolnshire Regiment as they did so. The day before the attack, Jack Denning wrote to his parents:

> This may be my last letter to you as we are for it tomorrow. I sincerely hope it will be successful. At all events I am determined to go in and win as I know you would have me do...But you may rest assured that should I get pipped [killed] I shall have done my duty...'

That night, reconnaissance patrols were sent out to check the enemy wire and to confirm that it had been cut by the artillery. Finally, on the morning before the assault, guns of all calibres directed their fire on the enemy's trenches, softening up any resistance. Zero hour was set at 12.35pm.

At 12.33 the 1st Lincolns stood ready. Bayonets were fixed, each man carrying an extra bandolier of ammunition and one Mills bomb. At the allotted time, Captain Denning sprang onto the parapet and encouraged his men over. Further to the left, A Company attacked at the same time. Two long lines of men, fifty yards apart, began to advance. Ahead, the 1st East Yorks and the 10th KOYLI had already moved off. After thirty seconds, Jack's men came under a barrage of shellfire, but in spite of heavy losses his men pushed on. However, as they reached the British front line, they discovered to their consternation that the trench was still occupied by men of the East Yorks and KOYLI. They had launched their assault but had been driven back, having found, to their complete surprise, that the enemy wire was not only uncut but very thick. The enemy trench, which was in a slight hollow, could not be seen from the assault trenches and the combination of wire, heavy enemy machine gun and shellfire, ensured a rapid retreat either into shell holes or back to their front line. The Lincolnshire Regiment's War Diary noted:

> It became apparent that they had been unsuccessful and fallen back to their original positions. Captain JENP Denning and the senior NCOs of C Company had been wounded during the advance.

The surviving men of C Company crowded into the front line trench and a hasty re-organisation took place under exceptionally trying circumstances. The attack in this sector had stalled.

Jack Denning had been seriously wounded by shrapnel in his stomach. It was three hours before he was picked up by battalion stretcher bearers and carried to a Regimental Aid Post from where he was sent to the 64th Field Ambulance (64th F.A.). The F.A. had established two posts, one on the northwest corner of Bernafay Wood, the other on the Longueval Road. Either way, it was a good couple of miles behind the line. The War Diary of the 64th F.A. records that 'walking cases arrived in large numbers early yesterday afternoon'. In the next twenty-four hours, 1,303 men arrived for treatment, overwhelming the medical staff, although, on this occasion, there was no shortage of medical supplies. The lightly wounded either waited or, after cursory treatment, were moved on to a Divisional Collecting Station, while more attention was given to the seriously injured. But these more pressing cases were slow to arrive. They relied on regimental stretcher bearers handing over to those of the RAMC at designated relay points. The problem was that the stretcher bearers of the Field Ambulance had tried to go out when the advance took place but had been stopped by an enemy counter-barrage. It meant that men like Jack would not be seen until much later in the day, possibly after dark. When he did arrive at the Field Ambulance, his tunic was cut away and he was given emergency medical attention before he was loaded on to a Motor Ambulance Convoy and transferred to the 36th Casualty Clearing Station at Mericourt-L'Abbé.

That day, 644 officers and men were admitted: Jack was one of thirty-one officers to be treated. He had arrived well over nine hours after being injured and there was little doctors could do other than relieve the pain. After a night in and out of consciousness, Jack Denning died, one of two officers who succumbed to their wounds. A Chaplain later wrote to Jack's parents, 'I prayed with him...He was very grateful for my ministrations and died a good soldier of Jesus Christ.'

On 28 September, a telegram arrived at the Denning home. 'Mother opened it with trembling fingers,' remembered Tom sixty years later.

'Deeply regret to inform you that Captain JENP Denning Lincolnshire Regt. Died of wounds Sept. 26.' Mother swooned to the floor. I can see it now. Father stooped and took her in his arms. Tears in his eyes.

Jack's effects were sent home. They were forwarded from the 64th F.A. in October and included his blood-stained tunic and his private possessions removed from his pockets: one notebook, one compass case and strap, one tobacco pouch, one pipe, one whistle and lanyard, a few letters and two pencils. He was buried in Heilly Station Cemetery, aged twenty-three years old. He was the first of Tom Denning's brothers to die in the war, a brother he had adored. Gordon, who served in the Navy, died on 24 May 1918. He was the closest in age to Tom and had contracted tuberculosis in the course of his service. The 'best two' of a remarkable family were dead.

It may have been just a coincidence, but around the time Gordon died, Tom Denning was sent to hospital from his unit, 151st Field

Company, Royal Engineers. He had not been wounded but was noted as being 'sick' in the unit War Diary. It also recorded that he had rejoined his unit 'at the end of the month'. The death of the second of his brothers was a terrible blow not just to Tom but to his parents back home in Whitchurch, who were left to bury their son Gordon in the local cemetery.

It would be many months before Tom could pay his respects at Gordon's grave but he could at least visit his brother Jack. While out at rest, he had ridden twenty miles to Heilly-sur-Somme.

> His was the only grave on which any flowers were growing. They were two wild flowers. One red and one purple. I picked them and sent them home to father and mother.

It was some consolation, and they kept the flowers pressed in the folds of a book until the petals finally fell apart. Tom also got his sappers to make a new wooden cross to replace the rough wooden one which bore his brother's name on a thin strand of tin. Later, when the War Graves Commission replaced the wooden cross with a stone, the Denning family added the inscription from Jack's last letter, 'You may rest assured that I shall have done my duty.'

* * *

Second Lieutenant Tom Denning was nineteen when he was sent to France on 13 April 1918. He was glad to join the 151st Field Company, RE attached to the 38th (Welsh) Division and proud to wear the Welsh dragon as a patch on his sleeve. He sailed from Southampton and was sent to what he called 'the hot sector' on the Somme, opposite the town of Albert, which was held by the Germans. There, they dug in night after night under continuous shellfire; he later recalled that the Welsh regiments were the best of diggers – they had had practice in the coal mines of their native country.

Albert, for so long behind British lines, had fallen in the first days of the German offensive in March. In the end, the Germans had advanced to within striking distance of Amiens but the line had held and in the second week of April the Germans switched the direction of their assault further north. For now, the men holding the line on the Somme could breathe a cautious sigh of relief.

It was symptomatic of the time that men not usually required to undergo intensive weapons training were taken to the ranges to practise. 151st Field Company was no exception. Throughout late April and into May, the training of sappers in pontoon building went hand in hand with musketry, referred to in the War Diary as 'rapid loading and fire control'. Most of those who proved proficient were taken to the ranges, but 10% were deemed to require instruction in the use of the rifle and in aiming. It is also interesting to note that even into June, as the German offensive in the West petered out, the fear of a renewed campaign was not dismissed. In the village of Toutencourt, sappers were sent forward to demolish wells in Mesnil and both wells and pumps in Engelbelmer and Forceville, villages very close to the line, thereby denying the enemy any resource which could prove useful should they mount a successful attack.

For much of the time, sappers were sent to wire the front line, also digging dugouts for battalion headquarters. Denning had applied to join the Royal Engineers because he felt that his mathematical abilities might be useful (he later achieved a First in Mathematics at Oxford), and he was correct in this: on one occasion a deep dugout had to be constructed behind the front line. A tunnel had to be driven from two different points to meet in the middle; he worked out the directions and, to his evident joy, the two ends met exactly.

For three months after his arrival on the Somme, the line held with little ostensible movement. By mid August, the Allies were preparing an offensive. Orders were received that all possible points at which infantry could cross the river Ancre were to be reconnoitred. For several nights, Denning and his fellow officers went ahead to establish the lie of the land. The major obstacle remained the River Ancre which had flooded in numerous places, and there were no bridges; the enemy held the opposite bank in force.

All available sappers were immediately engaged in building footbridges from wood salvaged from a nearby village. Meanwhile, Lieutenant Denning was ordered to see if he could get an infantry patrol across the Ancre using a portable boat. The experiment was 'quite useless', stated the War Diary, 'twenty-five men detailed for the purpose failed to get it along the main road.'

It was not Denning's fault. Some sixty engineers from the US Army [part of 318 American Infantry Regiment] had been attached to 151st Field Company, being divided between two sections for instruction. Half came under Tom Denning, who was ordered to take these men to the Ancre. 'They dropped the portable boat every time they heard a shell coming,' he wrote sourly. His own men would have got it there, he believed, but they were busily building footbridges. These were used a couple of nights later to cross the river.

The War Diary states that: 'Lieut. Denning and 6 RE with light bridges got the infantry patrol across.'

There was a relative calm before the storm which was to break over the German trenches a week later. Between 21 and 24 August, the REs played a critical part in the success of the offensive. When it came, the infantry made the crossing of the Ancre, wading over at night with water up to their chests, and under fire all the time. Denning recalled:

> We, the sappers, followed up, making footbridges across the river and the swamps – and repairing them – under continuous rifle fire. Then there was the task of getting the wheeled transport across – the guns and the ammunition transport.

The History of the 38th Welsh Division states:

> ...two battalions of 115 Brigade had crossed the Ancre at

Aveluy, over a bridge made by the 151st Field Company, RE, under the supervision of Lieuts. Denning and Butler, and formed up on a one battalion frontage…At 1am the attack was launched and 114 Brigade stormed the heights and took Thiepval… By 4pm the Division… had captured in this day's operations 634 prisoners and 143 machine guns.

On another occasion, their bridge received a direct hit. They had been making a roadway over the marshes with logs and sleepers and anything else that they could get hold of, erecting trestles and crossbeams and road-decks to get across the river itself. They were under constant shellfire as Denning noted:

Whilst we were working an enemy aeroplane came over about 500 feet up, and going not more than 100 miles an hour – these were early days of aeroplanes. They signalled to their gunners where we were. They got a direct hit on the bridge and we had to start all over again. We did it in time. The guns and wagons went across it day and night.

Denning was able to write home to his mother about this action, giving no details because of censorship. His mother kept the letter, written in blue pencil on thin paper. It said simply: 'We have been very busy building a bridge – two days without sleep – and afterwards maintaining it.'

The British Army had launched a succession of convulsive attacks all along the line, the First and Fourth Armies throwing the Germans back across the battlefields they had won at such high cost earlier in the year. On the Somme battlefields the success was remarkable. On the first day, the 22nd, neighbouring divisions had made significant inroads into the enemy defences and the 38th Division were called upon to follow up. On 23 August Usna Hill fell, then La Boisselle, and the Ovillers Ridge. The enemy fell back on Contalmaison, but after short if stubborn resistance they were pushed out and the village captured in the afternoon. To any man who had served in the first battle of the Somme two years earlier, the names of these hills, woods and villages were all too familiar. On the 25th, Mametz Wood fell to elements of the 38th Welsh Division which had taken part in the attack and capture of the wood in July 1916. By the 26th, the men were close to the western edge of Delville Wood and Longueval, a poignant place for Tom Denning had he had time to stop and remember his brother Jack. Three days later, the British Army was on the outskirts of Morval. The Somme Battlefield had been more or less crossed in less than a week.

Later, Earl Haig was to describe the actions of these few days as:

> a most brilliant operation alike in conception and execution which, with the days of heavy but successful fighting that followed it, was of very material assistance to our general advance.

The successful crossing of the River Ancre was followed by the Canal du Nord. Again, all the bridges had been destroyed and the enemy were holding the opposite bank. Denning recalled:

> They smothered the canal valley with gas shells. Our task was to get the pontoons up and across the canal. We worked under shellfire and had to perform the whole operation in gas masks. At one point one of my men pulled off his mask and said, "The gas is coming through my mask." About half a dozen others pulled theirs off too. We went on without them – and completed the job.

Other river crossings followed, over the Selle and the Sambre, and there was heavy fighting all the way.

> I can still see the line of infantry advancing under heavy fire –
> first one falling and then another – with us following close
> behind them. I can still see the battlefield strewn with hundreds
> of our best officers and men – lying dead – shot down as they
> went forward. I can still see the dead horses lying in piles beside
> the roads; and dead Germans black in the face. Such is war.

In November, the Armistice was signed, but Denning felt no rejoicing,
only relief. On 8 November he had been taken ill with influenza and
transferred by ambulance train to a base hospital at Rouen. Over the
next few days he witnessed soldiers dying one after the other of the
illness, while nurses struggled to cope with the sheer number of sick
men. Tom Denning was fortunate, but he was acutely aware that so
many others, who had been within touching distance of the end of the
conflict, were tragically lost.

* * *

Alfred Thompson Denning was born at Whitchurch in Hampshire on
23 January 1899, the fourth of five sons born to Charles Denning, a
draper, and his wife Clara, who had been a schoolteacher. Both his
parents were highly intelligent and well read: his father especially
quoted constantly from a wide range of literature, a habit picked up
early by his fourth son. They complemented each other: Charles was
not only a great reader but an amateur musician and would-be poet;
Clara was hard-working, unsentimental and determined that her
children (their oldest child was a daughter, Marjorie) should succeed.
It was a happy home, without what Denning called 'the complications
of modern business' – such as a typewriter or telephone – but with a
great deal of affection and deep religious faith, which Tom Denning
himself maintained all his life. Charles Denning had just one brush
with the law: he was called upon to do jury service at the Assizes in
Winchester for a week, at his own expense – which he could ill afford.

After attending the local primary school, Tom and Gordon won free places at the grammar school in Andover. There, Tom did well, regularly winning prizes; when he was about ten years old, he announced to his mother one evening, 'I think I'll be a barrister', although he later confessed that he had not been at all clear about what a barrister did! Gordon, twenty months older than Tom, left at fifteen to go to sea as he had always wanted to do. His younger sibling stayed on to work for a scholarship in Mathematics, although under some difficulty: the experienced male teachers mostly left to join up in 1914, and the women who took their place lacked the expertise to work at his level. Tom had to study hard by himself. Nevertheless, he won an exhibition to Magdalen College, Oxford, worth £30 a year. This was not much, but he was determined to manage, and the College President was sufficiently impressed by the young man's ability and determination that he had the award increased to £80, which was just enough for him to survive on, as long as he was very careful.

While at the College, Denning started military training with the OTC, and in June 1917, having passed his first year examinations with flying colours, he was called up into the army.

He was demobbed on 6 February 1919, and only four days later was back in Oxford. Whatever the traumas left by the War, Denning was ready and delighted both to study and to enjoy the social life; he was awarded his First in Mathematics and tried teaching. This was not a happy choice of career, and when one day he went to sit in the public gallery at the Assizes in Winchester, he knew that the law was for him. He went back to Oxford with a scholarship, and in due course obtained a First in Law and set off for London and a career as a barrister.

From an early age, Tom Denning had admired Mary Harvey, daughter of the Vicar of Whitchurch. She refused him, but they remained good friends and wrote to each other regularly. He was determined that he would win her and would consider nobody else, and at last, in 1930, they became engaged. Shortly afterwards, Mary was diagnosed with tuberculosis, the disease which had already killed

Tom's brother Gordon. He was devastated. But two years later, she had recovered sufficiently for them to marry, and in 1937, their son Robert was born. Sadly, the TB returned, and Mary died in 1941.

Meanwhile, Tom Denning's career at the Bar flourished. He took silk in 1938, and was appointed a High Court Judge and knighted in 1944. During the Second World War, he became legal adviser for the north east region of the country. If for any reason areas of the country were cut off from each other, each had in place a Regional Commissioner and a legal adviser, so that government and justice could continue. Denning had to travel regularly to and from Leeds, often arriving back in London under Blitz conditions. Much of his work was involved with detaining people who might prove to be a danger to the state, possible 'fifth columnists'; they could have no legal representation, and he had to question them and make a decision by himself.

In 1945, Denning remarried. His second wife, Joan, was a widow with three children. It was as happy a marriage as his first had been, and they were inseparable until Joan's death in 1992.

Denning was appointed a Lord Justice of Appeal and a Privy Councillor in 1948, and in 1957 he was given a life peerage as Baron Denning of Whitchurch. He became Master of the Rolls (after the Lord Chief Justice, the most senior judicial appointment) in 1962, and the following year came to public notice with the publication of the Denning Report into the Profumo scandal. In 1997, he received the Order of Merit. In his retirement, he continued to make statements – often provocatively – on current legal issues, as well as presiding over the local cricket team in his beloved Whitchurch. He died in March 1999, a few months after his hundredth birthday.

Lord Denning was one of the most outspoken, controversial and influential judges of the twentieth century. His judgements were pithy and sometimes mischievous, and his down to earth approach and style made him something of a legend in his long lifetime and beyond.

* * *

The family into which Tom Denning was born was indeed a remarkable one, and their military service outstanding. John (Jack), the eldest of his brothers, was not the only one who saw extended service on the Western Front, while two other brothers served in the Royal Navy

Reginald [Reg], the second son, had seen action with the Queen's Westminster Rifles in the Ypres Salient since the winter of 1914/15. He was later commissioned and served at the Battle of the Somme; on 15 July 1916, his Battalion, the 6th (Service) Bn Bedfordshire Regiment was almost wiped out. Reg was wounded so badly that he was left for dead, but many hours later a corporal found him still alive and carried him back. He was repatriated to England, where he was still in hospital when he heard the news of his elder brother's death. During the Second World War, by then a brigadier, he was in charge of the administration of the defence of the southeast of England, and was party to the preparations for the D Day landings. Subsequently, he was involved with the plans to recapture Malaya and Singapore, and when the Japanese unconditionally surrendered, General Denning was one of the officers receiving the sword of a Japanese General – a trophy which he kept for the rest of his life.

Gordon Denning was the third brother, and as a youngster he and Tom had been inseparable. Joining the Merchant Navy at fifteen, he was transferred to the Royal Navy soon after the outbreak of war. In March 1915 he, along with seven other midshipmen, was appointed to HMS *Hampshire*. In June the following year, she hit a mine, sinking and taking with her not only Lord Kitchener but six of the seven friends Gordon had known. He survived with one other, because they had been posted to another ship. Weeks later, Gordon took part in the Battle of Jutland, serving with distinction. Immediately after the engagement he was promoted to Sub-Lieutenant. But by the end of the year he was obviously ill, and tuberculosis was diagnosed. He loved the sea and his ship, and was heart-broken to be put on the Retired List at only nineteen. He died just before his twenty-first birthday.

The youngest of the five Denning brothers was Norman, born in 1904. After leaving school in 1921, he also joined the Navy, as a Paymaster cadet. In time, his abilities as an Intelligence officer were recognised, and he worked in Naval Intelligence in the Second World War. By the time he retired, he had become an Admiral.

CHAPTER SIXTEEN

JRR Tolkien

—⚬⚬—

Hurrying forward again, Sam tripped, catching his foot in some old root or tussock. He fell and came heavily on his hands, which sank deep into sticky ooze, so that his face was brought close to the surface of the dark mere. There was a faint hiss, a noisome smell went up, the lights flickered and danced and swirled. For a moment the water below him looked like some window, glazed with grimy glass, through which he was peering. Wrenching his hands out of the bog, he sprang back with a cry. 'There are dead things, dead faces in the water,' he said with horror. 'Dead faces!'

JRR Tolkien, *The Lord of the Rings*

OR A MAN WHO WROTE SO MUCH, John Ronald Reuel Tolkien left remarkably little in the way of his own Great War recollections. Undoubtedly traumatised by his time in France and devastated by the loss of two of his three closest friends, he took instead to 'escapism' or, as he suggested, 'really transforming experience into another form and symbol…' That experience of the 1916 Somme Battle is largely gleaned through his internationally renowned and revered work *The Lord of the Rings*.

Tolkien found the real world of war utterly oppressive and he was always reluctant to look back on this time. Instead, he preferred another, fantastic world, into which he could draw aspects of his own story. In the book's Foreword, he described his epic tale as 'A history of the Great War of the Ring.' And he acknowledged Sam Gamgee, one of its central characters – 'My Sam Gamgee' as he called him –

as 'indeed a reflection of the English soldier, of the privates and batmen I knew in the 1914 war, and recognised as so far superior to myself.' What sights he later ascribed to his character Sam Gamgee, were no more or less than reflections of his own acquaintance with the Western Front:

> It was Sam's first view of a battle of Men against Men, and he did not like it much. He was glad that he could not see the dead face. He wondered what the man's name was and where he came from; and if he was really evil at heart, or what lies or threats had led him on the long march from his home; and if he would not really rather have stayed there in peace.

* * *

It was a long circuitous march that originally brought the Germans to the Somme. That was back in late 1914, eight months before the British arrived to face the enemy north of the river, replacing French forces in the process. Soon afterwards, a plan was devised to attack the enemy on both sides of the river, in an Anglo/French offensive that proved complex in the planning, vast in the execution. When the Great Push, as the offensive was known, began, artillery pounded the enemy for a week before the infantry attacked on 1 July 1916.

For anyone who arrived after that date, it was obvious that at most points north of the River Somme the initial 'push' had been a failure bordering on a disaster. On 6 July JRR Tolkien arrived to witness the carnage for himself. A Second Lieutenant in the 11th (Service) Bn Lancashire Fusiliers, he was held in reserve with his comrades in B Company, but he saw the hundreds of wounded men returning and there was a sinister smell of decay in the air. In a brief interlude of peace, he had the pleasure of a visit from one of his oldest friends, Geoffrey [GB] Smith, who was recovering from sixty hours under fire, and together they walked in a field of poppies and talked not so much of war as of poetry and the future.

It was indeed a short respite, for on 14 July Tolkien and B Company went into action. It was a horrendous experience. Tolkien was a signalling officer, and had been trained under clean, well-ordered conditions; what he found was a tangled confusion of wires, field telephones out of order and covered with mud, and a prohibition on using the wires for any important messages, as it was known that the Germans had intercepted crucial orders earlier in the attack. The signallers had to rely on lamps, flags, runners and carrier pigeons. No Man's Land was littered with corpses, often horribly mutilated. Tolkien described what he saw as 'the animal horror of trench warfare'.

His company was to support 7 Infantry Brigade for an attack on the ruined village of Ovillers, which was in enemy hands in spite of the fact that thousands of troops had been killed there on 1 July. Once again, the wire had not been properly cut and there was flanking machine-gun fire from a labyrinth of German trenches. The attack was unsuccessful, and as dusk fell, the survivors, including Tolkien, struggled back to La Boisselle. It was a moonlit night as the wounded were evacuated from the battlefield, but shortly before midnight 7 Brigade again launched an attack, and at 2am Tolkien's Company was ordered to join them. The ground they had to cover was little more than an obstacle course: the original farmland had been terraced, the Germans covered it with barbed wire and the British ploughed it up with huge shell holes.

Tolkien's job was to try to set up and maintain communications through all this turmoil. There were now surface lines running back to La Boisselle and field telephones, but the surface lines could be tapped, and any attempt to use lights or flags simply drew the enemy's fire. Most messages had to be sent by runner, and orders from the Generals at HQ could take eight hours to reach the attacking troops. The three battalions fell back, and on 15 July the Lancashire Fusiliers returned to La Boisselle, which was no longer under shellfire.

They were filled with horror at what they had seen: in the first attack on 1 July, it had been impossible to rescue the wounded, and their bodies lay, more than two weeks later, crowded into the shell holes where they had crept for cover. The air was thick with the stench of decay. At La Boisselle, Tolkien found a space in one of the abandoned German dugouts, and at last managed a few hours' rest. The following evening, they were again called out, with no more success than before. The Warwickshires, to their right, had advanced only to become stranded in a trench northeast of Ovillers.

Throughout 16 July, Tolkien's brigade tried to reach the Warwickshires, and eventually, towards evening, managed to break the deadlock. The garrison of Ovillers surrendered: two officers and 124 men were taken prisoner. The Lancashire Fusiliers pressed on, and managed at last to reach the Warwickshires; they were relieved after midnight, and Tolkien was able to reach Bouzincourt, and – after fifty hours – to sleep. A few days later he received a postcard from GB Smith, telling him of the death of a mutual friend, Lieutenant Rob Gilson, described by his surviving batman as 'a very good officer and a good leader.' Gilson's death came as a heavy blow to Tolkien.

The 11th Bn Lancashire Fusiliers had themselves suffered heavy losses: 267 casualties within a fortnight. Tolkien was appointed Battalion Signals Officer and probably Lieutenant. He was in charge of all the unit's communications, with a team of NCOs and privates to work for him as runners, wirers and telephone operators, and to help him set up signal stations. He had to let the brigade know of any unit movements or signalling problems, but without allowing the enemy access to any of this information. It was a challenge.

On 24 July, Tolkien's unit was ordered to the northern sector of the Somme front, on the old front line facing Beaumont Hamel, to be met by shellfire as they were settling in. At Battalion HQ, Tolkien worked alongside the CO, the Intelligence Officer, and Acting Major John Metcalfe, who had served in France since September 1915. At barely twenty, Metcalfe was young, even by Great War standards, to be second in command of a battalion, a battalion he would briefly command a couple of months later. For five days, Tolkien organised communications, before being pulled back into reserve near Mailly-Maillet and then to a camp further back, where he was able to attend mass (he was a lifelong Roman Catholic) at Bertrancourt; he moved on to Acheux, where he was able to meet GB Smith once more.

GB Smith had managed to write poetry while at the front; he encouraged Tolkien to publish as soon as he could, but Tolkien found it extremely difficult to write under these circumstances.

> You might scribble something on the back of an envelope and shove it in your back pocket, but that's all,' he wrote later. 'You couldn't write…You'd be crouching down among flies and filth.

Nevertheless, he was aware of turning his ideas over in his mind, almost without realising it, though he confessed that this 'did not make for efficiency and present-mindedness, of course, and I was not a good officer'.

The 11th Bn Lancashire Fusiliers reached Bouzincourt at 1.30am on 27 August, only to be sent back to the front line after less than twenty-eight hours' respite. He was now on the other side of the old No Man's Land, in trenches that had been seized only hours earlier. The dugouts were strewn with the bodies of German soldiers; there were also prisoners, many of them wounded; they were under constant shellfire and it poured with rain. As Rob Gilson had once written, 'I could almost cry sometimes at the universal mud and the utter impossibility of escaping from it.'

At last, after two months of fighting and trench duty, Tolkien was given the chance of a real break, in the form of two weeks for resting and training. Afterwards, he went back to the Somme front with half a dozen men newly trained in visual signals, and was reunited with an old friend, twenty-one year old Leslie Huxtable, whom he had met during his training at Cannock Chase. 'Hux', as he was known, had just arrived in France and would serve directly under Tolkien, ready to take over as Battalion Signals Officer should Tolkien be killed or wounded; the two were delighted to meet again, and shared a tent.

During Tolkien's absence, tanks had been deployed and the village of Thiepval had more or less been taken; Thiepval Wood was little more than a wilderness of tree stumps – a picture of desolation that perhaps remained in the writer's mind as he described the Dead Marches in *The Lord of the Rings*. Waves of troops swept on from Thiepval in the first major attack on the Schwaben Redoubt since 1 July. In an attempt to head off the Germans, who were making a getaway, three groups of Lancashire Fusiliers dashed across No Man's Land and captured an important salient in the enemy line. One of Tolkien's lance-corporals, after a shell shattered his lamp, improvised with a salvaged German torch and continued to send messages. More than thirty prisoners were taken. Tolkien, who spoke German, offered a drink of water to a captive officer, who corrected his pronunciation.

About this time, he acquired a useful addition to his signalling equipment: a Fullerphone. This was a portable Morse telegraph set which, unlike the conventional field telephone, could not leak its signal via the earth, and so could be used far more readily and safely. It was still in use in the Second World War.

On 10 October, a shell burst on the parados of the trench in which Tolkien's friend and deputy, Hux, was standing, partially burying him. He was rescued, but had shrapnel wounds in his calf; he was taken to a casualty clearing station and thence back home to England – a serious loss for Tolkien. Huxtable eventually returned to France and was shot through the chest in March 1918; he survived the war.

Eleven days later, in icy weather, Tolkien's battalion attacked again, and he was able to let HQ know that they were beginning to receive German prisoners – more than seven hundred in all. Forty-one Lancashire Fusiliers were dead or missing, and 117 were wounded.

It was almost the end of the Battle of the Somme for Tolkien. On

22 October, the Battalion came out and into rest close to Albert. Hot meals were served and the men had a chance to bathe and clean up. Inspections were undertaken by increasingly senior officers, including, on 25 October, Lieutenant General Gough, who complimented the men on the work they had done, and then, the following day, they were inspected by no less a personage than the Commander in Chief himself.

It was on the 25th that Tolkien began to feel ill, and two days later he reported sick with a temperature of 103°F. He was sent to No.1 Red Cross Hospital at Le Touquet where he remained for the next nine days; he was then sent from Le Havre to Southampton before being transferred to England and the 1st Southern General Hospital in Birmingham. Tolkien would never set foot on the Western Front again and on 18 November the battalion struck him off its strength.

It was also the end of the Somme Battle for the 11th Bn Lancashire Fusiliers, who were sent north to Ploegsteert Wood, a quiet part of the line frequently used to rest exhausted battalions or to induct new units to trench warfare. The Battalion strength was so low, just 278 men, that all four companies were needed to hold the front line. Even so, there seemed little danger of any action and in their first four-day tour of the trenches they suffered no casualties. The only item of interest, the battalion war diarist noted, was four Germans checking their barbed wire in full view of the Lancashire Fusiliers, while their own men did the same. No one fired a shot.

Tolkien had trench fever, the result of the omnipresent lice which passed bacteria into his bloodstream. He complained of headaches, and pains in his knees and elbows, and for the next few weeks he had further attacks of fever. The Army was not prepared to let him go easily, however, and his CO sent a message to say that the battalion was short of signalling officers and he was needed, adding that 'Lieutenant Colonel Bird [his previous CO] values the services of Lieutenant Tolkien very highly.' On 2 December, he was called in front of a medical board; he was pronounced still unfit for service, but told that he would be fit for action in six weeks. During that time, he started to write again.

* * *

John Ronald Reuel Tolkien was born in Bloemfontein, South Africa, on 3 January 1892. His father, Arthur, had emigrated in the hope of better career opportunities, but the young John Ronald, as he was known to family and friends, was only four years old when his father died and his mother, Mabel, brought him and his younger brother Hilary back to England. They settled in the village of Sarehole, near Birmingham, and subsequently in Edgbaston; Tolkien went to King Edward's School in the city itself.

In 1900, Mabel and her sons, and her sister May, were received into the Roman Catholic Church, a move which alienated both sides of the family. Only four years later, Mabel was diagnosed with diabetes, usually fatal at the time; she died in November of that year, leaving her two young sons destitute. Their parish priest, Fr Francis Morgan, took charge of the boys and effectively brought them up, although they were boarded first with their aunt and then with a Mrs Faulkner. Among the lodgers at the latter's home was a young woman called Edith Bratt, a pretty girl who played the piano well, and with whom Tolkien struck up a friendship. Fr Francis, disturbed by this, forbade his charge to see or write to her for three years; the young man obeyed, but inevitably became more deeply attached to her than ever.

While he was at school, Tolkien formed a close bond with a group of boys with similar interests: initially Christopher Wiseman, who was a year younger than Tolkien but shared his enthusiasm for Classics and intellectual conversation; then Robert Gilson, son of the headmaster, a talented artist with a lively mind; and, a little later, Geoffrey Bache Smith, who shared Tolkien's love of literature and wrote poetry. There were one or two others, but this was the inner group who remained friends until their band was devastated by war. At school, they formed the TCBS (Tea Club and Barrovian Society – in honour of Barrow's Stores, where they met).

In 1911, Tolkien went to Exeter College, Oxford, where he studied Classics, while immersing himself in a range of languages, especially the Germanic languages, Welsh and Finnish; he also started to create his own languages. Attracted by Old English, which influenced some of his early writing, he changed from Classics to English Language and Literature, which he found more congenial. He was still studying when war broke out, but he achieved a first class degree in 1915.

In January 1913, Tolkien had come of age, and celebrated by writing to Edith to tell her that he still loved her. She, meanwhile, had become engaged to someone else, but as soon as she and Tolkien met again, she broke off the engagement, and he was able to write to Fr Francis to say that he and Edith planned to marry.

The outbreak of war caused Tolkien considerable heart-searching. He wanted a career as an academic (and enough money to marry Edith), but his family had roots in Saxony and his name was Germanic (he refused to change it, saying later, 'I have been accustomed...to regard my German name with pride, and continued to do so throughout the period of the late regrettable war...' He loved the Germanic languages, and he later described himself as 'a young man with too much imagination and little physical courage' – in the light of his war service, an unfair characterisation.

On his arrival in Oxford, Tolkien joined the University OTC. He did not greatly enjoy it. 'We had a drill all afternoon and got soaked several times and our rifles got all filthy and took ages to clean afterwards,' he wrote to Edith. The pressure on him to enlist was growing: Smith and Gilson had both joined up, as had his younger brother Hilary, and in June he himself became a Second Lieutenant in the 13th (Service) Bn Lancashire Fusiliers.

Early in 1916, Tolkien decided to specialise as a signalling officer, as the idea of words, codes and messages appealed to him. As AA Milne, also a signalling officer, said, it 'was much the most interesting work in the infantry, with the great advantage that one is the only officer in the battalion to know anything about it.' In their training, both officers learnt to map read and to send messages in a variety of different ways, from Morse code to carrier pigeons. In spite of its inherent interest, Tolkien found the work cold and cheerless.

It was now obvious that he would soon be sent to France, and so on 22 March, he and Edith were married. On 4 June, he embarked for the continent, commenting later that 'Junior officers were being killed off a dozen a minute. Parting from my wife then...it was like death.'

The beginning of his overseas service was not encouraging: the whole of his kit disappeared on the journey to Etaples, he was transferred to the 11th Bn Lancashire Fusiliers, and found the other officers either very young or much older and set in their ways and outlook.

Initially, on reaching the area of the Somme, Tolkien undertook further physical training and bayonet practice, but on 30 June the battalion moved nearer to the front line, although it was still held in reserve on the fateful 1 July.

* * *

Throughout 1917 and 1918, Tolkien's trench fever kept recurring. He attended frequent medical boards but each time the diagnosis was such that any return to France was discounted: 'still pale and weak, appetite poor,' was typical of the doctors' reports, indeed a year later a doctor noted that Tolkien 'still looks weak'. At times he was well enough to do home service, being for a while stationed in Hull; he and Edith walked in the woods at Roos, in East Yorkshire, and she danced for him there, an incident which was the inspiration for a theme in his *Legendarium*. Their first son, John, was born in November 1917.

In March 1918 Tolkien became bed-ridden with influenza and in September he went into hospital with gastritis, losing two stone in weight. He was already looking for an academic appointment when the Armistice was declared. He worked briefly on the *Oxford English*

Dictionary before being appointed as Reader in English Language at the University of Leeds. He continued to write both then and when he went to Oxford as Professor of Anglo-Saxon, in 1925. He remained at Oxford until he retired in 1959.

In 1926, Tolkien met the newly-appointed CS Lewis, who became one of his closest friends; there was perhaps a special closeness between men who had both known the horrors of war. They talked of literature, especially the Northern poetry which they both loved, and of the Christian faith that Tolkien adhered to and, at that stage, Lewis rejected. Tolkien was a Catholic, Lewis had been brought up an Irish Protestant, but gradually Lewis began to change as he listened to his friend's conversation, until eventually he too became a Christian. Together, they established a group of like-minded friends, the Inklings, who, for Tolkien, perhaps took the place of the lost TCBS.

Tolkien's writing is well-known. In 1937, he published *The Hobbit*, in 1954 and 1955, *The Lord of the Rings*; he wrote scholarly articles, produced editions and translations of Middle English poetry, and after his death, his son Christopher edited and published his father's unfinished or previously unpublished work.

After his retirement, he and Edith moved to Bournemouth; after her death in 1971, he went back to Oxford; he died on 2 September 1973 and they are buried together in Wolvercote Cemetery in north Oxford.

JRR Tolkien and his great friend CS Lewis have both become more firmly established in the public mind since their deaths by the continuing popularity of their writing, not least in films of their most famous work.

* * *

The grouping of school friends which Tolkien helped to found, the TCBS, suffered grievous losses in the war.

Robert Gilson joined the 11th (Service) Bn Suffolk Regiment as a Second Lieutenant in November 1914. He was a sensitive young man, in many ways unsuited to military life, but he was friendly and was soon on good terms with his colleagues. He was sent to France with the battalion on 7 January 1916 and was appalled by what he saw in the trenches near Albert – 'I can hardly bear the horror of this war,' he wrote. He went over the top on 1 July, and a friend noted that he led his men 'perfectly calmly and confidently.' In this spirit, he took over when his senior officer was killed and was still moving forward when he and his sergeant-major were both hit. A witness, Corporal Hicks, who was just ahead of Gilson, claimed that he saw Gilson killed when a shell exploded at 'about 9am'.

Geoffrey Smith originally had a commission with the Oxfordshire and Buckinghamshire Light Infantry in December 1914, but managed to get a transfer to the 19th (Service) Bn Lancashire Fusiliers, known as the 3rd Salford Pals, hoping that Tolkien would be able to join him. For some time, Lieutenant Smith was stationed in Yorkshire and continued to write poetry, but when he knew that he was likely to be going to France, he wrote apprehensively, 'Who knows what is hidden in the black darkness between now and the spring?' He was soon in Albert, near the Somme. In spite of the horrors around him, he urged Tolkien to publish his poetry, and when they were able to meet, they discussed their writing with undimmed enthusiasm.

By the time he heard of Gilson's death, Smith, now Intelligence Officer for a battalion that had lost half its men, was questioning German prisoners as well as collecting papers and letters from the German dead; it was a great relief when he was able to meet Tolkien at Acheux and briefly think about their poetry rather than their war. By October 1916, he had been promoted to Adjutant and was finding it a dull and unrewarding job; on 29 November, he was supervising road repairs and drainage when he was struck in his thigh and right arm by fragments from a shellburst. He walked to the dressing station and wrote a note to his mother, reassuring her that his injuries were slight. Two days later, he had developed gas gangrene; he died on 3

December aged twenty-two.

From a trench in Thiepval Wood, Smith had written to Tolkien: 'May God bless you my dear John Roland, and may you say the things I have tried to say long after I am not there to say them, if such be my lot.' It was a premonition. When Tolkien received the letter in early December, his friend was already dead. In 1918, Tolkien and Wiseman published their friend's poetry.

Tragically, Geoffrey Smith's death was followed by that of his elder brother Lieutenant Roger Smith, who was serving with the 4th (Service) Bn South Wales Borderers. He was killed the following month in Mesopotamia, aged twentysix. Ruth Smith was not only a widow but had now lost both her sons.

Christopher Wiseman was one of Tolkien's oldest friends. They met at school in 1905 and immediately enjoyed their discussions. Wiseman was the son of a Methodist minister, a liberal by instinct and a good amateur musician – in these things a contrast to Tolkien – but they were both keen rugby players. As their friendship developed, they called themselves the Great Twin Brethren; Wiseman became a founder member of the TCBS. He went to Cambridge with a Mathematics scholarship (joining Gilson, who was studying Classics), and in July 1915, announced that he was going to sea, having heard that the Royal Navy needed mathematicians as instructors. Early in 1916, he reported for duty as a naval officer on the HMS *Superb*, berthed in Cromarty Firth, where a mysterious explosion, thought to be caused by a German submarine, had just sunk a cruiser, killing more than three hundred seamen. In spite of this, Wiseman started to enjoy life at Scapa Flow, especially when he could go ashore and indulge his passion for archaeology. But on 31 May 1916, the *Superb* was involved in the confrontation with the German fleet at Jutland; Wiseman's ship survived unscathed, but over six thousand British sailors died. Shortly afterwards, Lord Kitchener's ship struck a mine off Scapa Flow and he was lost. Wiseman had to take part in a depressing search for confidential documents that might have been washed ashore.

After the war, the bond between Tolkien and Wiseman gradually loosened. In December 1918, Wiseman went to Cambridge to train junior officers, and later he became headmaster of a Methodist public school, inspiring his boys with his own love of music. Tolkien named his second son Christopher in honour of his old friend, but they met only intermittently. The TCBS had finally come to an end.

CHAPTER SEVENTEEN

Winston Churchill

—₥—

In war, chance casts aside all veils and disguises and presents herself nakedly from moment to moment as the direct arbiter over all persons and events...You may walk to the right or to the left of a particular tree, and it makes the difference whether you rise to command an Army Corps or are sent home crippled or paralysed for life.

Winston Churchill, *Thoughts and Adventures*

O F ALL THE PEOPLE who appear in this book, Winston Churchill is undoubtedly first amongst equals. In polls, he is consistently voted the greatest Briton not just of the twentieth century but of all time. A colossus on both national and international stages, he was an individual possessed of the most remarkable powers of leadership, oratory (including great wit) and personal courage. During his lifetime, he was Chancellor of the Exchequer, Home Secretary and twice Prime Minister. He was a war correspondent and a soldier, an artist and a prolific writer who went on to win the Nobel Prize for Literature in 1953. Over half a century earlier, in 1900, he had been elected a Member of Parliament at the age of just twenty-five. He was the only MP to sit in the House during the reigns of both Queen Victoria and our present Monarch: nothing about this individual was ordinary.

Churchill was a complex and driven man, and even his most ardent supporters recognize that he had pronounced flaws, and could be maddeningly self-centred and irresponsible. Yet throughout his life he was never a man who could be ignored and he maintained an uncanny ability to find his way into the epicentre of events, whether they were political, social or military. For a man so clearly ambitious, it is remarkable that he was so willing to take chances with the unpredictable fortunes of war. He was present on the Northwest Frontier, then in the Sudan – at the Battle of Omdurman – and again saw action during the Second Boer War. Later, in 1915, he chose, indeed asked, to go to the trenches of the Western Front. On one occasion, he recalled in a letter home that he had gone out 'in front of our own parapet into No Man's Land and prowled about looking at our wire and visiting our listening posts.' This was no isolated occurrence, for he added, 'This is always exciting'.

Fortune favoured the brave, and Churchill survived six months in and out of the front line in Belgium and France. Yet being brave was one thing, being rash and impetuous was quite another and it was typical of the man that, as Prime Minister thirty years later, he had to be practically held back from joining the invasion forces in Normandy in June 1944.

The landings in France that summer were a considerable success, albeit a very hard-fought one. When plans were drawn up for the invasion of occupied Europe, lessons had been learnt from a far less successful amphibious assault back in 1915. Then, British and Allied forces, in an attempt to open a supply route to Russia through the Dardanelles Straits, had first bombarded, then later landed troops on, the strategically important Gallipoli Peninsula, a wide strip of land that at its tip overlooked the Straits and guarded the shipping lanes below. Ultimately, the intention was to knock Germany's ally Turkey out of the war, but as it turned out, the landings on Gallipoli soon foundered. The ground war never seriously threatened to break out of the Peninsula, let alone take Turkey's capital Constantinople, and after a nine-month campaign the Allied forces were evacuated, having got little further than a couple of miles inland.

The failure of the Gallipoli Campaign was heavily associated with, amongst others, Winston Churchill, who was then First Lord of the Admiralty. He had strongly supported the naval bombardment of the enemy's forts guarding the straits, and had enthusiastically backed the opening of an alternative front to that being fought in France and Belgium. The failure, and the 205,000 casualties suffered, hit Churchill hard; his wife Clementine knew how much the campaign haunted him. 'I thought he would never get over the Dardanelles,' she said, 'I thought he would die of grief.' In Parliament he was demoted to Chancellor of the Duchy of Lancaster (a post with little authority), and excluded from the Cabinet War Committee. Feeling that his abilities were not being sufficiently used, he resigned, choosing to fight for his country.

Winston Churchill rejoined the Army, although he remained an MP, and took the opportunity of serving as a Major in the Queen's Own Oxfordshire Hussars, the Territorial regiment he joined after the South African War. In November 1915 he crossed the Channel, to be met by a staff car and taken to regimental headquarters to have dinner with the Commander in Chief, Sir John French. It was at this meeting that he asked for a spell in the trenches, preferably with the Guards, so that he might get acclimatized before taking command, he hoped, of a brigade. When he joined the 2nd Bn Grenadier Guards, they were just about to go into the line. The War Diary records his arrival on 20 November:

> Major Rt Hon Winston Churchill, who has just resigned from Government, arrived to be attached to the Battalion for instruction and accompanied the Battalion to the trenches.

Churchill had in fact appeared with too much luggage and was told abruptly that most of it must be left behind. By the time he reached the trenches, he had very little kit indeed, arriving with only a spare pair of socks and his shaving kit.

At dusk that evening, he entered Ebenezer Farm, a shell-battered and rat-infested place where his quarters, only eight feet square, had to double as a signals office, shared by four signallers. His fellow officers were wary of this politician in their midst, and the first meal they shared was a silent and strained occasion. They were determined that during his introduction to the trenches they would walk him off his feet – and tried to do so – while he had to convince them that he was less an ex-Government minister than a genuine army officer, even if he was still an MP. With this in mind, he wanted to start work as soon as possible, and, having had enough of Ebenezer Farm, he asked to go into the front line the next night.

The trenches he entered had been neglected, and his first job was to make them worthy of a Guards regiment. A great deal of time, he wrote to his wife, had to be spent cleaning up and strengthening the trenches and parapets. It was unpleasant work, made harder by increased shelling, cold winds and intermittent snow. Bodies had been built into the defences, so that feet and clothing would appear through the soil. In spite of this discomfort, Churchill felt that he was at last being useful, and was happier in that knowledge than he had been for some time. After two days in the line, losing two men killed and another two wounded, the battalion moved back to billets, where Churchill, who missed his creature comforts, sought a hot bath and some superior food and drink. It was sixteen years since he had had to eat army rations and he quickly requested that his wife supply plenty of food parcels from home. It was a pleasure, too, for him to meet Lieutenant Raymond Asquith, son of the Prime Minister, who was also serving in the Guards about six miles away. They talked over tea, and Churchill recorded approvingly that the young man had developed into 'quite a soldier'; the following year, Raymond Asquith was killed in action.

During his second spell in the trenches, Churchill had the first of several lucky escapes. On 26 November, he was ordered to visit the Corps Commander, so he left his company HQ and walked three miles, in considerable danger from shelling. When he arrived, he found that the General had gone and so he returned, only to find that in his absence a shell had demolished his dugout, killing a mess orderly inside. 'How vain it is,' he subsequently wrote to his wife, 'to worry about things.' Churchill remembered this incident for a long time and brooded over it; it was lucky not only for him but also for his servant who had gone along with him to carry his coat.

Out of the line, at dinner with senior officers, it was suggested he should now stay out of danger and await a brigade posting but Churchill refused. 'I wouldn't miss a day of it,' he wrote to Clementine. 'Nor did I. I also scorned the modest comforts of Battalion HQ and lived in the wet and the mud with the men in the firing line.' He spent his 41st birthday there, and described the day with his usual *joie de vivre*:

> For about three hours the trenches were under bombardment at about two shells a minute. I had a splendid view of the whole entertainment. Splinters and debris came very close – inches – but we only had two men hurt in the company. They were all very glad to be relieved, however, and on our return celebrated my birthday with a most cheery dinner.

Any thoughts his fellow officers had once harboured that this was a politician rather than a true soldier had been dispelled.

Churchill was confident that he would be offered the command of a brigade, not least because the Commander in Chief had every confidence in him. However, Sir John French's role as C-in-C, after the perceived failure of the Battle of Loos, was coming to an end, and with it Churchill would lose a major supporter. Sir John urged Churchill to take a brigade as soon as possible and Churchill 'acquiesced', remaining at GHQ from where he spent time visiting other parts of the front. During a trip to Arras he borrowed a new French helmet, and liked it so much that he kept it and wore it regularly, 'It looks so nice and will perhaps protect my valuable cranium,' he wrote to his wife.

On 9 December, he went back to the trenches with the Grenadiers, and Lieutenant Colonel George 'Ma' Jeffreys offered to make him his second in command. He was flattered and considered the offer, but as Sir John French seemed to have a brigade in mind for him, he returned to GHQ where he heard that he would be offered 56 Brigade, in the 19th Division. He was elated, especially as he knew and had a high regard for its Commanding Officer, Major General Tom Bridges, the man who had so valiantly drummed and 'whistled' the Royal Warwicks and Royal Dublin Fusiliers out of St Quentin over a year before. For the last time, Winston Churchill returned to the Grenadiers in billets at Laventie.

But back in London, Churchill's political enemies were speaking of his promotion with hostility, to the point at which his supporters, and even his wife, were unsure that he should accept it. Even so, the news that the Prime Minister, Asquith, realized that the promotion might be controversial and vetoed it, suggesting that a battalion might be more appropriate, came as a terrible blow. Churchill, his family and his supporters, including French, were bewildered and angry. In depression and bitterness, Churchill wrote of Asquith's 'meanness and ungenerousness.' He seriously considered ending his military career there and then.

Sir John French returned to Britain in mid December and in his place came the new C-in-C, Sir Douglas Haig. A friend to the last, French spoke up for Churchill on handing over command to Haig, who said that a battalion at least would be no problem. He insisted on seeing Churchill quickly and repeated this message, adding that he had heard good reports of his trench duties and a brigade could well follow. Churchill was pleased, and soon heard that the 9th King's Royal Rifle Corps was to be his, but this was quickly cancelled as the unit was leaving France. Churchill waited and fretted.

He had not lost his political touch and was kept informed of the situation in London, through friends, his mother and most of all, his wife, who wrote regularly and whose advice was often soundly based on her instinctive understanding of the politicians she met and talked to. He still felt he had been made a scapegoat over Gallipoli, and that the war was being mismanaged. A few days later, Churchill moved to share quarters with his old friend Sir Max Aitken, a journalist who was acting as a Canadian eyewitness at the front. Aitken provided his friend with the support and encouragement he badly needed, urging him to believe in his political future at a time when he was almost giving up hope. The two men remained close friends for the rest of their lives.

At Christmas, Churchill was given home leave and briefly visited London to see his wife and family. He was also able to discuss the political situation with Lloyd George, who was frustrated by the delay in bringing in conscription, and held out hopes that in the future there might be a government in which Churchill could play a part. However, within days of returning to France, he heard that he had been offered the command of the 6th Bn Royal Scots Fusiliers in the 9th (Scottish) Division. It had suffered heavily in previous encounters, especially at Loos, where more than half its men and three quarters of its officers had been lost, and was now being rebuilt in a quieter sector. His job would be to restore its morale and fighting ability. It was a challenge that he relished, and that evening he dined with the Divisional Commander, Major General Furse.

On 4 January 1916 Winston Churchill formally took command, and his first job, as in the Guards, was to win over the officers. He wrote to Clementine:

> Now that I shall be commanding a Scottish battalion, I should like you to send me a copy in one volume of Burns. I will soothe and cheer their spirits by quotations from it.

He was not initially impressed by his new Kitchener battalion, describing its officers as 'small middle class Scotsmen – very brave

and willing and intelligent, but of course all quite new to soldiering.'
Their average age was twenty-three. Their initial hostility towards him
was increased by his unfortunate introductory speech:

> Gentlemen, I am now your Commanding Officer. Those who
> support me I will look after. Those who go against me I will
> break. Good afternoon, gentlemen.

As one of his audience later commented, 'Everyone was agreed that
we were in for a pretty rotten time.'

His first parade was also something of a disaster, as he had no idea
of the commands to be given to an infantry regiment and so ordered
cavalry moves which were quite impossible. The men had the sense to
stand still and do nothing.

The new Lieutenant Colonel had joined his men in reserve billets at
Meteren, and now set about winning their confidence. He did so to an
amazing extent after such an unpropitious start. 'It was sheer
personality,' one of them recalled.

> We laughed at lots of things he did, but there were other things
> we did not laugh at for we knew they were sound…No detail of
> our daily life was too small for him to ignore…he would stop
> and talk with everyone and probe to the bottom of every
> activity. I have never known an officer take such pains to inspire
> confidence or to gain confidence.

Churchill found that the morale of the battalion was low, as it had
suffered a hard winter in mud and long difficult treks back to rest
billets. And this on top of their mauling at Loos. He was greatly moved
by all that his men had undergone during the battle, and so when the
first defaulter came before him, he asked, 'Where you in the battle?'
When the man said yes, the charge against him was dismissed. The
other officers were amazed at this, and horrified when, inevitably,

'everyone then said they had been at Loos'.

The problem was, as one officer later recalled in his memoirs, Churchill frequently sided with the rank and file when men were 'run in' for serious insubordination. This was not because Churchill lacked any sense of discipline but because 'he considered that no man would wittingly incur the serious penalties inevitable in such a case.' Instead, Churchill considered it only fair to explain the infraction and invite the soldier not to do it again. This 'second chance' let the men realize 'that they might at least once indulge themselves in the luxury of telling their sergeants to go to hell!'

Training started immediately and Churchill set about it enthusiastically. It was tough, rebuilding a shattered unit, which, even with new drafts, was under strength with 30 officers and 700 men. Churchill knew it would return to the line in two weeks but could see that it had the making of a fine unit. Luckily, they were granted an extra week out of the line and their Colonel put it to good use both in training and in providing for their comfort. A delousing committee was set up and achieved some success when a deserted brewery was turned into a bath-house. They were among the first troops to get the new steel helmets; new uniforms were issued and there was a vast improvement in rations. Football matches were arranged against neighbouring units, and the Colonel took pride in his team and rarely missed a match. On 16 January, he arranged a combined sports day and concert: a piano was obtained and songs were practised and 'people sang with the greatest courage who had no idea either of words or tune'. The atmosphere was relaxed and a great time was had by all.

As the month ended, the battalion moved to Ploegsteert in Belgium – Plugstreet, as the soldiers called it. Churchill inspected it before his men went in and was impressed with its position. The communication trenches ran out almost from the village itself, which still wore a veneer of civilisation with bars and cafés. It suffered occasional shelling but its civilian population, who had petitioned the Belgian

King to be allowed to stay, had not been evacuated, although later in the year, under intense shelling, they were forced to leave. The nearby military cemeteries were grim reminders of war, however, the closest only a hundred yards from Churchill's first battalion HQ, in a convent hospice where the nuns were still living.

The battalion's move forward, relieving the 2nd Bn South Lancashire Regiment, was made at 3.30am amid fear that the Germans might be aware of Churchill's presence and bombard accordingly, but the move passed off without incident. They were in position just before 6am, Churchill taking Laurence Farm, 500 yards behind the line, as his advanced HQ. It had some shell damage but he had his own small room and a sandbagged shelter for better protection. One of his first jobs was to reconnoitre the ground his men now occupied, and while doing so he spotted what he considered a better HQ in cellars closer to the front and ordered them to be pumped out. Unfortunately, they proved to be too sodden and waterlogged to be used. The unit had been due to spend six days in the line, but it was ordered back after just two. Churchill was delighted that it had suffered no casualties.

As it turned out, the first casualty might easily have been the Colonel himself. Churchill described what happened in a letter to his mother. The Battalion had arrived back into billets and that afternoon

> I had just had a splendid hot bath – the best for a month – and was feeling quite deliciously clean, when suddenly a tremendous bang overhead, and I am covered with soot blown down the chimney by the concussion of a shell these careless Boches fired too short and which exploded above our roof, smashing our windows and dirtying me!

But overall, he was happy in his work and there was much to do in checking kit and carrying out repairs; a particular pleasure was the arrival from home of brandy and cigars.

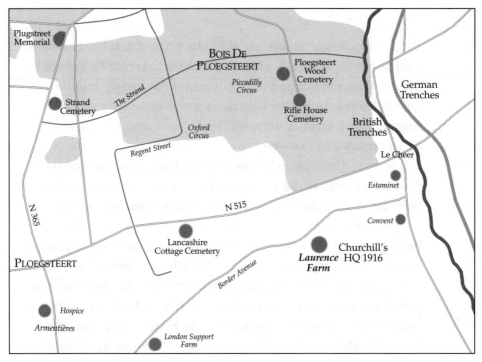

Laurence Farm: the location of Winston Churchill's battalion headquarters, 1916. See plate section.

Churchill simply ignored danger. He was known sometimes to stand on the firestep in broad daylight to encourage his men and to show how 'safe' it was. One officer recalled that he talked just a bit too loudly while out in No Man's Land, and moved like a baby elephant. He still wore his French helmet and appeared not to care a jot about his surroundings, neither flinching nor ducking at bullets or shells. He wanted the men to know that he shared their dangers and to trust him.

Back at Laurence Farm, he listened to the gramophone and even painted; a number of his works still survive. On 3 February a shell hit the farm but Churchill – who was enjoying coffee and port after an excellent lunch – emerged without injury. The torch that he had been toying with at the time was almost split by shrapnel, less than two inches from his wrist.

The news came through on 6 February that Churchill had been waiting and hoping for. A telegram arrived at Laurence Farm from St Omer, telling him to report back to take command of the brigade. But Churchill's delight was short-lived, as it was to be only a temporary promotion as a stand-in while the regular commander was away. The posting lasted only two days.

Despite his obvious ambitions, Churchill was a very conscientious commanding officer and felt deeply for his men, as they remembered later. On one occasion, the company runner met and saluted his Colonel, while walking along what had been Ploegsteert's main road. He had gone only a little further when he was called back and asked why he was limping. The soldier explained that his boots were in a bad way, and he had been told that it would be three months before he could have a new pair. Churchill immediately took a letter out of his pocket and wrote on the envelope that the bearer was to receive new boots immediately. The message was signed and sent at once to the Regimental Quarter Master Sergeant.

German shelling seemed livelier and more accurate and Ploegsteert was becoming a regular target. Churchill ordered the strengthening of the sandbagging around Laurence Farm which was frequently hit, but the sappers had done their work well and he considered it well-nigh impregnable. His view was tested when the Farm was peppered as several British shells fell short during a barrage and there were six casualties, among the wounded a newly-joined officer, Second Lieutenant Alastair Buchan, brother of the novelist John Buchan. He recovered then, but died of wounds received at Arras in 1917. On another occasion, the headquarters signallers were fortunate to escape when a shell burst in the signalling office just as they had vacated it. However, subsequently, three were mortally wounded when the Germans shelled Laurence Farm intensively at the end of February. The Farm was certainly a known target for the enemy and was hit on numerous occasions. It was with relief that Churchill came out of the line on 2 March with his leave confirmed and travel papers for

London in his pocket.

Churchill was still an MP and a deeply political man with re-invigorated ambition for high office, and in London he attended to his parliamentary duties. Life at the front had convinced him that the Government was prosecuting the war badly, and on 7 March he spoke in the Commons, attacking the Asquith administration and its war strategy, especially regarding the Navy. He landed some telling blows as he was obviously speaking from a position of authority, but his demand for the recall as First Sea Lord of Lord Fisher, an outspoken critic of Prime Minister Asquith, ruined everything. Far from his desired effect of speeding the Government's fall, it furthered his own estrangement.

Despite this blow, Churchill felt certain that his place was back in politics and not in the trenches. He wrote to Kitchener asking to be relieved of his command and in the meantime to have his leave extended, as he was due back in France the following day. Kitchener asked Asquith at Number 10, and he agreed. However, shaken by his Parliamentary set-back as he saw it, he subsequently withdrew the letter and left for the front once more and the trenches near Ploegsteert.

But politics was now consuming him and even his Divisional Commander, Major General Furse, told him that he would be of more use to himself and the nation back in Parliament. He was convinced, and planned to get back home as soon as he could; Clementine urged him to choose the moment wisely and not to risk making an unfavourable impression by leaving the army too precipitously. He wrote to friends, seeking advice, and they sided with his wife.

His chance to move permanently back to politics came with news that the 6th and 7th Battalions Royal Scots Fusiliers were to merge on 11 May, owing to both units being under strength. The Commanding Officer of the 7th was a regular soldier and Churchill was happy to let him take over. The arrangements took several weeks, and during this time Churchill continued with trench routine. Ironically, Sir Douglas

Haig now gave him his long-desired opportunity to command a brigade, but it no longer held any attractions for him. On 3 May, he and his men moved out of Ploegsteert, and he asked permission to leave the army as soon as his command was re-structured. Four days later, on 7 May, he paid an emotional farewell to his officers; the Adjutant responded that his leaving them was felt by every man there as a real personal loss. The War Diary, which had not deigned to record his unpopular arrival back in January, now robustly noted his departure.

* * *

Winston Leonard Spencer-Churchill was born in Blenheim Palace, Oxfordshire, on 30 November 1874, the son of Lord Randolph Churchill, third son of the Duke of Marlborough, and Jennie Jerome, the daughter of an American millionaire. He went to Harrow School, where he was not considered to be a bright boy but rather independent and rebellious, although he joined the Harrow Rifle Corps and was the school's fencing champion. His childhood was not a happy one; he frequently begged his mother to visit him but she rarely did, and his relationship with his father was always distant. He also had a slight speech impediment, although opinion is divided as to the form this took.

After Harrow, Churchill went to Sandhurst and was commissioned as a second lieutenant in the Queen's Own Hussars in 1895. He immediately asked to be posted to areas of action where, against all custom, he earned extra money as a roving war correspondent. He went initially to Cuba, where the Spanish were fighting Cuban guerrillas, and was apparently delighted to come under fire for the first time on his twenty-first birthday.

The following year, he was posted to India, where he was noted as one of the best polo players in his regiment. His account of a battle between three brigades of the army and a Pathan tribe brought him £5 per column from *The Daily Telegraph*. In 1897, he was engaged in the fighting, and on one occasion showed typical presence of mind. His men were hopelessly out-numbered and his Commanding Officer ordered Churchill to get them to safety, but before he left, the young officer asked for a note from the CO so that he would not be charged with desertion. It was duly given to him.

It was as a civilian war correspondent that Churchill went to report on the South African War. During the fighting between British and Boers, he was captured and held in a POW camp; he escaped and managed to travel almost 300 miles to Portuguese territory. This made him a war hero at home. He continued to be a war correspondent, but at the same time gained a commission in the South African Light Horse and was one of the first troops into the besieged towns of Ladysmith, and Pretoria. He and his cousin, the Duke of Marlborough, got ahead of the troops in the latter stronghold and received the surrender of 52 Boer guards of the prison camp there.

Back home in 1899, Churchill stood unsuccessfully as a Conservative candidate in an Oldham by-election, but in the general election the following year, he was elected for the same constituency. His early career in the Commons was almost as turbulent as his military adventures: in 1904 he crossed the floor to sit as a Liberal, campaigning for free trade, and by 1910 had risen to the office of Home Secretary; a year later, he was appointed First Lord of the Admiralty, expressly in the hope that the Navy could be strengthened to withstand any attack from Germany. He was in favour of better relations with that country, and did his best to secure an agreement that the two navies should co-operate rather than oppose one another; right up to the outbreak of war in August 1914, he hoped that a European conflict could be avoided.

Nevertheless, alongside the First Sea Lord, John 'Jackie' Fisher, he had strengthened the British Navy and helped to develop its resources, notably the change from coal to oil powered battleships, and in the final weeks before the war, he took rapid action to protect British interests, with guards on ammunition supplies and oil depots, and on all coastal defences. The Home Fleet was moved into position in the North Sea to deter any attempt at invasion. By the time that war was declared, Churchill felt that the British Navy was ready for the conflict, and, however enthusiastic he had been for peace, he was now 'interested, geared up and happy', as he wrote to his wife, and the preparations for war held a 'hideous fascination' for him.

After his military service during the war, Churchill served as Minister of Munitions under Lloyd George, and thereafter was regularly in offices of state, notably, in 1921, as Secretary of State for the Colonies, when he signed the Anglo-Irish Treaty establishing the Irish Free State (Eire). He lost his seat the following year, and, disenchanted with the Liberals, sat in 1924 as an Independent with Conservative backing. In 1925, he formally rejoined the Conservative Party, commenting that 'Anyone can rat [change parties] but it takes a certain ingenuity to re-rat.' He was then appointed Chancellor of the Exchequer under Stanley Baldwin, overseeing Britain's return to the Gold Standard, a disastrous move which led indirectly to the General Strike of 1926 – he was not an economist, and, as he later admitted, had been given bad advice.

Churchill was about to start his 'wilderness years', estranged from the leadership of his party and concentrating on his writing. Gradually, however, he began to pay attention to the rise of Adolf Hitler in Germany and the danger of German rearmament, and he was vigorously opposed to Neville Chamberlain's policy of appeasement. At the outbreak of war he was appointed First Lord of the Admiralty, just as before the First World War, and the Royal Navy, according to the probably apocryphal story, sent out the signal 'Winston is back.'

The rest of the Churchill story needs little repetition. Chosen to be Prime Minister in 1940, his determination and courage inspired the British people through the period when defeat seemed likely, and his speeches have gone down in history. After the war, he was defeated in the General Election, and then became Prime Minister once more in

1951. He had a stroke two years later, but remained in office until he retired in 1955.

Winston Churchill was more than just a military leader and politician. He was a prolific painter, starting to paint in order to help himself to get through the disaster of Gallipoli in 1915, and finding much pleasure and relaxation in his art until the last years of his life. His writings are major historical works: the citation for his 1953 Nobel Prize for Literature reads: 'for his mastery of historical and biographical description as well as for brilliant oratory in defending exalted human values.'

In 1963, President Kennedy made him the first Honorary Citizen of the United States.

He died in 1965 at the age of ninety, and was given a state funeral.

Late in his life, there was a little reminder of the past. Cruising in the Mediterranean with friends, he found that the yacht had to pass through the Dardanelles. Churchill gave orders that it should do so during the night, to avoid disturbing the guests – and himself? – with unhappy memories.

CHAPTER EIGHTEEN

Henry Moore

—⚊⚊—

You jumped down into a trench, stabbed a sack of tight straw
and climbed up the side of the trench again. I had to teach
the recruits how to do it, viciously and violently. Sometimes
they were young officers. One was so polite and gentle.
Instead of getting down there and saying 'You bloody
bastard!' or something, he said 'Bother you!'

Henry Moore

H E WAS ONE OF THE NATION'S greatest artists, perhaps its greatest sculptor of the twentieth century, yet when asked whether his artistic sensibilities were affronted by what he had seen at the Battle of Cambrai, Henry Moore almost took umbrage.

I wasn't a sensitive man. I meant to win a medal. I meant to do the best I could to win a medal because one believed in the cause for England. I mean, people were patriotic. I was a boy of eighteen and it was an adventure and I enjoyed it all.

Not the very last days perhaps, which, if prompted, he might have conceded were very unpleasant indeed: shelled by artillery, strafed by aircraft, gassed and invalided home. Yet there was no doubting his desire to serve his country. He did not wish to sit back and wait to be conscripted. Instead, in early 1917, he hunted round for a battalion that would let him volunteer, and found one in the Civil Service Rifles. Had he waited of course, he might not have gone to France in 1917, thereby avoiding injury, the effects of which, while never life-endangering, did prove lifelong. However, had he waited he would surely have gone to France the following year, and so run a reasonable chance of being killed, robbing Britain and the world of his very special artistic gifts.

The Battle of Cambrai in November and December 1917 was one of the shorter offensives on the Western Front but many historians believe it was nevertheless one of the most interesting engagements of the war. For the first time, it utilised a huge number of tanks (378 in total with another 54 in reserve) in a brilliantly-conceived combined arms operation against the Germans. It proved that the formidable Hindenburg Line, the enemy's deeply-constructed system of trenches, could be unlocked, offering the prospect of open warfare once more. It also showed that the enemy had developed new methods of counterattack which rapidly unpicked all the success achieved by the British forces. All this in two weeks: not bad.

One of those who would witness that counterattack was nineteen year old Private Henry Moore. His battalion, the 1/15th (County Of London) Battalion (Prince of Wales' Own Civil Service Rifles), was out on rest on 18 November at Ecoivres. Two days later, during a rugby match, news arrived of the Third Army's remarkable success that morning at Cambrai, six divisions having smashed through the Germans' three defensive lines. In a thick morning mist, without the customary bombardment, the enemy had been taken completely by surprise and thrown into confusion. Over the next ten days, their forces were thrown back, in places to a depth of six miles, although Cambrai itself remained in their hands. The news of this success caused the hitherto silent church bells of England to ring nationwide in a celebratory peel.

Many years later, Winston Churchill was to point to the Battle of Cambrai as a shining example of what could be achieved. In criticising the losses of previous campaigns, he wrote in his book *World Crisis*:

Accusing as I do without exception all the great allied

offensives of 1915, 1916 and 1917, as needless and wrongly
conceived operations of infinite cost, I am bound to reply to the
question, What else could be done? And I answer it, pointing to
the Battle of Cambrai, 'This could have been done...'

Churchill, never a man to mince words, or, at times, to worry too much
about sweeping statements, nevertheless summed up the feeling that at
Cambrai something different had happened. The fact that this success
unravelled so quickly was a bitter blow, but a new military dawn had
broken.

The attack along a narrow six-mile front finally stalled on 29
November. In the north, the troops had come to a halt just outside the
village of Bourlon, with the men strung out in the nearby Bourlon
Wood. Three-quarters of the wood had been taken but the eastern
sliver remained in enemy hands. It was to this wood that Moore's
battalion, part of the 47th (London) Division, was ordered on 28
November, the day the offensive officially ended. They would relieve
the men of the 2/5th Bn West Yorkshire Regiment and some
dismounted cavalry, reaching their positions at 2am. That day the men
consolidated their stance while the wood was shelled by the enemy,
costing the battalion 55 casualties.

At 8.50am on 30 November, the Germans opened up a furious
bombardment on the wood and SOS flares soared up into the air to the
left and right of the Civil Service Rifles. They unleashed not only high
explosive and shrapnel but also smoke and phosgene gas. The weather
was perfect for such a weapon: the temperature had risen and the
winds that would otherwise have blown away the gas had dropped. It
was later described by one of the men who was there:

The gas in Bourlon Wood hung in the trees and bushes so
thickly that all ranks were compelled to wear their respirators
continuously if they were to escape the effects of the gas. But
men cannot dig for long without removing them...there was a

steady stream of gassed and wounded men coming through the regimental aid posts. Their clothes were full of gas…

Henry Moore was in the thick of it. He wrote:

> The field when we arrived was all grass but there wasn't a blade to be seen when we left. They'd begun to mix shells, gas shells along with high explosive so that we wouldn't know that the shell that dropped just back there was a gas shell until you smelt it. We didn't like the gas mask on, it was uncomfortable, so every now and then we would see if the air was clear by lifting the mask and sniffing a bit and if the gas was still there we would put the mask back. Well, after three days of gas shells mixed with high explosive, we didn't know but a lot of us had been gassed.

All morning the German infantry attacked, gradually driving units of the 47th (London) Division towards the western edges of the wood, where they dug in and held their ground, resisting all attempts finally to push them out. Two enemy balloons were seen to rise and several enemy aircraft buzzed up and down the line, strafing the men on the ground; the 1/15th Battalion suffered severely. Henry Moore recalled:

> We were being machine-gunned by aeroplanes flying over and I got fed up with this as we seemed to be doing nothing. I asked the officer of our platoon if I could fire the gun and he said, 'Yes, if you go away from us because we don't want them to pinpoint you near us, so if you go 100 yards away you can draw their fire, if you want to do it.'

The team moved off under the direction of a corporal and found a dugout from which to fire the gun, although the officer ordered them to move further away.

It was like trying to bring down a house that was moving over your head at 80mph, except that you could only hit one or two bricks: you had to get the pilot or the engine. We found a bottle of rum in one pothole. The corporal got tight and I had to take control.

Moore had another problem to contend with when one of the team had to be taken back with shell shock. Moore took him for treatment, then returned to the gun. 'I tried nearly a whole day and didn't hit anything,' he recalled in an interview sixty-five years later. He also noted that the corporal received the only medal awarded to the team, the medal that Moore might have liked. 'But I was young and it was all romantic, heroic excitement.'

All along the front line, the Germans pushed the British back, staggering their attacks and wrong-footing their enemy. The fighting in Bourlon Wood had cost the Civil Service Rifles dearly. At one point, some men on the Battalion's left were cut off and almost encircled, and the CO, Colonel Segrave, had to move the Battalion HQ and A Company across open country under heavy fire. The war diary puts the losses at 39 men killed, 120 wounded and 40 missing, with two officers killed and eight wounded, of whom six were gassed. Moore said that only 52 of 400 men were able to muster as they were relieved by the Surrey Rifles and withdrew to tents at Fémy Wood.

It was the end of Moore's war, though he did not realize this straightaway. He began to feel unwell from the effects of gas, reported to the Regimental Aid Post and then had to walk ten miles to the Field Hospital, activity which helped to work the gas thoroughly into his system and make the effects worse.

The next morning, after having a rest, an officer told us that anybody who was voice-affected by gas could report sick. Out of the 52 who had marched back, about 40 of us reported sick; my own voice had gone.

Moore was marked down for home and was evacuated as a stretcher case to England and taken to hospital at Lansdowne Road, Cardiff, where he spent six weeks recuperating. The effects of the gas lasted for the rest of Moore's life: he always talked with a husky voice, which occasionally failed him altogether.

After he was discharged, he was sent to a convalescent camp at Shoreham-on-Sea, where he was delighted to find an old friend, Douglas Houghton, with whom he had first joined the Civil Service Rifles in 1917, and who was recovering from the effects of trench fever. Both volunteered for a three-week physical training course for instructors at Mill Hill School in London, followed by a month in Aldershot. It was all very strenuous, with assault courses and bayonet fighting, which Douglas Houghton found highly unpleasant. His friend wrote:

> Henry got quite a lot of fun out of our experiences – and it built up his strength, which stood him in good stead later, when his sculpture sometimes involved heavy lifting.

Moore was still not fit enough for active service but joined the training battalion of the Civil Service Rifles at Wimbledon, his home for the next six months. He and Houghton were promoted to Lance Corporal and Moore became a specialist bayonet instructor. He described his duties:

> You jumped down into a trench, stabbed a sack of tight straw and climbed up the side of the trench again. I had to teach the recruits how to do it, viciously and violently. Sometimes they were young officers. One was so polite and gentle. Instead of getting down there and saying 'You bloody bastard!' or something, he said 'Bother you!'

Off duty, Moore started boxing and found he was rather good at it; an interest in the sport stayed with him for the rest of his life.

The Allies had already launched what proved to be a rolling series of offensives and by the time that Moore volunteered to go back overseas, the armistice was signed. He rejoined his unit at Ferfay, an uninspiring place although the mining area reminded him of home, and the French family with whom he lodged was good-hearted; he helped in the house and enjoyed practising his French in the local shops, but overall it was boring and he felt homesick.

Moore's war had been a short one, with only two months at the front and two days of real fighting. Nevertheless, it brought him maturity, the ability to learn from others and physical toughness. He seemed outwardly unscarred, but there are some who see in the recumbent and pierced figures he produced in the 1930s an echo of the sights he must have seen in Bourlon Wood.

* * *

Henry Spencer Moore was born into the small coalmining village of Castleford in Yorkshire on 30 July 1898, the seventh of eight children. His father Raymond was a coal miner, an intelligent, self-taught, driven man who read Shakespeare and played the violin. He was an ardent trade unionist and determined that no son of his should go down the pits. His wife Mary was also a strong character and influential in her youngest son's life.

Their home for the first twelve years of Moore's life was a two-up, two-down terraced house with no electricity nor running water but spotlessly clean and precisely run. At the age of three, Henry started elementary school and his mother sent him off in – ironically – a specially-made uniform of khaki coat and trousers. His talent for drawing was encouraged while he was still very young, and when he was only about ten, he heard about Michelangelo and decided to become a sculptor. He began carving in wood and modelling in clay.

In 1910, like several of his brothers and sisters, Henry Moore won a scholarship to Castleford Secondary School. The school was modern and progressive, and its head, TR Dawes, was an enthusiastic supporter of the arts. He particularly liked architecture and would take his pupils out on field trips to churches to show them the different styles; the young Moore was particularly attracted by large Gothic corbels with fantastic faces, and the stone effigies of knights and their ladies. It all fuelled his ambition. The new art teacher, Alice Gostick, whose French mother gave recitals at the school, was a generous and enthusiastic young woman, fond of the practical arts, especially pottery. She inspired her young pupils both in and out of the classroom, and for Moore, meeting her was the start of a friendship that lasted to the end of her life.

Young Harry, as he was known at school, was a good sport and a popular boy. His artistic skill was recognised and he received his first commission in 1913 when he was asked to produce a carved notice board for a school society. He was greatly influenced by his surroundings and was lucky to be able to explore the beautiful, wild Yorkshire countryside near his home. In 1911, the family moved to a larger house and in 1914 – unusually for their time – bought a home of their own.

Moore left school in July 1915, just four days short of his seventeenth birthday, declaring that he wanted to be a professional artist. Raymond Moore was worried about his son's choice of career, fearing that earning a living in this way might be precarious, and so he suggested that Henry get some teaching qualifications behind him first, just as another brother had done.

Moore therefore became a student teacher, and, as it was now wartime and many teachers had joined up, became virtually full-time at the same school at which he had so recently been a pupil. He hated every minute of it and found the children unruly and very hard to handle: the boys got up to tricks that he was too young to predict, and the girls, 'infinitely worse' to the young teacher, would find ways of embarrassing him. He was only seventeen, and lacked the maturity to assert himself and gain control.

One significant achievement in 1916, however, was to carve the inscription on the Castleford School Roll of Honour, and the dates, 1914 – 19..., the final date incomplete. His own name would subsequently appear on the board (H. S. Moore, Civil Service Rifles) along with those of ninety-five other old boys, in neatly applied gold paint. Eight of them would die in the war and many more, like Moore himself, would suffer its effects long afterwards.

Over two million men had joined the forces of their own free will, but despite this incredible number – the largest voluntary social movement Britain has ever witnessed – compulsory conscription followed early in 1916. The promise was made that although boys of eighteen-and-a-half would be enlisted, they would not be sent overseas before they were nineteen.

Moore was not averse to serving and readily took up a suggestion from his brother that he should not wait to be called up and so sent to any old unit, but rather that he should volunteer and have some element of choice. And so in February 1917, he boarded a train to London with the names of a few regiments he liked the sound of – particularly the Artists Rifles – and on the journey met a lad on a similar mission. He and Douglas Houghton became instant friends and vowed to stick together. Houghton was something of a driven character too, and later became an MP, Cabinet Minister and peer. At the age of 97, he was the oldest serving member of the House of Lords, and the last peer to have fought in the First World War.

The young Henry had never been to London before and headed immediately for the headquarters of the Artists Rifles, only to be told, much to his annoyance, that he was too short; the same happened at the Inns of Court. A variation of the theme, this time that he was too young, came from the Honourable Artillery Company, a regiment that still required a fee to join. 'They had a waiting list of over a year – it would mean [owing to conscription] that I would be called up before that time.' Perhaps a more accurate reason was the snobbery he noticed when they asked what his father did for a living. Houghton's father was a lace-maker, Moore's a miner; neither was an attractive proposition for the HAC.

Douglas Houghton then came up with a possible solution. He was a civil servant and had heard of a unit called the Civil Service Rifles which he thought sounded admirable. Like the others they were a Territorial unit, but the important thing for the two eager recruits was that at last they were accepted, and Henry Moore became number 534592 Private Moore, in A company, the youngest soldier, he believed, in the regiment. He was kitted out in an ill-fitting uniform and sent to camp at Hazeley Down near Winchester where there was much drill and he was detailed to carry out cookhouse fatigues. The camp was muddy, and he soon wearied of the constant cleaning of boots and washing up hundreds of tin mugs and plates. Writing to Miss Gostick, he described collecting his first army pay: 'We had to march up to a table, come to attention, salute, say our number, take our money, salute again and walk off (all for one shilling a day).'

To ease the boredom, he asked for his drawing things to be sent from home, though, predictably, he had little time to use them. Nevertheless, he had no regrets about joining up and called the men he served with 'grand fellows' and said everyone got on well together. When his kit was issued, he said he felt like a walking saddler's shop, all belts, buckles and straps. All in all, he decided that the life was far preferable to teaching.

Their training sergeant had seen service in the Boer War and wore an intimidating military moustache. Private Moore clearly had a good eye and steady hand, and was delighted when he passed the musketry course and was deemed a first-class shot – an achievement which, he reported, would earn him an extra sixpence a day after two years' service. But it was not all work and training, and there was a chance to visit London and revel in the museums and galleries as well as enjoying a spell of leave back home. The prospect of going to the front did not seem to bother him unduly. Indeed, he made a prediction of his war which turned out to be quite uncannily accurate. He wrote to Alice Gostick in jocular terms: 'Heigh Ho! For France and a jolly old blighty, fine time in hospital and then – the end of the war.'

Moore reached the milestone age of nineteen on 30 July 1917, old enough to be sent abroad, but he had to wait an extra twelve days before he crossed the Channel from Southampton with his good friend Houghton. He was sent to join the 1st Battalion of his unit, based at Arras, for training in trench warfare. It had been serving in the dreaded Ypres Salient and was resting and refitting.

Arras was not a quiet front and there were still duties to be carried out. Moore wrote soon afterwards to a friend:

> I'm in the front line trenches, I continue in some amazing way to get about two hours of sleep every night; the rest of the time is taken up in sentry duty on the firestep. Things were rather lively last night, both sides were strafing, I don't know if we did much damage, but they did not. The afternoon strafing is just subsiding (now about 3.30pm). There she goes, one of ours, an 18-pounder. Saw two aerial fights this morning and two aeroplanes brought down in flames, oh, things are getting exciting.

Moore was fascinated by what he saw and experienced. He recalled seeing the older men killing lice at night with the aid of a candle run along their shirts' seams and was given their rum ration so that they 'could take quite a delight in seeing me tiddly'. He also remembered seeing his first dead body. The corpse was in a dugout. 'I didn't know the person was dead until I went up and shook him and he fell over, which was a shock.'

Being obviously young, willing and bright, Moore was also given numerous little jobs.

> An officer spoke to me and said, 'We are going to be relieved, I

want you to go back and see the new battalion in. You remember the way.' I didn't tell him I couldn't because I haven't a very good sense of direction, so I said, 'Can I start out now to find the way back because I may have got it wrong?' and I spent the whole morning finding the way back to the relief point, carving a little cross on every corner with my bayonet. It was a quiet part of the line and I would have been ashamed to get it wrong.

Next time out of the line, he wrote again to Alice Gostick, calling a strafing 'hellish' and recounting the strain of even routine trench duties, such as standing sentry:

If one lets one's imagination run ahead, one can be quite convinced that the barbed wire posts are forming fours, or advancing in lines towards your trench. The only thing to do in that case is to divert one's gaze to some other object and it's ten to one that will also become animated; however, you've got to put up with it (unless the other sentry also thinks they are Huns) until the hour's duty is up.

Moore was surprised that he was feeling homesick and also distressed when he heard that the magnificent cathedral at Reims had been damaged by shellfire. Nevertheless, he reported to Miss Gostick that, in spite of some nostalgia for Castleford, he was 'ever so much more comfy out here than I thought I should be'. He seems to have been remarkably adaptable, and was soon saying what a 'jolly good time' he had had on a course at the brigade school. On 18 November, news arrived of the assault on Cambrai, and that reinforcements were needed.

Henry Moore's military service was short-lived; when he looked back, he commented that his time in France had been comparatively easy: 'For me,' he wrote, 'the war passed in a romantic haze of trying to be a hero.' Once he was home, his father expected him to resume his teaching profession, but his son refused.

> I wouldn't be without that two years' experience. I went away a
> boy, a child really and by the time I came back I was what?
> Twenty. And I was able to say to my father 'I don't care what
> you would like me to do. I now know that I am going to be an
> artist,' and he had to accept it.

Moore applied for an ex-serviceman's grant, a sum available to those
whose education had been interrupted by the war, and he became the
first-ever student of sculpture at Leeds School of Art in September
1919. He continued to live in Castleford and to go in the evenings to
Alice Gostick's pottery classes, until at the end of his second year, he
won a scholarship to London; it remained his home for almost the next
twenty years. He began to discover new sources of inspiration, and in
1924 was awarded a Royal College of Art travelling scholarship to go
to Italy for six months to study the Old Masters.

During his seven-year appointment as a sculpture instructor at the
Royal College, Henry Moore met a painting student called Irina
Radetsky, whom he married in 1929. He was starting to acquire an
international reputation, spending time each year in Paris, where he
was particularly influenced by Picasso and subsequently becoming a
member of the British Surrealist Group. He and Irina visited Spain in
1934; in the ensuing Spanish Civil War, his sympathies were firmly on
the Republican side – he remained faithful to his father's left-wing
politics. Even after his sculptures had brought him considerable
wealth, he and Irina – and later their daughter Mary – lived simply
and unostentatiously.

In the Second World War, Moore's reputation spread, especially
among American collectors. Oddly, his fame at home came initially
from a series of drawings, not sculpture; these 'Shelter Drawings'
showed the people of London huddled in the underground for safety
during the Blitz. The drawings were widely appreciated, and in 1941,

he was appointed an official War Artist.

After the war, Moore was repeatedly honoured for his achievements, being appointed a trustee of both the Tate Gallery and the National Gallery; in 1955 he was made a Companion of Honour and eight years later, was awarded the Order of Merit (though he refused a knighthood). Both the German Chancellor and the French President visited him at his home to award him honours.

A few years before his death, Moore gave the whole of his estate and collection of work to the Trustees of the Henry Moore Foundation, set up both to conserve the art and reputation of the artist and to promote sculpture in the future. He died on 31 August 1986, internationally acclaimed and honoured, and represented by his work in almost every important collection.

CHAPTER NINETEEN

JB Priestley

—⚏—

I think the real Jack Priestley died in August 1914 somewhere on the Western Front. He came out of it apparently without any neurosis but I think that he actually did die. But a writer was born and what all those millions and millions of words were really written for was so that he wouldn't remember the 1914-1918 War.

John Braine, writer

FRIENDSHIPS ARE GOOD IN TIME OF WAR, but when it came to the Great War, friends, sadly, did not always last very long. John Boynton Priestley, Jack as he was usually called, or JB Priestley as he is much better known, was one of the most prolific authors, dramatists and broadcasters of the twentieth century. Like so many of those who went on to become famous, his life was deeply affected by what he had witnessed. Few served so long on the Western Front, and because of that he became acclimatised to, but never used to, the loss of comrades. He served first as a private and then as a subaltern at a time when the life expectancy of junior officers was painfully short, whether they were killed or wounded. By September 1918, with the war so close to a successful conclusion, any loss must have been all the harder to accept and bear, but Priestley was to lose yet more of his closest companions.

Three years after Priestley had first gone to France, he was sent overseas again with a group of young subalterns. It was 7 September 1918 and Priestley was just days away from his twenty-fourth birthday as he crossed the English Channel on a ship packed not with British troops, but with strong-looking and enthusiastic American soldiers. As far as he knew, he and his convivial group were the only British men aboard, and they watched and listened in amazement as a large band played ragtime music on the top deck. It seemed to Priestley, a novel way of going to war.

His group, six officers in all, were destined to be reinforcements to the 16th Bn Devonshire Regiment, although not every one of them would leave the Infantry Base Depot at Rouen, their first port of call on landing in France. Three of the officers, 2nd Lieutenants Robert Cox, Cyril Reed and Frederick Schrader, would be held back until casualties in the battalion triggered their onward progression. The other three would make their way forward after just a few days. They had all been good friends since meeting at the regimental depot at Devonport, six months earlier. One was Ernest Farrer, a professional musician from Leeds who was in France for the first time. Another was Roy Machon, a twenty-six year old civil servant from Bristol. He had seen it all before, having fought with the 8th Devons at Bullecourt in March 1917, when he had been badly wounded in the knee. The third was Jack Priestley. He too had experience on his side, having first served in France as far back as 1915 before being wounded.

Priestley recalled how the three friends slogged up a dusty road in hot, sweaty weather, while seemingly endless streams of transport lorries and limbers rolled past. By 16 September, they finally found their below-strength battalion close to the front line; unfortunately for them, it was preparing to go over the top on the 18th to attack the outposts of the Hindenburg line, the most heavily fortified defensive position the Germans constructed on the Western Front. Experience or inexperience could make a marginal difference, and marginal differences mattered. Two days later, Priestley and Machon were wounded and on their way back down the line, while Farrer, the new boy, was dead.

The attack was part of a grand aperitif to the main meal which was the Allied forces' attack on the Hindenburg Line. The fighting that took place in the first weeks of September 1918 was designed to probe and weaken the enemy's defences and, in the case of the assault on 18th, to gain a position that afforded good observation points over the potential prize.

At 7pm, just hours after arriving at the battalion, Priestley and his friends were sent forward with their platoons in order to take up positions close to where they would attack. The timing was unfortunate, as none of the new officers had much time to meet the men under their command before leading them into battle. Priestley led his men to a narrow railway cutting where they halted. It was late evening and as they awaited orders, the Germans began dropping gas shells close by. It was Priestley's job to run round making sure the men under his command were wearing their gas masks. The men hated wearing them, finding them claustrophobic, and difficult to breathe in, especially when anxiety and nerves made the heart race that much faster. Priestley later speculated that gas might have seeped into his mask, as he felt nauseous, and this was made worse that evening, as the men filtered out of a railway cutting prior to their advance, and they were all given tots of rum.

How long the men waited in this cutting is unclear. Orders had been given that the battalion would be attached to another brigade for the forthcoming operations, timed to begin the following morning at 5.20am. In the meantime, the Devons were ordered to relieve another battalion in the front line, from where they would lead the attack at first light. Final instructions were received and disseminated to the men by their platoon officers. A creeping artillery barrage would screen the troops as they advanced and a machine gun barrage would hold back and harass the enemy in their trenches. Three objectives were marked on officers' maps as green, red and blue lines. The Devons, who were in trenches just to the southwest of the village of Rossoy, would advance with the 24th Bn The Welsh Regiment to take the green line. Once it was taken, fresh troops would sweep past: in the case of the Devons, a battalion of the King's Shropshire Light Infantry.

Such is the nature of warfare that most attacks lose direction and cohesion the further an advance is made. Objectives, clear and simple on paper, become confused and lost in the fog of war, as shells burst and shrapnel scythes the air. On the morning of 18 September, the troops had much more than just bullets and bombs to contend with. They advanced in heavy rain and an autominal mist that hid the attackers from all observation. As far as brigade and divisional headquarters were concerned, the men had simply disappeared. Command and control was in the hands of the officers on the ground.

The attack was launched in the early morning on a wide front, and very quickly Priestley became disorientated. He later declared that he could not decide whether he had been careless, affected by the rum, or was suffering from gas poisoning. Even though the noise of battle was everywhere, he felt alone and dazed and began to wander about in the hope that he would eventually find where to go.

The King's Shropshire Light Infantry, who were close enough to see something of the battle, witnessed the confusion. 'The Devonshires whom we supported entirely lost direction,' their War Diary noted. Lieutenant Farrar may well have been killed at this point, while three other officers were wounded or soon to be so. As many as fifty other ranks were also casualties.

To all intents and purposes, Priestley appeared lost to the immediate battle; Machon had fallen once, but with only minor injury, struck in the back by a flat piece of shell casing. It was a lucky escape but he was in considerable pain. Nevertheless, he continued to lead his platoon forward and took his objective, capturing several prisoners and a machine gun. A 77mm gun was also taken, before those Devons who were still together attempted to consolidate the ground won. The mist remained thick and in places still kept visibility to just a few yards. Priestley must have been going broadly in the right direction, for out of the fog a German appeared, aged no more than sixteen. Priestley gesticulated with his revolver, and the boy raised his hands in the air and began to get visibly upset, gibbering. He ought, Priestley later acknowledged, to have been in school, but here he was on a battlefield and Priestley, while attempting to look stern, pointed in the direction the young boy should take, all the while hoping he was indeed sending him back into captivity and not towards the German lines. Off the boy ran, leaving Priestley once more alone and wondering where the battle might have got to.

Throughout the morning, messages from the fighting slowly filtered through to divisional headquarters, despite the fact that at one point all telephone lines to every battalion committed to the action had been cut. Only at 7.40am did definite news arrive that the green line had been taken. The Devons could halt while fresh battalions passed through them to continue the attack on the second objective. This too was reached, but consolidation proved difficult and only by early evening was news received that the whole of the second objective had been secured. Any further advance was now halted, at least for the night.

The battle was over for the day with nearly nine hundred prisoners taken, including, it is to be hoped, the young German that Priestley had sent back. As for the battle, Priestley never found where it had been. His head began to spin, he found himself short of breath, and took to a shell hole where stretcher bearers found him. It was to prove the end of his war.

Priestley and Machon were both evacuated down the line to a base hospital by the 55th Field Ambulance. Although Priestley was always under the impression that his friend had been killed, Roy Machon had little more than a badly bruised back. Five weeks later, he rejoined his unit and saw out the war. In 1919 he was awarded a Military Cross for his 'gallantry and devotion to duty,' that day in September.

The body of Second Lieutenant Ernest Farrer was found and buried close to where he had been killed. He lies today in Rossoy Communal Cemetery, along with a number of other men who were killed in the attack.

Perhaps it was Farrer that Priestley was thinking of when he later wrote that the best men had been killed in the war. Farrer was thirty-three and had married his sweetheart Olive in 1913. The son of a vicar from Leeds, he had attended Leeds Grammar School and the Royal College of Music. He became a composer and organist and, by the time he had joined up in December 1915, was a professional musician. Under the Derby Scheme, he enlisted as a private in the Grenadier Guards , which allowed him to remain in civilian life until he was needed. In August 1916 he was mobilised, training for 18 months before being discharged to take up a commission. In the end he had lasted just ten days in France. After he was killed, his identity disc and visiting card were recovered from his body, but his wrist watch and gold signet ring were not found, much to the distress of his wife.

The battalion had lost one officer killed and six wounded in the fighting. Second Lieutenants Cox, Reed and Schrader, the three remaining officers at Rouen, were needed up the line much earlier than they perhaps expected. As for Jack Priestley, the Army Medical Board decided that he was no longer fit for active service.

* * *

JB Priestley was born in 1894, in Bradford; his father, also Jack, was a socialist school teacher who passed on his left-wing ideals to his son. Young Priestley, who was later to use his native city as a background to much of his writing, left Grammar School to work as a clerk in the wool trade, but he already had dreams of becoming a writer. Patriotism was uppermost in his mind in 1914, and he was one of the young men who flocked to join the army when Kitchener made his famous appeal for 100,000 volunteers to enlist in his New Army. Later, in 1915, Priestley met Kitchener and was not very impressed, but he paid tribute to him for raising such a force from enthusiastic civilians.

Joining up in Halifax on 7 September 1914, Priestley was still a few days short of his twentieth birthday when he was posted as a private to the 10th Bn The Duke of Wellington's (West Riding) Regiment. This was the third Service Battalion in the regiment, for such had been the rush to enlist that the first two Service Battalions, the 8th and 9th, were already full by the time Priestley volunteered.

For the first few months, he and the other recruits slept in dripping bell tents, trained with antiquated rifles, and wore blue uniforms from which the dye ran in the rain. Nevertheless, the men were well trained, and gradually they attained the stature of real soldiers who could march twenty miles a day with full pack. At the end of August 1915 the battalion left for France, where they took over trenches in a then quiet sector near the village of Bois Grenier in northern France's industrial region of coal mines and brick works. In a letter home, which somehow escaped the eye of the censor, Priestley described the place as hardly more than a large cemetery with a front line that was just a three foot deep ditch and with no communication trenches behind. The weather was terrible, with snow and sleet, the men surviving on little more than a slice of bread as they lay down waiting to be relieved. After a couple of days, Priestley was sent out alone on a listening post. It was an educational experience, for while the enemy trenches were some distance away, any movement in No Man's Land was interpreted as a German soldier, whether it be a rustling hedge or swaying bush. The only thing to do was to shut his eyes briefly and hope that, when he reopened them, whatever he felt he had seen had disappeared. Priestley professed bravery in these early days of his war, a bravery that, he said, gradually diminished with every passing week, while the full weight of war was brought to bear on those in the trenches as shellfire tore the ground. Terror, he later asserted, came first through the ear.

Priestley had a lucky war, as he said himself. On the first day of the battle of Loos, 25 September 1915, his battalion was waiting to go over the top, fully laden with extra ammunition and bombs, scaling ladders in position. However, the neighbouring attack by the 8th

Division had some initial success, supported by a bombardment of machine gun and rifle fire from the Duke of Wellington's front line. Owing to reports that the 8th Division were in the third line enemy trenches, the Duke of Wellington's proposed assault was postponed and the ladders removed. They were relieved the following day. In the months that followed, Priestley took part in trench raids and was shelled on numerous occasions, but it was the unrelenting misery of trench life during winter that caused his greatest suffering, when he slithered and slid his way down the line on working parties, always caked in mud and with hot food the stuff of distant memory. In October, he wrote to his father that he had been digging trenches, calculating that in the heavy clay soil each man was expected to dig a segment of trench 6ft long, 4ft broad and 2ft 6inches deep in an afternoon. It was, claimed Priestley, some of the hardest work he had ever undertaken. He was filthy, caked from head to foot in mud and had no opportunity to have a wash.

In early 1916, Priestley was slightly wounded in the hand by a rifle grenade, and was dispatched to a hospital for treatment before returning to the line and an extended period of trench life that sapped the resilience of the company. Casualties mounted steadily as the battalion was encouraged to bomb, strafe and raid the enemy, who were better placed to defend themselves than the British soldiers, who suffered heavily during the inevitable retaliation. About this time, Priestley came under pressure to take a commission but refused; he wanted to remain in the ranks with the men, many of whom had become close friends. Within a few months, nearly all of them were dead.

It was only a matter of time before Priestley was hit again, when he was helping to divide the platoon rations in a small dugout. It was June 1916, the weather was hot, and as the bread and meat were being cut up he heard the rushing sound of an enemy trench mortar. Priestley recalled that he had no chance to get away and felt a deep terror before everything about him went into slow motion and he felt strangely detached from events. Then the world as he saw it disintegrated.

The mortar landed three yards away. Two men were killed, one wounded and four more taken down the line with shellshock, including Priestley, who by stages was removed to a Field Hospital, arriving back in England and hospital in Leicester. His medical records note: '15.6.16 To hospital shell shock in the field.' Priestley's luck had held again. Had he been in the open and not in a dugout, he would have been blown to pieces.

Priestley's war was over for the time being. After hospital, where he was treated for delirium, he was sent to convalesce, then to Ripon where he resumed training to restore his physical fitness, and subsequently to Alnwick where he spent much of the first six months in a state of apathy, often drinking to excess. He felt at rock bottom, nothing mattered any longer. In late 1917 he applied for a commission, the opportunity he had been offered earlier in the war and regretted not taking.

Officer training ensured another six months in Britain, at a camp in North Wales. Priestley was worked hard, but began to enjoy it and lost the apathy into which he had fallen. He played football for his company team, and began to write some satirical pieces both for performance and for publication. He passed the course, and left as an officer, free from the cookhouse duties and carrying parties to which he had become so used. At the barracks in Devonport, he did his best to avoid drill, and as a punishment was told that he was to be in charge of funeral parties. On most days, there would be a death in the large military hospital in Plymouth, and there had to be a firing party for the cemetery or a guard to present arms at the station. An officer did very little, as a sergeant would drill the men and give all the commands. This suited Priestley, and after a funeral, he would often take the rest of the day off and stroll along Plymouth Hoe eying the girls.

It was three years after his first overseas service that he returned to France, the only small band of British officers on an American troopship. His active service with the 16th Bn Devonshire Regiment was brief, before the gas attack which finally saw him removed from the front line.

However, this was not his last visit to wartime France. Although downgraded as unfit for active service, he returned overseas to a Labour Corps Depot near Rouen, auditioning artists for concert parties, before taking charge of a mixture of eighty unfit British soldiers and between six and seven hundred German prisoners of war, charged with battlefield salvage.

To his surprise, Priestley enjoyed the logistical problems of moving so many men and finding accommodation for them; on one occasion, when the site chosen for a camp proved to be totally unsuitable, he took on higher authority and won his battle; not only did they escape the waterlogged place first suggested, but they were given the chance to develop something better. Speaking in German to his prisoners, he explained that they could build a decent camp for themselves in the ruins of a German hut encampment if they worked hard; many of them were skilled men, and they set to and built a new, solid, waterproof camp for themselves in the place he had chosen for them. He became aware of the normality of the German soldiers, and was, he commented later, perhaps a little in awe of them. At Christmas, he visited the German warrant officers' mess where he found them sitting round a small Christmas tree, illuminated for the occasion. As he walked in, the men all stood to attention, clicking their heels together. For the first time in his army career, Priestley felt satisfaction in a job which used his own considerable skills in a way that he had never before imagined.

He was still in his camp in 1919, when he applied for demobilisation and found that, as he had been wounded three times, he had some priority and his release came comparatively quickly. He was touched to be solemnly thanked by the German prisoners, who gave him two group photographs which he kept, and to hear one of the British troops comment that he was the only good officer they had had.

So he found himself back in civilian life. Like Dennis Wheatley, Priestley chose not to claim his medals and thought no more about military service, though he could never forget the war. No matter how low he felt, on may occasions, he recalled that he never once hankered after army life.

* * *

In 1919, Priestley became a student at Trinity Hall, Cambridge, studying Modern History and Political Science. While there, he gained valuable experience towards his ambition by writing for the *Cambridge Review*, and after his graduation, being determined to freelance in London rather than taking regular employment, he found work as a theatre reviewer for the *Daily News* and contributed articles to *The Spectator* among other periodicals. He also started writing books of criticism, and soon established a reputation as a literary commentator.

His first major success came with his novel, *The Good Companions*, in 1929. His explanation of why he chose to write about a touring concert party in a long episodic novel is interesting. He admitted that the book had a fairy-tale atmosphere which he ascribed to being a reaction to his war service when so many friends had been killed. He had suffered from bouts of anxiety and felt under strain and this departure in his writing came like a release, far away from all that had happened before. There must have been many people in the late 1920s who felt the same way, and the book was a huge success. It was followed the next year by *Angel Pavement*, and by the early 1930s he had become a well-known novelist; he then turned to drama, and wrote a wide variety of plays, some, such as *Time and the Conways*, dealing with a subject which he studied extensively – beliefs and theories about the problem of time. The play for which he is best-known is *An Inspector Calls*, which was first performed in 1945 and made into a film some nine years later.

By the outbreak of the Second World War, Priestley was a regular broadcaster, initially several times a week and always late at night, to America and the Dominions. These broadcasts were made during the Blitz in London, and on one occasion Priestley left his hotel to make an extra recording for Canadian listeners, to find later that the part of the hotel in which he had been staying had been destroyed. The broadcast had almost certainly saved his life. For BBC listeners at home, his radio programme *Postscripts*, which followed the nine o'clock news on Sunday evenings, became so popular that it was estimated around 40% of the adult population listened to it – indeed, as the writer Graham Greene noted: 'in the months after Dunkirk, [Priestley became] a leader second only in importance to Mr Churchill'. It is certainly significant that the Nazis banned all of his writing.

However, there were complaints from members of the Conservative Party that his views were too left-wing, and the programme was cancelled. Quite how this came about is unclear. Priestley received two letters. One was from the Ministry of Information, the other from the BBC, each organisation blaming the other for being responsible for taking Priestley off the air.

Priestley became an increasingly political figure. In 1941, he co-founded a new Socialist party, the Common Wealth Party, but at the 1945 General Election only one of its candidates was elected to Parliament, and it was dissolved, most of its members joining the Labour Party. Priestley himself continued to write on both literature and politics, and together with Kingsley Martin, the editor of the *New Statesman*, founded the pressure group Campaign for Nuclear Disarmament, in 1958.

The most famous – and lasting – of Priestley's writings date from the 1930s and 1940s, though he wrote other minor works later, especially with his third wife, the archaeologist Jacquetta Hawkes. He was described as a man of integrity, honesty and generosity, but who also had times of great melancholy, perhaps as the result of the two world wars he had lived through. He died in 1984. There was a memorial service in Westminster Abbey, but his ashes were interred where his story began, in Yorkshire.

CHAPTER TWENTY

Harold Macmillan

—⚬—

I had in my pocket Aeschylus's 'Prometheus', in Greek. It was a play I knew very well, and seemed not inappropriate to my position. So, as there seemed nothing better to do, and I could not move in any direction, I read it intermittently. The shelling went on from both sides with tremendous uproar, but since I was between the trenches, I felt I was perhaps in a good position from this point of view.

Harold Macmillan, *Winds of Change*

HAROLD MACMILLAN famously declared that 'to be alive at all involves some risk', but then there was risk and there was risk. As a young officer on the Western Front, he knew all about the fine nuance between courage and recklessness, the delicate balance between caution and cowardice. 'Courage is mainly, if not wholly, the result of vanity or pride,' he wrote of his time with the 2nd Bn Grenadier Guards.

> When one is in action – especially if one is responsible for men under one's command – proper behaviour, even acts of gallantry, are part of the show.

Yet when he was alone on the battlefield, badly wounded and removed from immediate concerns about duty or example, it was perfectly possible for fear, 'not to say panic' to take a cold grip. At the village of Ginchy, during the Battle of the Somme, panic seized Lieutenant Macmillan.

I was alone and nobody could see me. There was no need to keep up appearances, and I was very frightened. I remember running or at least stumbling through the village, and out at the southern end, to get away from the bombardment. How far I actually succeeded in going, I don't know.

The calculated gamble to run saved his life but the shock had been profound.

There was a strange sequel to this incident. In 1943, when Macmillan was in North Africa, he was in a plane that crashed near Algiers. He was lucky to get out alive, and was badly burnt. He was taken to a nearby French hospital, and it evoked a memory. When he was evacuated to the hospital in Abbeville in 1916, he had begged that a message be sent to his mother to say that he was all right. Now, seven years after his mother's death, he made the same request. For a day or two, he was again the wounded officer from the battle twenty-seven years earlier and the intervening years – even his marriage and the memory of his children – had gone from his mind.

The Guards Division, in which Macmillan served, had not taken any active part in the early days of the Somme offensive of 1916. It had remained in the Ypres sector while the fighting raged to the south. Only at the end of July did it move by stages towards the battle, arriving in the vicinity in late August.

Another two weeks would pass before the 2nd Battalion became actively engaged in the fighting. On 15 September, the Division would take part in a renewed offensive in which tanks would be used for the first time in action, although the presence of these new machines had been a closely guarded secret, as Macmillan remembered:

Rumours had been going about regarding some mysterious engines of war. Nobody had actually seen them, and every kind of distorted account was given of these portentous monsters.

In the event, the ten tanks allotted to the Guards Division made little impact on the battle and around Ginchy, where the Coldstream and Grenadier Guards would advance, they either broke down or arrived too late.

Two days before the attack, a number of small raids were undertaken to straighten the line and remove obstacles that might endanger the general advance. At Ginchy, an enemy machine gun was pinpointed in an orchard in the northeast corner of the village, and two platoons of D Company were ordered to knock it out. Harold Macmillan was to take up two platoons from B Company in support and to protect the left flank. It was a bright moonlit night and the attackers suffered a number of casualties as they made their way across the shell-pocked ground. Nevertheless, B Company was successful and the machine gun post cleared, the survivors digging in on the edge of the wood and completing a short stretch of trench by the morning. Macmillan's party moved up just in case a counterattack materialised. The following day, the Germans shelled the trench before all four platoons were relieved and joined the battalion well to the rear of Ginchy, where the men were given hot food and a rum ration. Meanwhile, the 2nd and 3rd Coldstream Guards took over the front line as they were due to spearhead the attack in the morning, followed by the 2nd Bn Grenadier Guards.

Despite Macmillan's exertions, his day was not quite over. That evening he was ordered to go back up to the front line to note the direction the Grenadier Guards would need to take in the morning. It was important he made sure of the route and, with an orderly for company, he looked for markers that would help pinpoint the way.

> We passed a dead German lying in our path with his arm held
> out in a gesture of greeting...the corpse was a good landmark
> for the return journey.

Early the following morning as Macmillan's company filed back up towards Ginchy he looked out for the body.

> I watched with interest and amusement and great confidence
> that practically every man shook the dead German by the hand
> and said 'Goodbye Fritz, meet you soon.' That meant they were
> in good heart. Wonderful. They would be all right then.

The men had put on a collective brave face. They had endured
sporadic enemy shelling for most of the previous day and they were
about to go over the top. In such moments, as the pressure grew, men
were prone to ask or say the most unusual things. Sixty-five years
later, Harold Macmillan recalled one such odd request:

> We were walking along and a Corporal Newton said to me,
> 'Can you give me anything of yours, Sir?' and I gave him a silk
> handkerchief. The handkerchief was returned by Newton's
> family fifty years later.
>
> On the way up the men got a bit separated. I remember one
> officer, an awfully brave chap. He knew he was going to be
> killed, and indeed he was, and he had to help the men out, to
> keep them together. Then we formed up. This is an awkward
> moment. If the attack was at 6.20am, you had to be there about
> two hours before. Then you had to wait.

At the allotted time a creeping barrage began, and the Coldstream
Guards started their advance. Almost immediately they came under
intense machine-gun and rifle fire. Around 350 yards behind, the
Grenadier Guards moved off, led by their CO, the idiosyncratic
Colonel de Crespigny.

As Macmillan recorded in an interview:

> I can see him now in his irregular dress. A gold-braided peak
> hat and gold spurs which he always wore contrary to rules; he
> was never wounded in the whole war.

The German barrage dropped on Ginchy before the Grenadier Guards had even reached the shattered village. They had no option but to push on, losing men as they went, including Captain Marteine Lloyd, a twentysix year old regular who had gone to France in 1914. Once before he had been reported 'killed in action' only to turn up alive, if not entirely well. There was to be no second reprieve. Another officer, Lieutenant John Arbuthnott, a twenty-two year old serving in Macmillan's company, was mortally wounded in the stomach. He was almost certainly the man who had predicted his own death just hours before.

Despite the casualties, the War Diary would later marvel at how few men were killed or wounded passing through the ruins of Ginchy. The

The assault of the Guards Division, 15 September 1916. Coldstream Guards (C.G.) and Grenadier Guards (G.G.) suffered grievous casualties in taking their objectives.

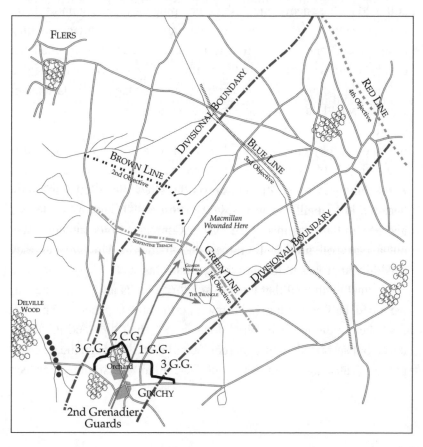

enemy shelling caused considerable confusion, but many lives were saved by the soggy ground into which the shells plunged, many failing to explode. At one point Macmillan was hit just below the knee-cap by a small piece of shell case, a minor wound which he ignored at the time but which would cause considerable pain later in life.

As the Grenadier Guards reached the northeast edge of the village, a problem became apparent. Neither battalion of the Coldstream Guards was anywhere to be seen. Much later it was discovered that their attack had veered off to the left. As their whereabouts were sought, the battalion could only wait for twenty minutes, (although Macmillan recalled that it felt much longer), before the decision was made to continue the advance towards the first objective assumed to be in British hands. Unfortunately the target, named Serpentine Trench, and a neighbouring strongpoint known as the Triangle, were still held by the enemy, and with no creeping barrage to support them, the Grenadier Guards had no alternative but to attack against unsurpressed enemy fire. It was remarkable that they reached the enemy positions, which were taken after a short but vicious struggle.

The original operational order envisaged that the 2nd Bn Grenadier Guards would take over the trench system from the Coldstream Guards, who in turn would advance sixty minutes after zero hour onto the second objective. This plan went totally awry. Instead, the Grenadiers held onto the first objective but were under continual fire. A machine gun which opened up on the Grenadiers' left flank soon became, in Macmillan's words, 'very tiresome'. It had to be silenced and Macmillan was instructed by his Company Commander to take out a party of three or four men and silence it. However, as they stealthily approached the gun, Macmillan was shot.

He later estimated that he was just thirty yards away when he was wounded, half crouching, half crawling; the bullets penetrated his left thigh below the hip. He rolled down into a shell hole and lay there, dazed but surprised at the apparent lack of pain. Although the machine gun was subsequently knocked out, Macmillan was stranded between the first and second objectives, while fierce fighting on his left continued unabated.

> I had in my pocket Aeschylus's 'Prometheus', in Greek. It was a play I knew very well, and seemed not inappropriate to my position. So, as there seemed nothing better to do, and I could not move in any direction, I read it intermittently. The shelling went on from both sides with tremendous uproar, but since I was between the trenches I felt I was perhaps in a good position from this point of view.

While Harold Macmillan lay immobile, one company of the Grenadiers pushed on towards the second objective, but this did not fall and during the course of the afternoon the Germans launched their own counter attacks which in turn were driven off.

> I could just look out of the corner of my eye and see the Germans running round the lip of my shell hole.

There was nothing Macmillan could do but lie 'doggo' and feign death, fervently hoping no German would take shelter in his shell hole.

> I lay out all day, indeed for over twelve hours, thinking of many things and nothing. My chief worry was the fear that I had been hit in a vital place, for everything seemed numbed. I bled very little, at least externally.

Macmillan's right knee was stiff and painful and his left leg completely useless; his water bottle had been hit by bullets and he had nothing to drink. He could only trust that if he held on until darkness, there was a chance of being picked up. Dazed but quite conscious, he waited until Company Sergeant-Major Norton, 'a splendid man', arrived with a search party. Norton had already performed one great act of heroism, having led a bayonet attack against an enemy bombing party which had been driven off. Now he carried Harold Macmillan back to Serpentine Trench. From here, stretcher-bearers arrived to move him and another wounded officer named Ritchie to the dressing station at Ginchy, but this, as they discovered, had been abandoned owing to heavy enemy fire. The two officers discussed the situation and decided they should not risk other men's lives any longer; Ritchie had only been wounded in the arm and they could move on by supporting each other. They sent the stretcher-bearers back to the battalion.

The shelling in Ginchy, which had slackened off, started again, and in the darkness and confusion, the two officers became separated. Macmillan admitted that this was his lowest point. Despite his wounds, he found the strength infused by fear to get out of the village, eventually rolling into a ditch. Here he was later found by transport men from the Sherwood Foresters, who took him to a dressing station.

His wounds meant that he had to be evacuated, involving a long journey to Abbeville by barge, about which he remembered very little. The French hospital there was under great pressure and his wound was not carefully tended; when abscesses formed under it, the decision was made to send him back to England. He believed that what happened next saved his life. He refused to go to a military hospital and insisted on going home instead. He made such a fuss that he eventually got his way, and his mother made alternative medical arrangements. Even so, it was more than two years before he was finished with treatment and almost two more before the wound totally healed.

For the Guards Division, 15 September ended with only mixed success though this was not for want of trying. Events conspired against them, but they upheld the Guards' traditions and did all that was expected of them, albeit at a terrible cost. The 2nd Bn Grenadier Guards lost 359 killed, wounded and missing, well over half of those who took part in the attack, including three officers killed or died of wounds and another nine injured. The two battalions of the Coldstream Guards suffered even more.

In all, Harold Macmillan had served six months in France.

> I suffered none of the long-drawn-out pressure which weighed so heavily on officers who had to undergo, without relief, long periods of trench warfare. It is not to be wondered at that, in those days, to get wounded, 'to get a Blighty', was regarded as a piece of good luck rather than a misfortune.

All the same, that 'lucky' Blighty gave him discomfort and pain for decades to come.

* * *

A great deal had happened in the thirteen months since Harold Macmillan first embarked for France in August 1915 to join the 4th Bn Grenadier Guards. After landing at Le Havre in high spirits, the Guards had passed through Saint Omer, and settled for several weeks at Blendecques. Here life was comfortable, although they all knew that they were preparing for a large-scale operation: the Battle of Loos.

A description of the intended battle was given by the Corps Commander to all divisional officers in a village square. Macmillan was curious.

> He made us a speech in which he described at some length and in some detail the battle... Since the civilian population were freely admitted to this open-air lecture, from the security point of view this seemed a somewhat odd procedure. Indeed, it was alleged by some of the more cynical of our officers that smiling patrons, leaning out of the windows of the houses, could be seen releasing pigeons at a frightening rate.

The 4th Bn Grenadier Guards, part of the 3rd Guards Brigade, were not called upon to take part in the first assault on 25 September which, after initial and in some places dramatic success, was repulsed. The enemy, after recovering from their initial surprise, turned stout defence into counterattack, regaining much of the land lost. Despite repeated and at times lengthy delays, the 4th Bn Grenadier Guards marched up to the front, taking over some old trenches near the village of Vermelles where they spent the night in comparative safety. There were disadvantages, however. Their section of trench ran through the old French churchyard, and as Macmillan later recalled:

> The coffins and bodies of the dead had received rather rough treatment. Here a skeleton, more or less entire; there a hand or head or leg. I thought, naturally, that this might have some effect on morale. But quite the opposite. Our Guardsmen thought this a most amusing coincidence, and there was much joking about it. 'That's where you'll be tomorrow, mate!' 'Lor! It's all got ready for us!'...as if their billet had been a sly joke of higher command.

The next day the brigade was ordered to attack. This included a march of up to two miles to the village of Loos along a road under shell fire. It was a remarkable example of discipline, for while the battalion was broken up into irregularly spaced platoons, the men marched in fours and broke only once when a hare temptingly ran between them. It was the first time Macmillan had been under fire and 'I must confess that for many months and even years I would dream of it.' The ground was littered with the dead and wounded from earlier attacks and machine gun and shell fire claimed more casualties before the perfectly ordered troops arrived at the destination. The 4th Bn Grenadier Guards was then split and at least half the battalion, in the absence of definite orders, attacked with the 2nd Bn Scots Guards. Harold Macmillan was amongst those who advanced.

There is a kind of daze that makes one impervious to emotion. Anyway, it was my first experience of a battle, and I could not suppose that this was any worse than usual.

When the Scots Guards were driven off, the officer in command, Captain Morrison, ordered the men to lie down and crawl back to a road and dig in. Morrison was a proud and corpulent man and chose not to crawl but walked about apparently impervious to danger. Inadvertently, this display put Macmillan under pressure to follow suit, and he did, trying 'to look self-possessed as possible under a heavy fire.'

As darkness fell that evening, Macmillan was hit in the hand by a stray bullet. Earlier in the day he had received a sight wound to the head which brought on a feeling of concussion. This coupled with an extremely painful hand and a much swollen arm, made the next few days something of a blur. Macmillan was ordered to a dressing station from where he was sent down the medical chain until he eventually returned to England and a hospital in London. Here he stayed until discharged just before Christmas, when he was given leave. In the New Year, he was posted to the Reserve Battalion at Chelsea Barracks, with routine duties. His wounds healed, but he never recovered full strength in his right hand.

The months of convalescence gave him time to see old friends, but by April 1916 he was fit for overseas duty once more, and was posted to the 2nd Battalion, led by the eccentric but fearless Lieutenant Colonel de Crespigny. This man was loved by officers and men alike; his chief interests were hunting, gambling and fighting, but he was a fine regimental officer, and prone to a subversive attitude to authority. On one occasion, an order from General Headquarters had come down that a record of the number of rats in the trenches was required for submission. 'Crawley', as he was known, organized a rat shoot on a massive scale. Sandbags were filled with the bodies of rats, left a day or two to ripen, and then, at dead of night, piled up outside Brigade Headquarters.

In spite of the clear difference in their characters, Crawley was very kind to Macmillan, whom he regarded as a strange animal who loved books and arguing about philosophy, and Macmillan was always pleased if he felt that he had won the older man's approval.

The next three months were spent in or around the Ypres Salient. The regimental historian wrote that 'the monotony of trench life was relieved by the exciting but dangerous ventures of patrols.' On one such occasion, Macmillan was sent out by night with a private and a corporal with the objective of seizing a German in order to get information. There were difficulties: their own wire, the flares, and, if they got far enough, the enemy wire. They soon ran into a German patrol, one of whom threw a bomb that exploded on the side of Macmillan's tin hat. The man responsible was attacked by Macmillan's Corporal, and killed or wounded.

Macmillan's party managed to get back to their own lines, but he had severe concussion and could not give a clear account of what had happened. The Corporal summed up his share of the action: 'I 'it 'im [the German] and 'is 'elmet came off. Then I 'it 'im again and the back of 'is 'ead came off.'

Macmillan received another wound stripe, a friendly compliment from Crawley, and a message of congratulations from the Brigadier. He also had facial wounds which should have been treated in hospital, but as all medical facilities were being cleared in preparation for a major offensive, he was just kept out of the line until he recovered. That major offensive would be the Somme.

* * *

Maurice Harold Macmillan (he never used his first name) was born in London on 10 February 1894, the youngest of three boys. His mother was American and his English father was involved with the flourishing family publishing business. It was a comfortable existence, with a London town house for the week and a country retreat in Sussex at the weekends. There were servants and a nanny, and the young Harold was initially educated at home before going to preparatory school in Oxford.

Soldiering made an early mark on him, and he recalled being mightily impressed by the Guards on royal duty in London, the celebrations following the Relief of Mafeking during the Boer War, and even seeing the Kaiser in the funeral procession for Queen Victoria. Nevertheless, it seemed likely that he would be destined for the family business when he grew up.

In 1906 he went to Eton, but developed pneumonia which eventually took him out of the school and back home, where his education was continued by private tutors. Both his parents were hard taskmasters and expected the best from their children. Young Harold did not disappoint them, and won a classical scholarship to Balliol College at Oxford where he threw himself into student life. One particular friend was Gilbert Talbot who was to die at Ypres in 1915 and who has a living memorial in the Toc H movement, which, during the war, provided a place of rest, comradeship and Christian fellowship for officers and men alike. An Oxford Union photo from 1912 shows them together, and Macmillan would later meet Gilbert's brother, Neville, who was a senior army chaplain on the battlefield. At Oxford he also met the poet Rupert Brooke, and in a strange foreshadowing of his later life, visited 10 Downing Street with Prime Minister Herbert Asquith's son, Cys, who was another Balliol friend. Another of Asquith's sons, Raymond, serving with the 3rd Bn Grenadier Guards, was killed on the Somme in 1916 in the same attack in which Harold Macmillan was wounded. A third son, Arthur, lost a leg during the war.

Despite his interest in current affairs, Macmillan said the war came as a complete surprise. As he wrote later:

Had we been told, when we were enjoying the carefree life of Oxford in the summer term of 1914, that in a few weeks all our

little band of friends would abandon for ever academic life and
rush to take up arms, still more, that only a few were destined
to survive a four years' conflict, we should have thought such
prophecies the ravings of a maniac.

Germany, they considered, was led by men of solid reputation and a
civilized background. When war broke out, their view was that it
would be over by Christmas and that they must on no account miss it.

For many of his peers it was easy to enlist, as they had served in the
Territorial Force or in the College's Officer Training Corps.
Macmillan had been more interested in academic life, and had
neglected to join. But he had also just undergone an operation for
appendicitis, a serious matter in those days, involving a lengthy period
of convalescence, and so he had to submit to what he saw as the heart-
breaking experience of seeing his friends join up without him.

For the time being, all Macmillan could do was to read about the
news from the Front, limited though this was. Yet staying passively at
Oxford did not seem to be an option, and in the autumn of 1914, he
was accepted into the Artists' Rifles, and began to drill in the Inns of
Court, without uniform or rifles. The remaining obstacle was the
medical examination: he was now fit, but his eyesight was likely to
prove an insuperable barrier. Fortunately, with the pressure of men
coming forward, medical officers were inclined to be lenient, and he
found himself a Second Lieutenant in a New Army battalion of the
King's Royal Rifle Corps. Subsequently, he had no problem with his
need to wear glasses and carried a spare pair with him. Gas masks did
present a challenge, but, as he wrote, 'I do not believe anybody could
see much out of gas masks, with or without spectacles.'

He joined his battalion in Southend for training, and in spite of the
lack of kit, their good humour and enthusiasm went a long way. Their
commanding officer was an old retired Boer War veteran, who seemed
surprised by the motley collection he found himself leading, some
with tunics and civilian trousers, others with khaki trousers but

civilian coats. The Adjutant had been a regular soldier and so had one or two NCOs, but nobody else seemed to have any military experience. It all seemed fun, although tempered for Macmillan by the appearance of his friends in the casualty lists; he felt he must get out to join them as soon as possible.

In the meantime, they concentrated on drill, in an open field on the cliffs outside the town. It poured with rain, the field turned to mud, and the men were soaked through every day. In the evenings, they studied books abut infantry training and military law, but by the time Christmas came, they were beginning to lose heart.

With his 21st birthday approaching, Macmillan tired of what appeared to be playing soldiers and decided it was time to use his connections to get an interview with the Grenadier Guards. He made a good impression and after a few weeks of nervous waiting, was told he had been gazetted into the Reserve Battalion. It was March 1915 and the war seemed at last to be getting nearer.

He was sorry to leave his comrades in Kitchener's Army, and looked on them with great admiration later, when they fought in the battles of the Somme and Passchendaele. But for the time being, he was delighted to be among smart, highly-disciplined soldiers. He discovered, rather to his surprise, that drill was less of an ordeal if it was well done; when, many years later, he became Prime Minister, one of his greatest pleasures was watching the rehearsals for the Queen's Birthday Parade: the drill had developed, he wrote, to something like the beauty of a ballet.

At Chelsea Barracks, spit and polish were much in evidence. He was told to buy a new uniform from an approved tailor, and to add a sword to his acquisitions. The sword never made it to the Western Front but he kept it as a souvenir into old age. He was still living at home, and so able to meet old friends as they came on leave or went back to the Front; life was strenuous but pleasant.

When it was decided to form a Guards Division, Macmillan was posted to the new 4th Battalion of the Grenadier Guards and they moved into camp. The weather was superb for training and there were frequent trips to London. 15 August was a longed for day – departure to France – and it was done in style. When they had embarked and seen that the men were well settled, the officers were ushered into the saloon for refreshments. To their amazement, they found a full luncheon in the style of a peace-time party, served by waiters from the Ritz; there was a fine selection of food and wine, and they enjoyed it all 'in a kind of rapturous silence,' wrote Macmillan. All this was provided by Captain JA Morrison commanding A Company, a man of equal wealth and generosity.

> How he arranged it, I don't know. But this splendid send-off put us in very good heart. We little thought then that within a month Captain Morrison would find himself commanding the battalion at the Battle of Loos, after the loss of four officers killed, two gassed, five wounded and casualties in other ranks amounting to over 350.

* * *

Harold Macmillan's injuries received at Ginchy in September 1916 were not the end of his army career. Between his stays in hospital, he carried out light duties at Chelsea Barracks, overseeing recruit training, and briefly was an adjutant at a school of drill for young NCOs and officers. He was always a bit limited in the official duties he could carry out because the wound in his left thigh meant that he could not wear a sword.

He became haunted by memories and fear, and the loss of his friends. The battles of 1917 depressed him and made him bitter that he was at home when others were in the trenches. When the Armistice was announced, he was in hospital but able to walk with sticks. He watched the ecstatic crowds, but was conscious chiefly of the losses.

Macmillan could not face going back to Oxford, a 'city of ghosts' which held too many painful memories. Nevertheless, he felt that he had gained a great deal from his time in the army: good fellowship, the generosity and broad-mindedness of many of his fellow officers, and the meaning of courage. He had also, he thought, gained both confidence and humility, and a sense of obligation to those who had died, to make good use of the life that had been spared.

While others threw themselves into a social whirl in order to forget, Macmillan had neither the strength nor inclination for such distractions. He started to read political biographies and memoirs, and felt that the old political and social order must change. His army service remained a great source of pride to him, and it gave him an interesting insight. In the Second World War, which he spent largely in North Africa, he felt that everyone, from the High Command to the fighting troops, was united by a common respect and affection. This, he recognised, was largely due to the fact that many of the leading generals had served as regimental officers in the First World War, and had not forgotten their experiences. They appeared frequently near the front line, and were well known to the men. In this respect, they had an advantage over those with whom he had fought in the earlier conflict.

After the Great War, Macmillan's interest in politics developed and he became Conservative MP for Stockton in 1924. He was greatly affected by the poverty and hardship he found in the area, and was determined on social reform – he was seen at the time as something of a left-wing radical. Years later, perhaps influenced by his memories of the First World War, he stood out against the appeasement of Nazi Germany, and this opposition kept him on the backbenches through the 1930s. Not surprisingly, when war broke out again, he was asked to serve in the wartime Coalition Government at the Ministry of Supply and in the Colonial Office. In 1942, he went to North Africa as British representative to the Allies in the Mediterranean, where he met and became close friends with General Dwight Eisenhower, a connection which was maintained when Eisenhower became President of the United States.

From 1945, Harold Macmillan served in a wide range of offices of state, perhaps most notably as Minister of Housing under Churchill in 1951, when, remembering his early experiences in Stockton on Tees, he promised to build 300,000 houses a year – and kept his word. In 1957, after Eden's Suez fiasco, he became Prime Minister; he was re-elected in 1959 after declaring that 'most of our people have never had it so good' – generally misquoted as 'you've never had it so good.'

The Macmillan Government was perhaps most notable for an economic policy that had employment at its root, and by moves towards independence for former British colonies in Africa – 'the wind of change', as he famously said, blowing through the continent.

Harold Macmillan resigned as Prime Minister in 1963, and took up the Chairmanship of Macmillan Publishers, the family business. His wife Lady Dorothy Macmillan, whom he had married in 1920, died three years later. Much of his time was now taken up with writing, especially a huge six-volume autobiography, which his political opponent Enoch Powell described as inducing 'a sensation akin to that of chewing on cardboard'. His wartime diaries, published after his death, had a more friendly reception.

In 1984, Harold Macmillan was given the title of 1st Earl of Stockton; the town had long since made a deep impression on him, and in the last month of his life he commented that 63 years earlier, the unemployment rate in Stockton had been 29%; in 1986, it was 28%. It was, he said, 'a rather sad end to one's life.'

CHAPTER TWENTYONE

Peter Llewelyn Davies

—ɯɯ—

He [Peter] *had been through something more than a furnace, and what was left of him was for a long while little more than a ghost; a shattered remnant that even Barrie couldn't help.*

Denis Mackai, novelist and friend to the Barrie family.

I F IT WAS INTENDED TO BE A SECRET, then it was the world's worst kept. The German offensive in France of March 1918 had been expected ever since Russia had withdrawn from the war in the previous year. 1917 had also been the year in which the United States entered the war on the Allies' side and Germany knew that if it was ever going to win, it had to strike before American troops began to arrive in any great numbers. Russia's capitulation enabled Germany to transfer a million men from the eastern to the western front. This would be their final chance of victory.

On the Western Front, British soldiers had been preparing for an enemy offensive for a couple of months, although a shortage of troops had imperilled the effort. It was just a question of exactly when, not if, the enemy would attack.

On 12 March, by brigade order, a small group of men serving with the 7th (Service) Bn Kings Royal Rifle Corps [KRRC] crept out under cover of darkness and placed a notice on the German wire – a risky but by no means unique occurrence. The Germans, the note said, would be ill advised to attempt any attack, in fact, a general invitation for their surrender was extended. It was not taken up. The Battalion

War Diary recorded the ominous silence. 'The ensuing tour of six days was notable only for extreme quietness. Active patrolling of No Man's Land was carried out nightly from dusk to dawn.'

The message from brigade had been sent up the line and passed to the battalion's adjutant, Captain Peter Llewelyn Davies. Even war had its lighter moments, but the note placed on the enemy wire, for all its feigned bonhomie, had a serious point. It let the enemy know that their attack was indeed not only awaited but anticipated, and heavy casualties were bound to ensue.

The offer to take all the Germans prisoner was a bit of additional jest, boyish fun that might have appealed to Peter; after all, he was one of JM Barrie's famous boys, and while he may have been only a part of the amalgam that was Barrie's greatest creation, Peter Pan, he had, at least, given him the name.

Although so closely associated with Peter Pan, and frequently teased, Peter Llewelyn Davies, unlike his namesake, was a boy who had to grow up quickly, like all young officers sent to the Western Front. He had been in France since 1916 in the full knowledge that he might not see home again. His elder brother George had been killed in March 1915, and, with the German attack imminent, there was every likelihood that Peter's name was about to be added to the long casualty lists.

On 21 March 1918, the 7th KRRC were in support; 'nothing could have been more peaceful' wrote the battalion war diarist. At 3.30am the Colonel, after going round to inspect the companies, returned to headquarters and lay down for a few hours' sleep. Everyone expected to remain in position until dawn.

He had been asleep for only an hour when he woke. In an instant he was up and about. An almighty barrage was landing on the trenches and communication with the front line was immediately cut before any report could be received.

After an intense bombardment that engulfed the entire battle zone, the Germans attacked. Owing to fog, visibility was down to less than fifty yards, and the front line was quickly over-run, the Germans advancing on brigade headquarters. The 7th KRRC took up the fight, but found that the Germans, rather than attacking head on, were appearing from trenches in the rear. By 11am, A and C Companies were practically surrounded. The survivors of the battalion fell back to a sunken road and took up positions with the remnants of neighbouring battalions. By the afternoon, the fog lifted and enemy aircraft began flying up and down the line, and a further retreat was required. At least thirteen officers from the 7th KRRC had been killed, wounded or taken prisoner, and by dusk only six officers, one of them Peter Llewelyn Davies, and 130 other ranks remained with the battalion.

By the morning, the battalion was in support close to a railway line at the village of Jussy. Most of the day was spent digging in as the enemy crept ever closer, spraying the village and the roads with machine-gun fire. The day was fine and clear, and it was not until the evening that the enemy renewed the attack. The situation was critical, but Peter, with great skill, helped organise the defence. At one point the enemy crossed a nearby canal, only to be thrown back again by a counter attack of mixed units led by a Major St Aubyn, one of the last senior officers in the battalion, who was killed just as the skirmish ended.

At dawn on the 23rd, the weather turned misty again, and reports were received that the Germans were once more in the process of surrounding what was left of the battalion. In conjunction with a battalion of Cameronians, the remainder of the 7th KRRC manned an embankment. The Germans shelled the line and advanced to a point so close that bombs could be thrown over and down the embankment. Supplies of ammunition were running low. One limber was sent up at the gallop to bring fresh supplies, reaching the men just as a shell landed and killed both horses.

By late morning the position was again untenable, but as the troops withdrew, the fog lifted and the Germans opened fire, inflicting a number of casualties including the Colonel, who was seen to be hit in the face by shrapnel, while another officer, temporarily attached to the battalion, was killed. It was at this point that Peter Llewelyn Davies, as the most senior officer left, took command. Under him were just two junior officers and seventy other ranks. For the next two days, Peter led the men to one position after another, digging in only to be ordered back once again. The men were exhausted and slept when possible, an hour or two here, an hour or two there, before the march continued.

By the 26th a few men had rejoined the battalion from leave, as well as a few from the transport. However, the battalion was almost spent as a fighting force. An extended note in the War Diary sums up the next weeks in a few extended paragraphs. On 5 April, the 7th KRRC suffered its last casualties. The nucleus of officers and men who were left formed a training staff for Americans at a base camp. In early May, Peter left to join the British Mission attached to the French 10th Army. The survivors were soon sent to a new battalion, the 34th (County of London) Bn London Regiment, and the 7th KRRC ceased to exist. It had been the oldest of Kitchener's New Army battalions, formed two weeks and a day after the outbreak of war, and had served in France since May 1915. 'The battalion fought with distinction through some of the hardest fighting of the war, and were finally overwhelmed,' wrote the *King's Royal Rifle Corps Chronicle* after the war.

Peter Llewelyn Davies's devotion to the task in hand and to the men under his command had been inspirational. He had turned twenty-one less than a month before the German attack, but his front line experience had been immense: it was nearly two years since he had first stepped into a front line trench. His expertise had been employed to the fullest extent imaginable and it was no surprise to anyone when he was awarded the Military Cross. The citation appeared in the *London Gazettte*. It noted:

For conspicuous gallantry and devotion to duty during recent operations. He displayed untiring energy, and set an example to the men of the battalion. He repeatedly rallied men and led them into suitable fire positions. During a very trying time he carried out all his duties as Adjutant most thoroughly and assisted the junior officers, who were (owing to casualties) in temporary command of companies. By his coolness under fire and good example he steadied the men on several critical occasions.

* * *

In August 1914, three of the five Llewelyn Davies boys, George, Michael and Nicholas (Nico), were on their traditional holiday in Scotland with the writer J M Barrie, who had adopted them after their parents' death. They were in such a remote location that they did not immediately hear about the declaration of war, until seventeen year old Peter, the third son, who was still at Eton, arrived from London with the news. He also had a letter from the Adjutant of the Cambridge OTC, to which George belonged, declaring that at this time of crisis all undergraduates knew their duty. On reading this letter, George returned to London with Peter, both determined to join up.

They were advised to head for Winchester to enlist in the Rifle Brigade, the Adjutant's old regiment. George was nervous as he had been unwell on his way to the depot, but on arrival he and his younger brother marched in and found themselves in front of the Commanding Officer of the 6th (Special Reserve) Battalion of the King's Royal Rifle Corps. Initially, the officer's manner was gruff, but when they gave him the Adjutant's name, his attitude changed: they had been at Cambridge together. He addressed George, and found that he had been at Eton and played cricket. His manner became ever more genial, and by the time he found that George had made a valuable 59 at Lord's in 1912, in a match that he had himself witnessed, little more needed to be said. That Peter was his brother was a good enough recommendation, so he gave them the appropriate forms, and they were in: two Second Lieutenants designate.

They returned to Scotland and on 9 September they received orders to report to Sheerness. As part of George's hasty preparations, he got engaged. At a time when many men were trying to get into the forces quickly, fearing it would be 'all over by Christmas', he wrote that he thought it would be long and hard. In December, he was posted to the 4th Bn Rifle Brigade.

Peter went through the same training at Sheerness as George, but it was accepted that – to his disgust – he was not likely to go overseas before his 19th birthday. 'I do hope,' he wrote to Barrie, 'Uncle Jim', as he called him:

> that you haven't taken any steps to prevent my going before I'm 19. I've had so much training that I am quite fit to go, apart from my age, and I assure you that it's much more of a strain waiting here than going to France.

George wrote to Barrie from the trenches in mid-January 1915, telling him about life at the front and saying he was taking every precaution.

> The hardships are the things that count, and one gets into the way of taking them as they come…Don't get worried about me. I take every precaution I can, and shall do very well.

Nevertheless, the awful weather conditions resulted in illness, and George had to spend some time out of the line, cheered by a Fortnum and Mason hamper from Barrie. George's letters remained relatively brief but cheerful, but Barrie had another source from within the family, George's uncle, Guy du Maurier, the Commanding Officer of a battalion of Royal Fusiliers which was then also in the Ypres salient. He was more outspoken about the conditions the men were enduring, and it was through him that in February Barrie heard that George had been slightly wounded in the leg.

While he tried to be optimistic in his letters, George was clearly a reflective and sensitive man and on one occasion he describes being deeply moved by the sight of a ruined château and especially a small shrine in its garden:

> On the altar, just in front of the figure of Christ, there was a charger of four cartridges. To a sentimental civilian like me, not yet hardened into a proper mercenary, this had a rather striking effect.

In a letter of early March, George described the death of a man who had been killed at his side when he stuck his head above the parapet. The top of his head had been shot off, a dreadful sight, as George wrote. The letter elicited a heart-rending response from Barrie. He had just heard the news that George's uncle Guy du Maurier had been killed, and fear for his boy swept over him.

> Of course I don't need this to bring home to me the danger you are always in more or less, but I do seem to be sadder to-day than ever, and more and more wishing you were a girl of 21 instead of a boy, so that I could say the things to you that are now always in my heart... I don't have any little iota of desire for you to get military glory. I do not care a farthing for anything of the kind, but I have the one passionate desire that we may all be together again once at least.

'Surely,' wrote Peter many years later:

> no soldier in France or Flanders ever had more moving words from home than those in this tragic, desperately apprehensive letter... Plenty of other people, no doubt, were thinking and writing much the same sort of thing, but not in such perfection.

Indeed, taking all the circumstances into consideration, I think it must be one of the great letters of the world…Far the most pathetic figure in all the world was the poor little genius who wrote these words, and afterwards, no doubt, walked up and down, up and down his lonely room, smoking pipe after pipe, thinking his dire thoughts.

Life and death were indeed a lottery at the front and on 14 March, George replied to Barrie's letter.

14th March
Dear Uncle Jim

I have just got your letter about Uncle Guy. You say it hasn't made you think any more about the danger I am in. But I know it has. Do try not to let it. I take every care of myself that can be decently taken. And if I am going to stop a bullet, why should it be with a vital place? But arguments aren't any good. Keep your heart up, Uncle Jim, & remember how good an experience like this is for a chap who's been very idle before. Lord, I shall be proud when I'm home again, & talking to you about all this…..

Yours affectionately
George

The following day the battalion was ordered to take part in an advance to push the enemy out of the small town of St Eloi. Prior to the attack, the Colonel talked to the officers of C Company. They were sitting on an embankment listening intently when George was hit in the head by a stray bullet and killed almost immediately. His body was buried in a field on the left hand side of the road, his grave adorned with violets.

In a letter to Barrie written a few days afterwards, a fellow officer made it clear that, on the way up to the line, George had had a premonition of his own death. George wished that his body would not be taken to some village in the rear but buried outside the trench where he fell; a finer death he could not wish for. He was the first officer to die that night and they had not even reached the front line.

The news of George's death reached Barrie in a telegram, to be followed by others of sympathy and condolence as friends heard the bad news. Along with the telegrams and letters came one small white envelope containing George's last letter, written on 14 March. JM Barrie later wrote at the foot of the first page, 'This is the last letter, and was written a few hours before his death. I knew he was killed before I got it.'

Peter Llewelyn Davies was in training at Shereness when he received a telegram from Barrie: 'GEORGE IS KILLED – HOPE YOU CAN COME TO ME.' Peter was granted compassionate leave and hurried back to London.

> I remember arriving at the flat in Adelphi Terrace…and it was all very painful….The effect on J M B was dire indeed, poor little devil. Oh, miserable Jimmie. Famous, rich, loved by a vast public, but at what a frightful private cost.

* * *

The following year Peter was sent to the front, joining the 1st Bn King's Royal Rifle Corps in billets, 'in a small smelly village, made up of a few battered cottages, and a large number of exceedingly noticeable dunghills'. Within a week, he had gone up to the front line in what was a quiet section of the front.

> It was hard to realise that we are in mid-summer. Everywhere it is more like November. I don't think there is less than a foot of slush anywhere in my trench, and it rains continuously, cold all the time… none of those beautifully sandbagged and floor-

boarded affairs one sees in photographs (usually taken in England). No beautiful dugouts with vast oaken supports and iron roofs.

Preparations for the Battle of the Somme, to be launched later that month, were in full swing, but Peter's unit was not involved in making the initial assault and his main concern at this time seems to have been trying to get a transfer to the 2nd Bn of the KRRC where he had several friends; this came through towards the end of the month. On his last night before the move, he vividly described in a letter his activities and his cheerful state of mind:

I and a corporal and a rifleman crawled out through our wire and across to within about fifty yards from the German trench. It was a full moon, and the lightest night I have ever seen, so you can guess I was flat on my belly the whole way. I was very thankful for the numerous shell holes which, muddy and half full of water though they were, came in very useful as cover. I could hear the Huns slushing up and down their trench and coughing. They didn't spot us at all, and I really rather enjoyed it: but there was some horrible debris between the lines.

On 18 June, Peter transferred to the 2nd Bn KRRC. He was delighted with the move, being made Signalling Officer, 'a very pleasant job' according to his report. He messed with a small group of officers at battalion headquarters and had better rations than other company officers. On 24 June he wrote to Barrie that he had dined on caviar and paté de foie gras the evening before, luxury even out of mess tins. The weather was good, and he commented that this

brought out aeroplanes of both sides in swarms. The blue sky is dotted all over with the bursting anti-aircraft shells which never hit anything but are exceedingly picturesque.

Given the disastrous opening of the Somme fight and its subsequent grinding continuation, Peter's unit was not likely to avoid it for long, and by stages from early July, it moved up as part of 2 Brigade of the 2nd Division from Lillers to Candas then to the battlefield around Contalmaison. Yet even before he reached the Somme, his attitude to war had begun to change.

> Not long ago I can remember rather looking forward to taking part in a fight. My curiosity has been satisfied, and I shall never have any such desire again. Modern artillery fire is damnable beyond all powers of description. There is none of the exhilaration there may have been in pitched battles of a few years ago. You crouch down in the bottom of your trench and listen helplessly to the whispering noise which comes before the crash of each heavy shell. Each near one seems to be coming straight at you.

On 23 July the 2nd KRRC took part in an attack on a German trench known as the Switch Line. The attack went in at 12.30am but the men were spotted immediately and the Germans let rip with devastating machine-gun fire. Though they entered the enemy trenches, lack of support meant that they could not hang on and were forced to withdraw. Among the 230 casualties was their commanding officer, Lieutenant Colonel Bircham DSO, who was severely wounded and died two days later. Peter wrote to Barrie:

> He was all that one could desire in a battalion commander, and I don't suppose there was a braver man alive. He simply didn't know the meaning of fear. The last I saw of him was his figure disappearing into the darkness as he walked over the top from one trench to another while bullets and shells of all descriptions were flying all around.

The tone in Peter's letters was changing. While the men's morale, he insisted, had not fallen in any way, war could still be detested. Shortly before the attack on the Switch line, a new officer had arrived with whom Peter formed a great bond. His name was Captain Wilson and the two had much in common.

> His dislike of war and fighting is quite as intense as mine. Everyone hates it, of course, but there are degrees, and I think he and I have reached the superlative. He was a scholar at Winchester, and is as different as possible from the professional fighting man.

The two men exchanged ancient Latin and Greek tales, much to the amusement and amazement of fellow officers and men. It would be a short-lived friendship.

Not just the tone but the content of Peter's letters changed. He hated war and in his surviving letters his thoughts often turned to home, and he wrote about friends and family and the gossip he heard, and the parcels he received. If he spoke about the war, it was often about the shellfire, bad enough for any individual soldier, but to Peter of especial significance because bombardments broke telephone wires and, as the Signalling Officer, it was his job to go out and ensure that the signallers had done their work and that the lines were mended, a difficult and very dangerous job:

> As the [shell] fire grows more intense, the linesman feels sorrier and sorrier for himself, for he knows that he must mend it in spite of the shells. My men did magnificently and I am recommending two of them for medals, which they deserve a hundred times over.

On 12 August, Peter was one of an advance party which moved up by Mametz Wood to the trenches facing High Wood, a place of fearful renown. It was one of the hottest spots on the front, and before its relief a week later, the 2nd KRRC had lost 138 men, chiefly to shelling. The unit's new commanding officer had been wounded, and so was Peter's closest friend, Captain Wilson. He wrote to Barrie:

> There is very little hope for recovery. I saw him [Wilson] just after he was hit and he was then already that horrible colour of dirty chalk. I shall miss him far more than all the other officers we have just lost – he was a man in a thousand.

On 9 September, Peter took part in yet another attack to the east of High Wood. He went in with twenty signallers; nine came out. After just three months, the machine gun officer and the adjutant were the only officers who were still with the battalion since Peter had arrived in mid-June, and a few days later Peter too left. He was suffering from impetigo, a skin condition brought on by the filthy conditions and the strain. He was taken to hospital at Etaples, and wrote that he felt there was a strong chance that he would be sent home. The impetigo had spread over his face and looked disgusting, and the renewed offensive on the Somme in mid-September meant that beds were at a premium.

Peter was right; he was returned to England. But he was not suffering only from impetigo but from shellshock as well, and required a long period of recuperation. He recovered from his mental wounds to the point where he could return to the Western Front the following Easter, but he, of all the brothers, had been and remained the most deeply wounded by the death of George. While Peter had been concerned over Barrie's state of mind after George's death, Barrie had been anxious about Peter's. 'I feel painfully for Peter between whom and George there was a devotion not perhaps very common among brothers,' he wrote to a friend.

Peter had lost his parents and a brother by the age of eighteen. In the spring of 1917, while back in England, he met and fell in love with an older married woman called Vera Willoughby. This, as he confessed, 'shocked Uncle Jim to the core' and led to a temporary rift between them. Peter was more isolated than ever, and for a time his letters to Barrie ceased.

In 1917, Barrie received permission to visit George's grave in Belgium; he visited it alone. Peter, on his return to the Western Front, also managed to visit his brother:

> I had the place to myself, and never remember feeling more alone. It was a grey, lowering, dismal sort of day, shivery too…All sorts of vague thoughts came and went in my head, of dust and skeletons and the conqueror worm, and old, unhappy, far-off things, and older days that were happier. What with one thing and another I am not ashamed to admit that I wiped an eye.

Peter returned to his unit and never failed to do his best in the service of his country. He remained abroad for the rest of the war, enduring with total professionalism all that could be thrown at him, but his disgust at the carnage never abated; rather, it deepened. In a letter to Barrie on 5 July 1918 he wrote:

> My dislike of it all is infinitely greater than it ever was before, and I often feel as though I should wake up a raving lunatic at the end of my night's rest (which usually occurs between six and 11 in the morning). More bored, more easily tired, and more firmly convinced of the hopeless and grotesque folly of the war…that's how I am progressing.

Peter would survive the war but, like so many of his generation, he was not allowed to escape it.

* * *

Arthur Llewelyn Davies, a lawyer, and his wife Susan had five sons:

George, Jack, Peter, Michael and Nicholas. When George was five, in 1897, he introduced himself and two of his brothers to the writer JM Barrie in Kensington Gardens, and a friendship developed between Barrie and the boys and their mother. Barrie was at ease with children; he was a natural storyteller and played amusing tricks for his small friends which delighted them. George was a particular favourite – 'never a cockier boy' wrote Barrie, who used him as a model for a character in his book *Little White Bird*, published in 1902.

Barrie was in some ways a sad figure. He had had a brother, David, to whom he was devoted, but at the age of thirteen, David died in a skating accident. He felt that the only comfort was that David stayed a boy: he would never have to grow up. This was perhaps the germ of the story of Peter Pan, the boy who never grew up, an idea developed between Barrie and the Llewelyn Davies boys. A comment of George's, 'to die will be an awfully big adventure' was quoted when the show was first performed in 1904 (although dropped, for reasons that might be guessed, in 1915).

Barrie's friendship with the boys and their mother developed, but in 1906 the boys' father Arthur was diagnosed with cancer of the jaw, and he died the following year. Three years later, their mother, Susan, died of the same disease. George was now seventeen and at Eton, where he was a good sportsman and popular with the other boys. Jack was sixteen, Peter thirteen, Michael ten and Nicholas (known as Nico) was only six. Barrie, whom they called 'Uncle Jim', became their legal guardian.

In 1908, George and Peter had seen Highland troops marching, and been very impressed. George joined the OTC at Eton and he enjoyed the military training. He played cricket for the school at Lord's – an achievement which later helped both him and Peter to be commissioned into the Army. Peter followed his older brother to Eton, but he was still grieving for his mother, who had only recently died, and he found it difficult to settle. He was also mercilessly teased about 'being Peter Pan', a burden he had to carry all his life, and he referred to the play and book as 'that terrible masterpiece.'

But he was an able scholar, and won a place at Trinity College, Cambridge; he was, however, on the Eton OTC's annual summer camp in August 1914. His older brother Jack had been to Osborne Naval College and had joined the Navy, and so it was only George, Michael and Nico who went to Scotland with Barrie for their traditional summer holiday.

By the end of the war George was dead, and Peter's younger brother Michael, perhaps Barrie's favourite and the one who is said to have most influenced the *Peter Pan* story, left Eton for Oxford. He was a highly intelligent and artistic young man, but deeply troubled. In 1921, shortly before his 21st birthday, he and his closest friend, Rupert Buxton, were drowned; their death has most frequently been claimed as a suicide pact, but it is possible that Rupert, a strong swimmer, was attempting to rescue Michael, who could not swim. Barrie wrote the following year that Michael's death 'was in a way the end of me.'

In 1929, Barrie gave the copyright of *Peter Pan* to Great Ormond Street Hospital for Sick Children in London. When he died in 1937, the remaining brothers were very distressed to find that they had been cut out of his will, and that everything had been left to his secretary. One of Peter's sons felt that inheriting from Barrie would have recompensed him for the notoriety he had experienced because of the link with Peter Pan – a connection that he hated.

There are various possible explanations for what happened to Peter. He was haunted by the deaths of his brothers and the long shadow cast by the First World War; he discovered that his wife and sons all suffered from a genetic disease. He started to collect the family papers into a document that he called 'The Morgue', but as he reached the story of Michael's death, he committed suicide by throwing himself under a train at Sloane Square station. 'Peter Pan's death leap', 'Peter Pan commits suicide,' ran the newspaper headlines; they were journalistic and eye-catching, but to Peter they would have been nothing more than insult heaped upon mortal injury.

Acknowledgements

We should like to thank everyone at Pen and Sword Books: Charles Hewitt for commissioning the project; John Wilkinson for his expert cover design; the inimitable Roni Wilkinson for his expert text layout; Dominic Allen for the maps and Marie Parkinson for the picture section; Paula Brennan and David Hemingway for their help and encouragement

On a personal level, we would also like to thank Taff Gillingham for his expertise and advice with the script, and Richard's mother, Joan van Emden, for her investigative skills and her superb editorial work. We are also grateful for the support given to us by Jeremy Banning, Peter Barton, and Paul Reed, and to Claude Verhaeghe of the Auberge Ploegsteert and to the battlefield guide, Peter Williams.

With a project as wide ranging as this, there are of course many other people we wish to thank. However, in particular we are grateful to Nicolas Ridley, son of Arnold Ridley, for all his support and interest in the project and for his kind permission to quote from his father's unpublished memoirs, *The Train and Other Ghosts,* and to use the picture of his father in uniform taken in early 1916. Rachel Hassell, Assistant Keeper at the University of Bristol Theatre Collection, was most helpful during our research and the Theatre Collection kindly gave permission for us to reproduce the image of Arnold Ridley taken while filming *Dad's Army.*

Ned Walsh and Dominic Walsh, the nephew and great nephew of Ned Parfett, were generous with their time and kindly permitted us to reproduce personal artifacts and images of Ned.

We are also grateful to Marista Leishman, daughter of Lord Reith, who kindly allowed us to use extracts from her father's memoirs, and to Wheatley Productions for the requisite permission to reproduce images and words.

Unstinting in his help with the Llewelyn Davies brothers was Andrew Birkin, whose superb book *The Lost Boys* was of great help, as was his equally good website for JM Barrie. Andrew also put us in touch with Laura Duguid, a member of the Llewelyn Davies family, who gave us permission to us both the image of Peter Llewelyn Davies and quotations from his wartime letters. The photograph of George Llewellyn Davies at Eton is reproduced by kind permission of Great Ormond Street Hospital for Children, London.

The photograph of Dennis Wheatley in uniform is reproduced with the kind permission of Leeds University Library. The picture of Basil Rathbone, taken in 1917, was reproduced with the kind permission of Major Ian Riley, the Honorary Secretary of the Liverpool Scottish Museum while quotations taken from Rathbone's autobiography *In and Out of Character* are reproduced by permission of Limelight Editions. We are grateful to these individuals and organizations, and similarly to the many people who have helped us along the way, including Dr Luckett at Magdalene College Cambridge University for permission to reproduce the war letters of George Mallory, and to Phillipa Grimstone, Sub-Librarian, for her generous help. Mary Metz at Mountaineers Books and writer Audrey Salkeld gave us useful information for the chapter on George Mallory.

We are grateful to the National Archives for permission to reproduce JRR Tolkien's Medical Return, Rob Gilson's Post Office Telegram, the letter from Nigel Bruce to the War Office, Basil Rathbone's application to join an Officer Cadet Battalion, and John Christie's Active Service Casualty Form.

Getty Images kindly gave permission for us to reproduce the following photographs: JRR Tolkien: Photographer Haywood Magee, image no. 3429462, George Mallory: Photographer David Hahn no. 51068265, Basil Rathbone and Nigel Bruce, image no, 2763144, Ned Parfett, image no. 2666163, and John Christie, image no. 3324088 and 2630120.

We acknowledge the following sources, and are grateful for permission given in each case:

The Letters of J.R.R. Tolkien, Edited by Humphrey Carpenter.

copyright holders to images. Although every effort had been made to fulfil requirements with regard to reproducing copyright material, the authors and publisher will be glad to rectify any omissions at the earliest opportunity.

Finally we must make especial mention of our long-suffering wives Anna (van Emden) and Diane (Piuk) who have both put up with much during the writing of this book and always remained patient, calm and supportive.